D0367241

Other titles by Katherine Ramsland

BEATING THE DEVIL'S GAME:
A HISTORY OF FORENSIC SCIENCE AND CRIMINAL INVESTIGATION

THE C.S.I. EFFECT

THE FORENSIC SCIENCE OF C.S.I.

THE HUMAN PREDATOR:
A HISTORICAL CHRONICLE
OF SERIAL MURDER AND FORENSIC INVESTIGATION

INSIDE THE MINDS OF MASS MURDERERS:
WHY THEY KILL

INSIDE THE MINDS OF SERIAL KILLERS:
WHY THEY KILL

INSIDE THE MINDS OF HEALTHCARE SERIAL KILLERS:
WHY THEY KILL

A VOICE FOR THE DEAD
(with James E. Starrs)

THE SCIENCE OF COLD CASE FILES

THE UNKNOWN DARKNESS:
PROFILING THE PREDATORS AMONG US
(with Gregg McCrary)

THE CRIMINAL MIND:
A WRITER'S GUIDE TO FORENSIC PSYCHOLOGY

PIERCING THE DARKNESS

TRUE STORIES OF

C.S.I.

The Real Crimes Behind
the Best Episodes
of the Popular TV Show

KATHERINE RAMSLAND

BERKLEY BOULEVARD BOOKS, NEW YORK

THE BERKLEY PUBLISHING GROUP
Published by the Penguin Group
Penguin Group (USA) Inc.
375 Hudson Street, New York, New York 10014, USA
Penguin Group (Canada), 90 Eglinton Avenue East, Suite 700, Toronto, Ontario M4P 2Y3, Canada
(a division of Pearson Penguin Canada Inc.)
Penguin Books Ltd., 80 Strand, London WC2R 0RL, England
Penguin Group Ireland, 25 St. Stephen's Green, Dublin 2, Ireland (a division of Penguin Books Ltd.)
Penguin Group (Australia), 250 Camberwell Road, Camberwell, Victoria 3124, Australia
(a division of Pearson Australia Group Pty. Ltd.)
Penguin Books India Pvt. Ltd., 11 Community Centre, Panchsheel Park, New Delhi—110 017, India
Penguin Group (NZ), 67 Apollo Drive, Rosedale, North Shore 0632, New Zealand
(a division of Pearson New Zealand Ltd.)
Penguin Books (South Africa) (Pty.) Ltd., 24 Sturdee Avenue, Rosebank, Johannesburg 2196,
South Africa

Penguin Books Ltd., Registered Offices: 80 Strand, London WC2R 0RL, England

This book is an original publication of The Berkley Publishing Group.

This book was not authorized, prepared, approved, licensed, or endorsed by any entity involved in
creating or producing the *C.S.I.* television series.

PUBLISHER'S NOTE: While the author has made every effort to provide accurate telephone
numbers and Internet addresses at the time of publication, neither the publisher nor the author
assumes any responsibility for errors, or for changes that occur after publication. Further, the
publisher does not have any control over and does not assume any responsibility for author or third-
party websites or their content.

Copyright © 2008 by Katherine Ramsland.
Text design by Kristin del Rosario.

PRINTING HISTORY
Berkley Boulevard trade paperback edition / September 2008

Library of Congress Cataloging-in-Publication Data

Ramsland, Katherine M., 1953–
    True stories of C.S.I. : the real crimes behind the best episodes of the popular TV show / by
Katherine Ramsland. — Berkley Boulevard trade paperback ed.
        p. cm.
    ISBN 978-0-425-22234-8
    1. Crime—United States—Case studies.   2. Murder—United States—Case studies.   3. Criminal
investigation—United States—Popular works.   4. CSI: crime scene investigation (Television
program)   I. Title.

    HV6529.R36 2008
    364.10973—dc22

                                                                                        2008013050

PRINTED IN THE UNITED STATES OF AMERICA

10   9   8   7   6   5   4   3   2   1

For my father,
Henry Johnston,
who's always been enthused
to watch me grow and succeed

CONTENTS

TRUE STORY: In 2003 in Philadelphia, a teenage boy was murdered by a gang of his friends, and they used his money to shop and buy drugs.

ten (109)

C.S.I.: **"Overload":** An unlicensed therapist using a rebirthing treatment for reactive attachment disorder kills a boy and claims that he had a seizure and hit his head against the floor. Blanket fibers on her sweater and his underwear give her away.

TRUE STORY: Candace Newmaker, 10, was smothered as a result of "rebirthing therapy" in Colorado.

eleven (119)

C.S.I.: **"I Like to Watch":** A rapist gains access to a woman's apartment by posing as a fireman.

TRUE STORY: In 2005 in New York City, Peter Braunstein impersonated a fireman to gain access to a woman's apartment, where he molested her.

twelve (131)

C.S.I.: **"Face Lift":** Nadine Weston is burned to ash in her home, with only a foot remaining, yet her chair and the surrounding furniture have barely been damaged. In the ceiling overhead, the fire made a sizable hole.

TRUE STORY: The FBI investigated an apparent case of spontaneous human combustion in Florida.

thirteen (141)

C.S.I.: **"Crash and Burn":** An angry female driver crashes into a restaurant to kill as many employees of an insurance company who dine there as she can, as payback for the company's poor treatment of her.

TRUE STORY: Priscilla Joyce Ford crashed through two blocks of streets in Reno, Nevada, in 1980, killing seven and injuring two dozen more, as payback for the city's treatment of her.

fourteen (147)

C.S.I.: **"Meet Market":** A burnt body on a shop floor opens up the gruesome world of illegal trade in cadaver parts when an autopsy reveals that the bones were removed and replaced with pipes, broomsticks, and other items. Skin tissue is missing as well, leading the investigators to a mortuary harvesting body parts without consent.

TRUE STORY: When the news came out in 2005 that the bones of Alistair Cooke had been plundered at a funeral home, the investigation turned up a partnership of funeral directors in the greater New York area who were illegally removing bones and tissue from dead bodies and selling them to tissue-processing companies.

fifteen (157)

C.S.I.: **"The I-15 Murders"**: A trucker driving along Interstate 15 murders several women, and after each one someone leaves messages on the doors of restrooms. The team uses handwriting analysis to pin down the suspect.

TRUE STORY: Keith Jesperson, the "Happy Face Killer" from the Pacific Northwest, left messages in restrooms about committing several murders along his truck routes.

sixteen (167)

C.S.I.: **"Unfriendly Skies"**: The entire team investigates the death of a passenger aboard a flight, which involved several of the other passengers ganging up on him.

TRUE STORY: In 2000, Jonathan Burton died aboard a flight after passengers subdued him and beat him up to keep him from bringing down the plane.

seventeen (175)

C.S.I.: **"Who Are You?"**: A plumber finds skeletal remains in a crawlspace that turn out to be those of a twenty-year-old female murdered by a man working on a construction site. Her remains were sealed into the concrete, and forensic art revealed her.

TRUE STORY: The identity of a middle-aged woman, murdered and buried in a cement foundation, is revealed via a police sketch and a unique fingerprint analysis.

eighteen (183)

C.S.I.: **"Burked"**: The son of a casino mogul lies dead on the floor of his home, the apparent victim of a drug overdose, but clues point to the possibility that he was murdered with a procedure known as "burking."

TRUE STORY: The death in 1998 of former Las Vegas gambling executive Ted Binion appeared to be a homicide by burking, and two people were tried for the crime.

nineteen (191)

C.S.I.: **"Empty Eyes"**: Six showgirls who live in the same house are murdered.

TRUE STORY: In 1966, Richard Speck slaughtered eight nurses in Chicago.

ACKNOWLEDGMENTS

Ever since *C.S.I.* was first televised in 2000, I've been writing about its background stories, so I have a long history filled with people to thank for leads, affirmation, and information about forensic investigation. Most have been thanked in previous books for specific contributions, but I want to reiterate that the opportunities that my Crime Library editor, Marilyn Bardsley, afforded me have probably been the most significant. Not only did she give me access to plenty of sources and opportunities to write about some of the stories within these pages, but she's also contributed over the past decade to my unflagging enthusiasm for this subject.

I'm appreciative of James Starrs's efforts to help me with membership in the American Academy of Forensic Sciences, where I've met a considerable number of knowledgeable forensic experts.

Just as important are the people behind the scenes who provided opportunities, feedback, and support. Ginjer Buchanan, my editor, has been terrific about encouraging my ideas and getting the manuscript through its many stages. It's great to have her enthusiasm behind my projects.

I can never say enough great things about my agent and trusted friend, John Silbersack, of Trident Media Group. He always groks what I'm thinking about any given project and helps decide just how it's best presented. More important, he's been the best supporter I've ever had in this business, and he makes it fun.

My family, too, keeps up with what I'm doing and cheers me along the way.

INTRODUCTION

A deaf serial killer. Dollhouses of death. Grifters, impersonators, and killer priests. These are among the actual stories that inspired the writers of *C.S.I.: Crime Scene Investigation*, which entertains millions of viewers every week. Sometimes it's not enough to watch the episode; sometimes you want to know what really happened.

There's little doubt that *C.S.I.*, along with its spinoffs and the programs it has influenced, has had an impact on the way people think about crime stories. It's almost impossible to even consider crimes involving perpetrators and victims without also thinking about the forensic science or investigative angle needed to solve them. When *C.S.I.* first began in the fall of 2000, it was easy to spot the episodes that were inspired by actual cases, although the writers usually added a fictional twist. They identified tales that intrigued people and made headlines, or that had a unique motive, context, or setting. That's why we want to know more.

I've often been asked by *C.S.I.* viewers whether a given incident actually happened. Would a woman really kill to get someone's organs, or is there actually a business in harvesting bones from corpses? I enjoy filling people in on stories behind the episodes, and now I have the opportunity to fully lay out a collection of my favorites. In addition, I explored a few tales that were new to me and equally intriguing. What follows are the cases that either directly inspired an episode or were so similar to the episode details that the facts involved shed more light on motives, profiles, or victim impact.

Some cases, such as the trial in Ohio for the murder of Sister Margaret

Ann Pahl, took place after *C.S.I.* had made a huge splash, so attorneys and expert witnesses even discussed the show's influence on jurors. This is known as the "*C.S.I.* Effect," and it can't be discounted as a social influence. It has even figured into the plans of a few offenders, who believed they could use what they'd learned from watching the program to pull off a perfect crime.

But this book is strictly about crime stories that have occurred across the country, providing ideas for plots. Readers who want to know what actually happened, and whether a crime was solved and the perpetrators convicted, will find that information here. In many cases I placed psychological concepts or interesting facts in sidebars to offer more background, such as what we know about female mass murderers or what head injury has to do with violence, but for the most part I just tell the story. It is, after all, the reason we get hooked on popular television shows like *C.S.I.*, which will probably be around for a long time to come. As Gil Grissom says, let's follow the evidence.

one

C.S.I.: "Bite Me": A woman dies at the bottom of a staircase, and the shock-ing amount of blood contradicts her husband's claim that she had accidentally fallen.

TRUE STORY: The 2001 investigation of the death of Kathleen Peter-son, found at the bottom of a staircase in her home, was ruled a homicide.

Around 2:45 in the morning on December 9, 2001, an emergency call came in from 1810 Cedar Street in the Forest Hills section of Durham, North Carolina. It was Michael Peterson. "My wife had an accident," he said in a rushed voice. "She's still breathing." He explained, when prompted, that she had fallen down the stairs and was not conscious. He urged the dispatcher to send someone. When asked how many stairs she had fallen down, he seemed confused, but estimated it had been about fifteen or twenty. He seemed to be pant-ing as he urged someone there with him—apparently his injured wife—to breathe. He then hung up. Within moments he called 911 again, asking where the ambulance was. His wife was no longer breathing, he said. Then he hung up again. The dispatcher sent police units as well, in case she died.

Paramedics responded to the Cedar Street address, a million-dollar mansion, entering the home and finding Kathleen Peterson, a forty-eight-year-old executive with Nortel Networks, sprawled on her back in the well of a stairway. The walls were covered in blood. Michael Peterson, too, had blood on him, and was walking in circles and sobbing. His adult son, Todd, came in to attend to him.

The paramedics were astounded by how much blood they saw on the stairwell walls. A pool of blood encircled Kathleen's body, and her shoulders were hunched and her hands clamped. Apparently someone had attempted to clean up some of the blood, as a roll of paper towels lay close to her. There was also blood on a nearby white leather athletic shoe.

Kathleen had no pulse and no blood pressure. She was dead. As emergency personnel looked around, there seemed to be something wrong with this scene. A police officer noted that the blood on Michael Peterson's clothing appeared to be dry, which, if true, would mean that he'd been aware of his wife's accident longer than his emergency call indicated. Blood on the stairwell wall was also quite dry. Other officers who arrived agreed that it did not look like the scene of an accident. Oddly, there was even blood on the porch and sidewalk outside, as well as on a cabinet door apart from the area of the body. Luminol allegedly revealed a set of bloody footprints, now wiped clean, that had gone from Kathleen's body into the laundry area, then into the kitchen. Michael Peterson was the only other person in the home besides the victim.

A family member who came mentioned that Kathleen had been drinking quite a lot that night. Even so, the position of Kathleen's body did not appear to have been from a fall down the steps. Her neck was not broken.

Peterson asked if he needed a lawyer and was told to wait until more personnel arrived to process the scene. He went to the computer to check his e-mail, then talked with his brother, a civil attorney, on the phone.

Although the medical examiner, Dr. Kenneth Snell, initially decided that the death was consistent with an accident, when he spotted lacerations on Kathleen's scalp, he advised officers to look for a long, rodlike implement. Later, the autopsy indicated that Kathleen had seven deep scalp lacerations on the back of her head as well as bruises on her face and head. Her manner of death was ultimately determined to be from blunt force trauma to the head that was inconsistent with a fall. This case was a homicide.

The police got a warrant to search the home, seizing Peterson's computers and more than sixty other items. They also videotaped the scene and collected the clothing Peterson had worn that night. They failed to find a rodlike implement.

Peterson hired attorney David Rudolf to represent him. He was arrested and released on $850,000 bond, returning home to preserve every drop of blood within the stairwell for his own experts to examine. But there was more in his history that would add fire to the suspicions of investigators.

In Germany, he and his first wife had been friends with a woman, Elizabeth Ratliff, who had also taken a tumble down the steps in 1985. At the time, the authorities had concluded she died from a stroke. Yet Peterson was the last person to see her. He had walked her home after dinner on the evening before the nanny found her at the foot of the stairs in her home. She was still warm that morning, so presumably she had fallen recently, but the circumstances now looked more suspicious.

Ratliff had been the mother of two girls, Margaret and Martha, for whom Peterson was now the guardian. Throughout the ordeal, they would side with him while Kathleen's daughter, Caitlin Atwater, would stand against him. Many people decided right away that Peterson was a serial killer, using the same MO twice, but one can only assume that he was a rather stupid criminal for doing the same thing twice, so publicly. Pushing Kathleen down a set of stairs was a sure way to reopen the earlier case and have the finger pointed directly at him. Since Peterson was intelligent and quite literate, it was also possible to view the two deaths as terrible accidents, although the coincidence was admittedly startling. This ambiguity would hover over the case even after the trial was over.

*   *   *

In October 2002, District Attorney Jim Hardin Jr. announced his intention to exhume Ratliff's body for a second autopsy. In April 2003, he and the medical examiner stated that Ratliff had been the victim of a homicide. Now things looked bleak for the fiction writer—the last one to see two different women alive before they took a fatal fall.

Oddly, Peterson allowed a team of French documentary makers to film him, his attorneys, and his family members. They took more than 650 hours of footage that produced an eight-hour program, *The Staircase*, which followed everyone involved but focused specifically on the defense. Peterson seemed to believe that his attorneys were planning an effective strategy and that he would be exonerated. In the documentary, he was often in a positive frame of mind.

In July, after a lengthy jury selection process, Peterson's trial began for first-degree murder; it lasted four months. Hardin, joined by ADA (assistant district attorney) Freda Black, insisted that Peterson, a former Marine, had battered his wife to death with a fireplace "blow poke," which had mysteriously disappeared from the home, and then fabricated the story about his wife's fall. In light of the Ratliff autopsy results, Peterson's situation appeared highly suspicious. Hardin stated that he did not need to prove a motive, but he hypothesized that Peterson had earned little that year from his writing (he was the author of *A Time of War* and *A Bitter Peace*), and the couple had been spending beyond their means. Killing Kathleen would gain him a $1.8 million insurance payout, sufficient to settle debts and continue his lavish lifestyle. During the trial, Hardin added another motive: Kathleen, eleven years younger than Michael, may have learned about her husband's attempt that evening to arrange a secret homosexual liaison and had argued with him over it.

The defense team, led by Rudolf, insisted that Kathleen's head injuries were not consistent with a beating. She'd experienced an episode of hypoxia from head injuries related to the fall. Her inability to help herself was the result of a night of drinking at the poolside. They provided the following scenario: As her husband stayed outside at the pool area, near a running fountain that was on, Kathleen climbed the stairs in flimsy plastic sandals, blacked out, and fell backward and struck her head. She lay bleeding and then tried to get up. She slipped in her own blood and hit her head again. She struggled there, trying to get up, coughing and wheezing, expelling blood all over the stairwell. Their experts indicated that this could have taken place over a stretch of time, accounting for the amount of blood.

Since there was no evidence of violence between the Petersons and good evidence that he and Kathleen had experienced a warm relationship, it seemed unlikely that Peterson would just start beating his wife, even during an argument. Supposedly, Kathleen already knew about Peterson's bisexuality, and while she might be annoyed, it would hardly amount to a battle to the finish.

Rudolf claimed that the prosecution did not collect data to support its theory about motive until just before the trial, suggesting it was hurried, and in any event there would not have been sufficient financial gain for Peterson to justify this motive. He maintained that the Durham police had a vendetta against Peterson due to columns he had written over a period of years criticizing them for their inept handling of cases, so they were skewing the investigation toward implicating him. Given their shoddy work at the scene, their interpretations were not trustworthy.

The key factors in the trial were the amount and placement of the blood spatters (some ten thousand individual spatters), and the nature and number of lacerations on Kathleen's skull. (While police claimed to have discovered bloody footprints going from the body to a utility sink and other places via luminol, they had failed to take photographs of them.) Also at issue was whether Peterson had done other things as his wife lay dying rather than calling for immediate assistance, and why he had blood spatters inside the hem of his tan shorts. That meant involving experts on both sides to offer interpretations that would tip the scales in favor of homicide or accident.

A paramedic who arrived at the scene testified that he'd never seen so much blood. Some of it, he thought, was already dry. But he was not an expert and had only seen one other fatal fall incident. He thought Kathleen had died some time before he'd arrived, but the judge told jurors to disregard that comment.

The jury also saw a video of Kathleen lying at the foot of the stairs, shot by a crime scene technician. In that footage, Michael's socks and shoes were sitting next to the body, as were bloody towels. They learned that Michael had grabbed Kathleen and held her, and that his son had pulled him away. Under cross-examination, the crime scene tech, Dan George, was forced to admit to a number of errors in processing the scene and allowing it to become contaminated. Key items were not taken into evidence, and a few other items were mishandled. Notes were brief or nonexistent, and the police themselves had caused some of the contamination.

The prosecution's expert on Kathleen's injuries, Dr. Deborah Radisch, had performed the autopsy and also the second autopsy on Elizabeth Ratliff. Radisch testified to the similarities between the two deaths and said that from her experience with wounds, she believed

BLOOD SPATTER PATTERN INTERPRETATION

When bodies bleed while the heart is still pumping, the behavior of blood tends to be uniform. When blood flies through the air from an impact, the pattern in which it lands can determine its track and the location and position of the implement that inflicted the blow. Layered spatters can indicate how many blows took place, and the way it rests where it landed can indicate the weapon's momentum. Generally, multiple blows will result in "cast-off" blood, which flies away from the weapon as it is being wielded back at the victim. Blood that pools or drips tells a different story, and impressions can be left in blood that assist with reconstruction of the crime.

Defendant Michael Peterson listens as SBI special agent and blood
spatter expert Duane Deaver testifies during Peterson's trial.
AP/Wide World Photos

that Kathleen had been beaten to death, because the wounds were
too numerous to have occurred during a fall. She said that Kathleen
had defensive wounds on her hands and broken cartilage in her
throat, which also indicated an attempt to strangle her.

Peter "Duane" Deaver, the blood spatter expert from the North
Carolina Bureau of Investigation, who had run simulation experiments that got similar results, said that three distinct patterns indicated that Kathleen had been bludgeoned with a weapon: blood
spatter on the adjacent hallway wall as high as nine feet was possibly
cast off from a weapon being raised to hit again; other blood on the
door molding indicated that Kathleen had been standing; and eight
drops of blood inside Peterson's shorts offered proof that he was close
to her when she was hit. Also, it appeared that a blood pattern on the
stairs indicated that the weapon was placed there. He concluded that
Kathleen had been assaulted by someone using a fireplace blow poke,
and Kathleen's sister had allegedly given the Petersons a blow poke as
a gift. Thus, one had been in the home, but it was now missing.

For the defense, Dr. Jan Leetsma, a forensic neuropathologist, indicated that the speed of the fall and the angle of the head, among other factors, could cause death without leaving the effect of a *contre-coup* injury, expected from a blow to the back of the head. He had examined 257 beating deaths and believed that Kathleen's injuries were inconsistent with a beating. In his estimate, she had sustained four blows, not seven. He concluded that a beating death with a blow poke was inconsistent with his findings, while a fall down the stairs was not.

Then the renowned criminalist Dr. Henry Lee testified. As a former commissioner for the Department of Public Safety and chief criminalist and director of the Connecticut State Police Forensic Science Laboratory in Meriden, Connecticut, he had testified in numerous high-profile cases, most notably offering a consultation for the O. J. Simpson defense team that was instrumental in that acquittal. Chief emeritus for the Connecticut Division of Scientific Services, he helped set up the Henry C. Lee Forensic Institute, had consulted in all fifty states and thirty-nine countries, and estimated that he had assisted law enforcement in over six thousand cases around the world.

Lee stated that the blood spatter was consistent with a finding of accidental death, as Kathleen's repeated coughing as she lay dying could have caused that much blood to spray on the walls. He could not rule out a bludgeoning, he admitted, but did find inconsistencies with that theory. Most notably, there was a lack of the expected type of cast-off patterns and damage to the adjacent surfaces by the swinging of a forty-inch blow poke in a confined area. In defense of criticism that he did not conduct his own experiment to establish the point of origin of the blood, he attested that his experienced eye was as good as techniques using computers or string. Further, activities conducted by the state's crime scene investigators had altered the original pattern. He did not agree that the marks of blood high on the wall in the adjacent hallway indicated cast-off from a weapon, and he bolstered his testimony by coughing and spitting diluted ketchup onto a white poster board to show how it made different patterns.

Dr. Faris Bandak, a biomechanical research scientist, indicated that Kathleen had experienced a ground-level fall. He had used Kathleen's height and weight, with the dimensions of the staircase and stairwell, to calculate the incident, and showed the jury a computerized animation of what he believed had occurred. The animation depicted her walking up the steps, falling backward, and striking her head on a ridged molding on a doorjamb. Then her head grazed the wall as she fell, hitting a stair edge. She then tried to stand but slipped and fell again, with multiple impacts. Bandak disagreed that an implement like the blow poke could have caused the injuries, but seemed unable to explain the facial bruising.

Rudolf also had a surprise in store. The prosecution had claimed that the murder weapon, the fireplace blow poke, was missing, but Rudolf produced a blow poke that he indicated had been found in the Peterson's garage a few days earlier. It was an embarrassing moment for the investigators, and they were certain it had never been there. Nevertheless, the dust-covered implement had clearly not been used in a beating death, and the prosecution had no alternative weapon in mind. They offered the possibility that the blow poke Rudolf produced was not the only one in the house.

On rebuttal, Dr. James McElhaney, a professor emeritus of engineering, said that the injuries Kathleen sustained were not consistent with a fall. He believed that something light and cylindrical had caused them, and he had calculated the velocity needed, which was more consistent with a beating than a fall. Still, he conceded that the defense scenario was possible.

Also, Dr. Saami Shaibani indicated that from experiments he had done where he asked subjects to fall backward to see where they hit, Kathleen could not have fallen. However, Shaibani's credentials came into doubt during the trial, causing some havoc, and his testimony was stricken.

Chief medical examiner John Butts, who had supervised Dr. Radisch's autopsies, indicated that Kathleen had not had a sufficient amount of blood in her lungs to have aspirated so much onto the walls. He did admit, when pressed, that Kathleen had consumed a sufficient amount of Valium and alcohol to cause a blackout and fall.

Hardin's closing argument emphasized the fact that the victim had sustained thirty-eight separate injuries to the face, skull, back, hands, and wrists, for which he said that even two separate falls could not account. He believed the defense's argument was counter-intuitive. A fiction writer makes things up, and in this case Peterson had fabricated the scenario of an accident. Hardin was defensive about the blow poke, and reminded jurors that the two staircase deaths associated with Peterson were linked. He then said that Kathleen had grown angry over a homosexual liaison, adding that Peterson had checked his e-mail as his wife lay dead on the stairs—unexpected behavior for a grieving widower. He did not repeat the financial motive.

The defense witnesses had made some telling points as well. In closing, Rudolf reiterated that there had been no plausible motive and offered ten reasons for doubt. Among them were that the supposed murder weapon had not been used; there was no history of violence between the two; there was no brain trauma or skull fracture evident on Kathleen; the blood spatter was not the result of blunt force impacts; there was no spatter on Peterson's shirt or glasses; the spatter on his shorts was in the back; and the investigation was shoddy and the information it produced unreliable. He had intended to demonstrate with a blow poke and mannequin what would actually happen had this implement been used, but scrapped that plan. He also ignored the theory floated by some of Peterson's friends that an owl had committed the crime. (They thought some of the gashes on Kathleen's body resembled marks made by talons, and her struggle with the bird would explain all the blood; they could not explain how the owl got in and out or why it left no feathers.)

The jurors took six days to reach a conclusion, and on October 10, 2003, they convicted Michael Peterson of first-degree murder. He received life in prison without parole, to be served at Nash County Correctional Center.

The jurors then talked with the press, saying they were confident of their decision. They had not accepted the defense's theory about the amount of blood in the stairwell and the lacerations to Kathleen's head. Suspicious about the blow poke's sudden appearance after no one could find it, they believed that Peterson had attacked his wife and then could not stop before it became fatal. One woman said about Peterson's trial demeanor, "He didn't react the way you would think someone would react. Lots of times he seemed lighthearted."

The case was appealed, but in 2006 the state appeals court refused to overturn the conviction. Peterson had argued that he did not get a fair trial because of judicial mistakes, such as erroneously allowing evidence about his bisexuality, Ratliff's death, and the Petersons' finances, but two of the three judges on the panel rejected the reasoning. Peterson's appeals attorney, Thomas Maher, said he planned to go to the Supreme Court. The dissenting judge had noted that there was insufficient evidence to prove that Ratliff had been murdered and insufficient similarity between the deaths to even include the Ratliff case in the trial.

Kathleen's daughter, Caitlin Atwater, brought a civil suit against her stepfather for the wrongful death of her mother. That would give her attorneys a chance to question him about the incident in a way that the prosecutors could not during the criminal trial. However, the suit was settled outside the courtroom for $25 million, an amount that Atwater will likely never receive from the bankrupted Peterson. If his conviction is overturned at some future date, the deal is void, as it was not an admission of guilt.

It's interesting to note that the *C.S.I.* episode inspired by this case retained its ambiguity, while adding elements for its own twist.

SOURCES

"Appeals Court Refuses to Overturn Murder Conviction of Novelist Michael Peterson." CourtTV.com, September 19, 2006.

Fanning, Diane. *Written in Blood*. New York: St. Martin's, 2005.

"Friends of Convicted Novelist Argue Owl May Have Committed Murder." Associated Press, December 13, 2003.

"Jurors in Peterson Case Discuss Their Verdict." Associated Press, October 15, 2003.

"Lawyer Looks Forward to Questioning Peterson about Murder." Associated Press, December 28, 2006.

"Peterson Lawyer Says Blow Pokes Were Ordered for Closing Arguments." Associated Press, March 20, 2004.

"The Staircase Murder." Maha Productions, 2004.

North Carolina v. Michael Peterson. Trial coverage on CourtTV.com, 2003.

two

C.S.I.: "Felonious Monk": A group of monks is shot execution-style in a Buddhist temple, but not for robbery, and graffiti on the wall implicates a local gang.

TRUE STORY: Nine people, including six monks, were massacred at a Buddhist temple in Arizona in 1991.

The officer stopped a teenager driving on Luke Air Force Base west of Phoenix, Arizona. His name was Rolando Caratachea, age seventeen, and his teenage friend, who stopped behind him, was Jonathan Doody. It was a routine stop for "suspicious activity," and the officer spotted a rifle slung across the passenger-side seat. He made a note for his records but allowed the boys to continue on their way.

It was August 20, 1991, ten days after a horrific event in nearby Waddell in which this rifle had played a part, but the officer did not realize its significance. He had received no communication about looking for just such a weapon in the hands of a teenager.

On August 21, the boys were riding together in the same car and the same officer stopped them once again. This time the rifle was not present, so he asked where it was. Caratachea said it was in his car, parked at Doody's house, which was located on the base. The officer went to search the car, and when he found the rifle illegally concealed, he called a sheriff's deputy. The deputy came to the home and ran a check on the boys, who had no record and were not suspected of anything. He let them keep the rifle and decided not to write up the incident, but the base officer did. He did not realize then that a seemingly minor detail in his careful records would help solve a difficult case.

On Saturday, August 10, a woman arrived to deliver food to the monks at the Wat Promkunaram Buddhist temple. She noticed that irrigation water was running for the vegetable gardens, although none of the six monks who resided there was outside. Among them lived a monk-in-training, a nun, and her seventeen-year-old grandson. All were from Thailand, practicing Theravada, which required strict monastic discipline. They sought harmony within their existence and promoted good by helping others.

Letting herself into the L-shaped building, always unlocked, the woman prepared to assist with the morning meal. Soundlessly, she moved through the carpeted temple area, where a lifesize golden Buddha sat inside an alcove among a wealth of ornate religious items on a wide altar. Near the statue was a money tree, a regular feature in Buddhist ceremonies, and attached to its branches were dollar bills representing unlimited riches.

Opening the door to the living quarters, she was shocked by what she saw. In the small living room, next to a couch, all nine residents, dressed in their orange-yellow saffron robes, were arranged like the spokes of a wagon wheel, facedown on the floor. But this was no act of community devotion. Their clothing and the carpet around them were soaked in blood, and they lay completely still. The woman ran to call the police.

The Maricopa County Sheriff's Office sent out officers to protect the scene and detectives to start looking for leads. It was clear that this shocking mass slaughter would fast evolve into an international incident, so they called the FBI to request profilers. Special Agents Gregg McCrary and Tom Selp were soon on their way.

The lead investigator, Sheriff Tom Agnos, had never seen anything like this. It was an unspeakable act of brutality against seemingly gentle people, and one victim had been an elderly woman. All had been shot at close range to the back of the head, more than once.

Crime scene at the Wat Promkunaram Buddhist temple in Maricopa County, Arizona.
Gregg McCrary

It appeared to be an outright mass execution, and with the exception of a monk who was out of alignment with the others, they seemed to have accepted this fate without a fight. Their fingers were interlaced behind their necks, as if posed that way, and they had probably been on their knees. It looked as if some had died while praying.

It was soon clear that while these people had been killed with one type of weapon, a few had wounds on their arms from a different type. On the floor around the bodies were three shell casings from a 20-gauge shotgun, and around the scene were more casings from a .22-caliber weapon, but some were .22 shorts, some .22 longs, and some long rifle rounds. The shotgun load had been birdshot.

Looking for evidence, investigators spotted a full ashtray in the middle of the circle of death—surely not from the monks. They also observed that two fire extinguishers had been sprayed randomly around the home's interior as an act of vandalism. Two sets of footprints showed in the dust, and since the monks did not wear shoes, this was good evidence. A technician lifted the impression with an electrostatic dust lifter. In addition, a pile of keys lay on the kitchen table, and the word *bloods* had been carved crudely into one wall.

Among the dead, the temple abbot had been thirty-six. Most of the other monks had been in their thirties or forties, although the nun had been seventy-five, and her grandson a teenager. The murdered temple helper had been twenty-one. Each had a room with a single mattress on the floor and few possessions.

Since the victims were from Thailand, investigators believed there was a chance that at least one had been connected to drug imports, as there was a brisk heroin trade in the area via Asia. Maybe the goods had been distributed but the account not paid up. People were often executed for such oversights. However, this did not account for the vandalism or pile of keys. Drug-sniffing dogs also found nothing inside the austere residence. Two alerted on a ceremonial rug, but no narcotics were found.

Revenge was proposed, as investigators considered the possibility that one of the monks was having an affair with someone else's wife, since a red-and-white late-model Ford Bronco II had been seen leaving the premises around 7:00 A.M. that morning. Yet why would an angry husband execute everyone else, especially in this bizarre manner? And why pile up the keys or spray the fire extinguishers?

Then there was the wall-carving in letters two feet tall, *bloods*. The police knew of a gang in Phoenix called the Bloods, but there seemed to be no clear reason why they would target peace-loving monks living in a temple many miles from the city rather than another gang nearer to them. No one took this potential lead very seriously, although the *Arizona Republic* later mentioned it as a possibility.

A hate crime was also possible, since these Thai monks had settled into a conservative area, but neighbors reported being on good terms with them. Some said that the monks were always willing to help, even if the person in need did not belong to their religion. They gave out food from their gardens freely.

That brought investigators to the idea of robbery, although this had not been carried out with any great expertise. While a number of valuable items remained untouched in the temple, including the money tree, it turned out that items such as cameras and stereo equipment were missing from the bedrooms. The monks also had shared a communal van, and it was their keys to the van that lay piled on a table, as if the person sorting through them was looking for a specific key, perhaps to a safe. Yet a safe nearby was untouched.

Special Agents Selp and McCrary looked at all the evidence and walked through the crime scene before the bodies were removed. From an initial victimology, they determined that there was nothing that elevated the risk of this group attracting such a fate. They had no known enemies. It was the profilers' opinion that the massacre had been committed by two youthful offenders who knew or had known someone associated with the temple. They had used guns and ammunition from a basic hunting collection and had not known where to look for valuables, what few there were. The full ashtray indicated that the executions had taken place over a period of time, as if for entertainment. Selp and McCrary recommended to the sheriff that his officers canvass the area for teenagers using these types of weapons who had some association with the temple.

As a start, the police confiscated licensed weapons of the right caliber for testing, to at least eliminate them as the murder weapon. Sheriff Agnos set up an 800 number for citizens to call in. Other people involved in the temple were questioned, but none had any idea who might have done this brutal act. People in the temple congregation attested to the monks' willingness to help out at almost any time.

Agnos assigned a task force, the members of which began to learn everything they could about the monks. It was possible that something in one's background would generate more leads or even connect that person with someone who fit the profile. They soon discovered that the monks had worn jewelry, which was missing, so they listed this as an item for which to search in local pawnshops.

But the task force ran out of leads. Then an unusual phone call shifted the investigation in a new direction.

*   *   *

On September 10, investigators received a call from a man in the
Tucson Psychiatric Institute who claimed he could tell them exactly
who had been involved in the massacre, because he himself had been
the lookout man. He gave his name and hung up. It seemed odd that
he'd just turn himself in, but it had to be investigated.

Around the same time, the Office of Special Investigations at
Luke Air Force Base called the sheriff to report that base police had
come across a .22-caliber rifle. In their records were notations about
the traffic stops on August 20 and 21 involving the local boys, one of
which was of Thai descent. The task force got a search warrant and
seized the rifle, but one officer said it was then placed behind a door
and accidentally forgotten. Thus, it was not tested for six weeks.

However, the two boys with a gun no longer mattered. The sheriff believed he had a viable suspect who could provide details about
the crime. Members of the task force drove to Tucson.

The surprise caller had given his name as Michael McGraw, and
police found a Michael McGraw, 24, at the institute for drug treatment. Yet when they talked with him, he denied making such a call
and insisted that someone else had done it to set him up. The officers
nevertheless took him into an interrogation room and kept him there
for nearly two days. They said he mentioned the word "bloods,"
which made them certain they had the right person. (He'd actually
asked if there had been blood on the wall.) Eventually he broke
down and confessed to being involved in the temple massacre and
implicated four other young men: Mark Felix Nunez, 19; Leo
Valdez Bruce, 28; Dante Parker, 20; and Victor Zarate, 27. Two were
ex-cons.

These men were brought in and questioned while their homes
were searched. After long hours of exhausting interrogation, all four
confessed. Along with McGraw, they were detained for a grand jury
hearing, and the task force concentrated on getting physical evidence
to corroborate their story. On September 13, the Major Crimes Task

Force, composed of sixty-six investigators, announced the arrest of the five Tucson men. But they were in for a nasty surprise.

McGraw immediately called the press and recanted his confession. His interrogators had fed him information, he said, and had shown him diagrams and charts, insisting that he draw the same pictures and repeat everything they said back to them. "I did exactly what they told me to do," he claimed. For over forty-four hours, he told a reporter, there were as many as thirty investigators questioning and threatening him. He insisted he had not made the call that brought them to Tucson, and he'd been denied rest, food, and his requests for a lawyer. He'd been kept in the room the entire time, so he'd had to urinate into soda cans. His rights were violated, and he'd been humiliated.

The other four suspects recanted as well, insisting that they had been interrogated for so long, with no regard for their physical needs, that they had finally said whatever the police wanted to hear just to get a break. Two of them reported that before the interrogation, they were placed in a room containing charts and photographs associated with the massacre. From these they had gleaned enough information to tell their interrogators details about the crime. A couple said that the police had even read them the confessions of the others who had capitulated before them, so they could get the details "right."

However, the police countered their claims with the fact that the suspects had offered details about the crime not generally known and not available to them. Not only that, simple logic went against these men: Who in their right mind would falsely implicate themselves in a capital crime, knowing they could get the death penalty?

The police pointed out that the suspects had all agreed on what had occurred. Accordingly, on the afternoon of August 9, they had driven to Phoenix in two cars, a Ford Bronco and a Chevrolet Blazer. They had then met in south Phoenix with three young men from the area before going to the temple later in the evening to rob it. Parker even described a spiral-shaped ring taken from one of the monks that the deputies did not know was missing. He also described how one monk had resisted them and added that a nun had entered the room where they had rounded up the men and startled them. She, too, had been shot.

That seemed to bring an end to the many questions: This incident had been a robbery, with the elimination of witnesses. The police fully expected to find evidence to nail these men in court. Yet none of the shoes of any of the men fit the footprints lifted from the temple floor, and no one had a weapon that had been used that night. Then, to their embarrassment, videotapes exonerated Victor Zarate, showing that he was at work at Tucson Greyhound Park at the time he said he had driven to Phoenix. He was released, but the others remained behind bars. They came to be known via the press as the Tucson Four. Three grand juries were convinced that, with their confessions, there was sufficient preliminary evidence to hold Bruce, Nunez, and McGraw for trial. A judge decided that Parker should also be held.

On October 24, the Arizona Department of Public Safety announced its finding on the rifle taken from Rolando Caratachea, finally found behind the door: They had a match between the casings from the temple and the ones fired by this .22-caliber semiautomatic Marlin rifle. Caratachea said he had loaned the rifle to Jonathan Doody and his friend, Alex Garcia.

The task force got a warrant to search the apartment where Doody lived with sixteen-year-old Alessandro "Alex" Garcia. They were students at Agua Fria High School and participants in the Air Force ROTC program. The search turned up a 20-gauge Stevens shotgun, which was soon matched to the other shell casings found at the crime scene. The investigators also found two knives, a camouflage hat, two face masks, and gloves. In Garcia's parents' home they located duffel bags, one of which was filled with miscellaneous army equipment, and they got tips that certain items had been pawned.

When investigators talked with the families, they learned that

Doody had visited the temple when his younger brother, David, had been involved there. The information was consistent with the FBI profile—a couple of local kids with an association with the temple. The boys were arrested.

Yet Sheriff Agnos insisted that the Tucson Four not be released. He hinted that he had a source of information that would back away if that happened, and that he still had leads to follow. He pointed out that the FBI was still analyzing hair and fibers collected at the temple. Until those results were finalized, the men should stay in jail. He added that the confessions had been solid, because streetwise men—especially men who'd already been in prison—would not have admitted to something they didn't do, knowing it would have dire consequences.

Yet Maricopa County attorney Rick Romely examined the case and came to the conclusion that they had no solid evidence against the men. He questioned how the confessions were obtained, especially since the interrogators had used information from McGraw's confession to pressure the others. The interrogations lasted for so many hours that the men had been exhausted. But there was evidence that what one man said had conflicted with another's account, and these contradictions and errors of fact raised considerable doubt. No

There are three types of false confessions: voluntary, coerced-compliant, and coerced-internalized, and each involves a different type of psychology. With voluntary confessions, people sometimes confess spontaneously, especially when a crime has received a lot of attention, in part because they want to associate themselves with the fame. More common are confessions that are coerced-compliant, in which the suspect eventually complies and says what interrogators want to hear. He or she does not actually believe it but says it anyway, and the reasons range from fatigue to youth to the desire to escape pressure. The coerced-internalized is rare and occurs after suspects have been pressured to confess to something they did not do and then come to believe they did.

defense attorney would ignore that. Romely asked Agnos to read the confessions word for word, but Agnos remained firm. For all they knew, the boys had been in league with the men from Tucson. Romely believed a judge would probably dismiss the charges at an impending hearing, and he intended to make that decision himself.

On November 22 the Tucson Four were released and the charges dismissed without prejudice. That meant that the county attorney was admitting that his office had no solid evidence to detain the men, but should such evidence surface in the future, they could be rearrested. Within days one of them sued the county for false arrest. Two others would follow, all of them claiming that they had been falsely arrested, falsely imprisoned, treated inhumanely, and illegally denied access to an attorney.

Doody and Garcia also confessed, although each pointed the finger at the other as the executioner. Their boots matched the footprints from the temple. At first, Garcia said there was no one involved but them, and he drew a sketch of the temple to show that he had been there. He got the lesser-known details right, such as the fact that rice had been spilled on the storeroom floor and that the nun's dentures were on a table by her bed. But in a later statement he said that others had taken part—which raised the hopes of the task force about the Tucson suspects. Under interrogation, Garcia gave two names, "Willis" and "Bruce," and mentioned a "black man" but implicated only himself and Doody in the actual murders.

Doody, too, eventually offered a confession, but he described events quite differently. He said he and Garcia were part of a larger gang. All of them had initially met by the Agua Fria River around 8:30 that evening (not the same place as where the Tucson men had described a similar meeting), and then set off to rob the temple. One of the monks recognized someone in their party, so Doody said he was told to go outside. While away from the scene, someone—he did not know who—started shooting people. Doody said that the crime had begun as a "challenge" to see if they could beat the temple's sensor-alarm system, although he could not explain the reason for bringing guns, knives, and military gear. He said the group had threatened to harm his family if he told.

He also implicated some friends, notably Caratachea, who was detained, but the police turned up no evidence against him. The rifle was his, but he denied knowing how Doody was planning to use it.

Doody got a lawyer, who claimed that his interrogation was as problematic as those to which the Tucson Four had been subjected. He was just a teenager but had been held and questioned for fourteen hours, and during the first half of that time he had not admitted to anything. The interrogation had produced 950 pages of transcripts, an indication of how long it had been. Nevertheless, the physical evidence was strong. A judge soon decided that the boys would be tried as adults, with the potential penalty of death. They went to prison to await trial.

In 1993, Garcia struck a plea deal for life in prison in exchange for testifying against Doody. He described how Doody had shot the monks and returned to each one to repeat it. Three weeks later he admitted to another crime for which a mentally challenged man had been coerced to confess. In October 1991, two months after the temple massacre, Garcia and his fourteen-year-old girlfriend Michelle had murdered Alice Cameron, age fifty, in a campground. Garcia had goaded Michelle into pulling the trigger, supposedly to prove her love. They then stole the woman's money, about twenty dollars. Michelle pled guilty and received fifteen years. It was clear that Garcia was a dangerous young man, and had he not been arrested, he might have continued to kill.

At Jonathan Doody's trial in May 1993, Garcia revealed his version of what had happened on the night of August 9, 1991. The initial plan, he said, had been merely to rob the monks. He and Doody had obsessed about it for two months, after they heard from Doody's brother about the solid gold Buddha and a safe that supposedly contained $2,000. According to some reports, David Doody had said that the monks also kept money, cameras, and guns in their rooms. To the boys, it had seemed like easy pickings. Doody apparently had his eye on a car that cost $1,000, and after their "hit" he intended to buy it. To make it interesting, they turned their planned intrusion into a "war game."

They purchased military clothing and gear, including snow boots, camouflage hats, scarves, goggles, and harnesses with knives. Doody borrowed the rifle from Caratachea, and Garcia smuggled his uncle's shotgun out of his father's house. They added silencers and tested both weapons in the White Tank Mountains. The silencers failed, but they were too excited about the plan to give it up. The temple was fairly isolated, with no immediate neighbors, so whatever shooting they might do, they believed, would probably not be heard.

On the evening of August 9 they went to a party and then drove to the temple between 10:00 and 10:30 P.M. They watched for activity, left for a while, and then returned and burst in, ordering the residents to the floor. They arranged them in a circle, kneeling and facing one another, and for an hour one held them at gunpoint while the other searched for keys to the safe and committed general vandalism. To their surprise, the monks did not resist. At one point a nun came in to find out what was going on, and they forced her on her knees to join the men. Her nephew was already there.

The boys managed to grab over $2,600 in cash and change, along with cameras and stereo equipment, although they never found the key to open the safe. At this point, Garcia said, he wanted to leave, but Doody resisted. His plan was to eliminate witnesses, which meant killing everyone there. He was afraid some of them knew him because of his brother's association with the temple. Standing on a couch over his kneeling prey, he started shooting them. Garcia reluctantly used the shotgun to wound some of them, but he insisted that he had not killed anyone. Then, as an afterthought, he carved the word *bloods* on the wall in the hallway.

On July 12, 1993, over his attorney's continued protest about the interrogation, Jonathan Doody was convicted of nine murders and eleven other criminal counts, and sentenced to 281 years in prison. The prosecutor had sought the death sentence, but since Doody had his own version of what had happened, which exonerated him, the judge decided the situation of "he said/he said" was too ambiguous for such an extreme conclusion. No one could be certain which of the boys had actually pulled the rifle's trigger (although it was more likely that Doody, who had borrowed it, had used it). While the sentence erred on the side of caution, it ensured that Doody would never be free. Alessandro Garcia was sentenced to 271 years in prison, the maximum possible under his plea agreement, a deal that helped him escape the death penalty.

The Tucson men who had sued Maricopa County for false imprisonment and a violation of their rights received a settlement of $2.8 million. The man implicated in the campground murder, who had been imprisoned for a year and faced the death penalty, received more than $1 million.

In 1996 the Arizona Court of Appeals, examining the allegation that Doody's confession had been extracted without a parent present, upheld the conviction and the prison sentence.

SOURCES

"Buddhist Monk Murders." *Medical Detectives*, Medstar, Episode MD 504.

Cannon, Lou. "Sheriff Rejects 'Hate Crime' in Phoenix Temple Killings: 50 Officer Task Force, Aided by FBI, to Investigate." *Washington Post*, August 13, 1991.

Conti, Richard P. "The Psychology of False Confessions." *Journal of Credibility Assessment and Witness Psychology* 2, no. 1 (1999): 14–36.

Fitzpatrick, Tom. "Dealing with a Confessed Serial Killer." *Phoenix New Times*, January 13, 1993.

Kelleher, Michael D. *Flash Point: The American Mass Murderer*. Westport, CT: Praeger, 1997.

Martin, Philip. "The Sheriff's Suspects: The Whole World's Watching His Investigative Work in the Buddhist Temple Murders." *Phoenix New Times*, December 11, 1991.

————. "Teenage Wasteland: Death and Boredom in the West Valley." *Phoenix New Times*, February 19, 1992.

McCrary, Gregg, and Katherine Ramsland. *The Unknown Darkness: Profiling the Predators among Us*. New York: Morrow, 2003.

"Monks Mark Temple Slaying's Tenth Anniversary." *Arizona Republic*, August 10, 2001.

Pancrazio, Angela Cara. "Time to Remember 1991 Massacre at Thai Buddhist Temple." *Phoenix Gazette*, August 10, 2006.

"Twelve Years Ago, Nine Were Slain in West Valley Temple. *Arizona Republic*, August 5, 2003.

three

C.S.I.: "Shooting Stars": In an abandoned military compound, eleven members of a small cult are found dead, having committed suicide.

TRUE STORY: In 1997, thirty-nine members of a cult called Heaven's Gate committed suicide together.

Rio DiAngelo phoned the police on Wednesday, March 26, 1997. He had received videotapes by Federal Express from members of Heaven's Gate, all of whom were now dead inside a rented mansion in an area of San Diego, California, called Rancho Santa Fe. Believing they had shed their earthly "vehicles" to enhance their spiritual existence, he offered the address on 18241 Colina Norte so the bodies could be collected. He had already been there to videotape the scene.

Deputy Sheriff Robert Bunk went to the mansion that afternoon to check it out. The imposing building, surrounded by a tennis court and swimming pool, was eerily quiet, and an overpowering stench indicated the presence of corpses, just as the caller had said, so he called for backup and waited. Together, the two officers entered the home. Aware that a religious cult resided here, they recalled the mass suicide in Jonestown, Guyana, in 1989 and anticipated something similar, on a smaller scale. But the odor inside was intense. As they moved from room to room, they saw motionless human forms lying on bunk beds, shrouded with purple cloths. Two uncovered bodies

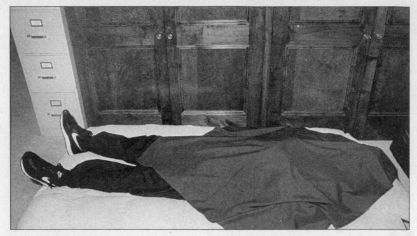

One of the thirty-nine bodies discovered in March 1997 in a mansion rented by the Heaven's Gate cult. The event was the largest mass suicide in the United States to date.
AP/Wide World Photos

had plastic bags tied over their heads, and they had clearly suffocated. One was in a bedroom alone, and all were in various stages of decomposition.

The officers counted thirty-nine corpses, all dressed alike in new black-and-white Nike tennis shoes, long-sleeved black shirts, and black sweatpants. On their left shirtsleeves were triangular armband patches emblazoned with the constellation Orion and the words "Heaven's Gate Away Team"—possibly a reference to the television program *Star Trek: The Next Generation*, on which a small crew, the "away team," went on planetary ventures. (One member had a sister who had played a role on this series.) Small overnight bags packed with clothing, lip balm, and spiral notebooks were at the foot of each bed. It was the largest mass suicide to occur to date in the United States, and it seemed likely that most had been assisted.

The San Diego County coroner arrived and went from one room to another, videotaping the scene before removing the bodies. Among the odd discoveries were twenty white plastic trash bags in the trash, along with elastic straps. On computer screens throughout the mansion were images of alien-human hybrids, along with one screen flashing a "Red Alert" from the Heaven's Gate website. Hundreds of videotapes found in the house featured cult members speaking to people they had left behind about how excited they were to be join-ing someone named Ti on a higher plane. Clearly, each person had died of his or her own free will and had wanted badly to do so. The member who had called in the incident, Rio DiAngelo, had lived among them, departing a month earlier, so he was able to report that the suicide had long been the plan, sparked by a recent astrological event.

After the autopsies, San Diego County Medical Examiner Brian Blackborne announced another shocking find: Seven members had been castrated, including the group's leader, Marshall Applewhite. In addition, inside the shirt pockets of each of the deceased the coroner found three quarters and a five-dollar bill. Investigators learned that members of the group had developed a habit of having this specific sum of money whenever they went out so that they would always have cab fare or change for the phone.

Among the victims, all Caucasian, were twenty-one women and eighteen men, ranging in age from 26 to 72. Unlike with other suici-dal cults, mercifully there were no children. Some research indicated that most of the deceased had joined Heaven's Gate during the 1970s, but eight converts were recent, including the sole survivor. He believed he was meant to be on earth to keep their message alive. The bodies were finally released to grieving and perplexed next-of-kin. Some openly said that their relative had done what seemed best, while others thought the cult member had been brainwashed and would otherwise never have committed such an act.

As many around the country wondered how people could so will-ingly take their own lives based on some man's belief that it was the right thing to do, they learned about the founders of Heaven's Gate. Marshall Herff Applewhite was the overachieving son of a Presbyter-ian minister. A class leader who could easily persuade people to accept his ideas, he had attended seminary but was dismissed from his teaching position at the University of Alabama School of Music over an affair with a male student. His wife left him, taking their two young sons, so he got another job, and yet again got entangled with a student, a young woman. In 1972 he admitted himself into a psychiatric hospital, according to some accounts, to cure his obsessions with sexuality. In his early forties he viewed himself as seriously ill. In retrospect he would regard this hospitalization as an interlude guided by higher powers.

Applewhite met a nurse, Bonnie Lu Trousdale Nettles, four years his senior and a member of the Theosophical Society. Her own marriage was falling apart, and she persuaded Applewhite that he was a powerful spiritual leader. They discovered a mutual fascination with UFOs, astrology, and science fiction, so Nettles urged Applewhite to read *The Secret Doctrine* by Madame Blavatsky. He believed what he read, and they opened a center in Houston for the study of metaphysics. They came to believe that they were the earthly incarnations of aliens millions of years old—the two witnesses mentioned in chapter 11 of the Book of Revelation, whom they believed had been on earth to save people. As "The Two," they embarked on an evangelical mission, severing ties with family and friends (she left her four children) and driving out of Houston to spread their message.

What they told people was similar to what many other end-times cult leaders preached: One day they would be persecuted and put to death by their enemies, their bodies would lie in the open for three and a half days, and they would prove their deity by rising from the dead and disappearing into a cloud. From there they would ascend to a higher level to be with God. They believed the biblical "cloud" was a spaceship that would welcome them aboard. It was their means of salvation from the "Luciferians," or evil aliens that enslaved humans through worldly concerns like jobs, sex, and families. They invited others to join them, and set up a press conference.

In Brownsville, Texas, Applewhite told a reporter that if he came to their meeting, they would give him the most significant story of his career. Believing it was about drugs, the reporter invited the authorities. When The Two spotted the police, they left, which aroused suspicions. Officers looked up the license plate number of their rental car, discovered that it had been reported stolen, and chased them down, placing them under arrest. They were charged with credit card fraud (charges were dropped) and car theft. Applewhite served six months in jail awaiting trial, and was convicted and sentenced to four more months.

Then he and Nettles went to Southern California to start spreading the word. They called their group HIM, for Human Individual Metamorphosis, and picked up twenty-five disciples. Their first official public meeting occurred in Waldport, Oregon, in 1975. For months beforehand, they had posted flyers on telephone poles urging people to attend the meeting to learn the truth. Two hundred people arrived.

The Two preached their message, insisting that to be saved, spiritual-minded individuals must recognize that few humans actually have souls. Only those who do can be harvested by God, and those people would recognize the truth of this message. Once they did, they would give up their worldly clutter at once, come under the control of The Two, and agree to follow a strict regimen. Using biblical notions about sexless angels and the praise Christ gave to those who sacrificed family life to follow him, they insisted that spiritual perfection came only at a price, but sacrifice was freedom.

Applewhite and Nettles didn't convince as many people as they had hoped, yet their strong belief in what they said, along with their intensity in delivering the message, proved compelling. The twenty people who followed them felt protected and reassured about their worth.

The Two gave several televised interviews about their beliefs and the miracles they would perform, which brought them nationwide attention. "We're going to stage, so that it can be witnessed," said Applewhite on a news broadcast, "that when a human has overcome his human-level activities, a chemical change takes place and he goes through a metamorphosis just exactly as a caterpillar does when he quits being a caterpillar and he goes off into a chrysalis and becomes a butterfly."

That did not mean they would leave their bodies behind in graves, he insisted. "We're going to be murdered and when we are, after three and a half days, we're going to walk up, just get right up, and you're going to watch us." During that same year, Applewhite and Nettles gave a date for their departure into outer space. The eager disciples learned that a spaceship was arriving to pick them all up, so they congregated on the specified night to await its approach. It didn't arrive at the expected time, so they sat up throughout the night and waited. Hours went by and nothing happened.

In the morning, Applewhite apologized for his mistake and invited anyone who desired to leave to go ahead. A few discouraged members returned to their families, but many remained. They had sacrificed too much to just walk away, and they wanted to achieve their higher destiny. Even when The Two reinterpreted their approaching resurrection to be metaphorical rather than actual, many followers still opted to await the next set of instructions. A peaceful and secretive group that participated in strict discipline, the members made occasional forays into recruitment, but most of their time was spent in rigorous training for reaching a higher consciousness.

Applewhite and Nettles followed this formula closely. They

CULT APPEAL

Groups such as Heaven's Gate that promise a higher order from extreme discipline appeal to people who feel frustrated with the way things are and are hungry for change. They also believe in the possibility of human perfection and an unprecedented social order. They like being ready for action because it feels as if total well-being is under their control and within their reach. Salvation is generally ensured through a charismatic leader who knows how to socialize converts, reinforce beliefs, and keep the group organized and focused. Monastic discipline, special diets, and social withdrawal cultivate dependence on the leaders and encourage the loss of individuality.

instructed their followers to cut their hair short, wear androgynous clothing—a uniform that would set them apart and also remove temptations of the flesh—and engage in daily training toward the end of becoming genderless, eternal beings. There was to be no more sexual contact and no personal privacy.

The members soon formed into an insulated community, sharing the same thoughts and repeatedly affirming the dogma and prophecies. They developed "crew-mindedness," as Applewhite called it, working together in a unified manner in the way they might have to function on a spaceship. Some of the men, like Applewhite, had themselves castrated to better resist sexual temptation.

Applewhite and Nettles also taught their disciples that they were all related. Applewhite was their "father" and Nettles, who posed as an alien that had inhabited an older human form, was their "grandfather." The Two renamed themselves variously as "Guinea" and "Pig," "Bo" and "Peep," and finally "Do" and "Ti." Disclaiming all earlier media reports about them, they went underground to fulfill their ultimate plan. Yet by the end of 1976, the group had diminished from 200 adherents to 80.

A legacy of $300,000 bequeathed to them allowed them to keep going. To attract more people, they promised spaceship rides for $433 and had dozens of takers.

In 1985, Ti grew ill from liver cancer and died. Applewhite promised she would be physically resurrected, but there was no sign of this miracle. Some followers began to question the doctrines, so Do continued to emphasize the discomfort that true believers have with mainstream American society. Ti was indeed alive, but was elsewhere. She had gone into space ahead of them to get things prepared. Now Applewhite described the bodies not as the means to get into heaven but as mere earthly vehicles that had to be shed. He promised that Ti herself would pilot the "mothership" that would carry them to a better place. Using *Star Trek* terminology during the television show's heyday made the idea even more familiar and inviting. The group continued, albeit a bit diminished. Applewhite tried to think of a way to recruit more believers.

In 1993 he launched a campaign for advancing into a form that was "more than human." Calling the group Total Overcomers Anonymous, he placed a large ad in *USA Today* to alert the American populace to the fact that the earth would soon be "spaded under" and they would have one last chance to escape. He went so far as to say that he had once lived as an alien inside the body of Jesus Christ, but during those days, the souls destined for saving had not been ready. Now they were and he was there, the same alien but in the body of Applewhite, to take those who were prepared. He managed to get a few more people aboard.

That year, Applewhite and his followers watched with the rest of the world as more than eighty members of the Branch Davidian cult in Waco, Texas, died after the ATF standoff. For the first time Applewhite began to collect guns and hint at a similar form of persecution aimed against him. Apparently he'd identified with David Koresh as a messiah figure, cut down by those who feared him. Several of his followers told a reporter for *LA Weekly* that they would all be departing soon. They were going to walk out to the Santa Monica pier and catch a ride into space.

However, that event did not take place, and in October 1996, they moved to Southern California, renting a 9,000-square-foot, nine-bedroom, seven-bathroom house in the wealthy community of Rancho Santa Fe. There they developed a lucrative computer business as website designers. They called the place "the Monastery" and their business "Higher Source." They also used the Internet's far-reaching communication capabilities to promote their beliefs and gather more disciples. At this time they took the name Heaven's Gate, and proposed to others that Applewhite was part of an evolutionary group that was "above human." His followers were students brought to earth from the kingdom of heaven. Some had crashed and the authorities had confiscated their bodies, but those who escaped took over human vehicles, tagged with special chips, and participated in their "classroom for growing a soul." They were preparing now to leave those vehicles so they could return to heaven. Indeed, earth would soon be destroyed, and those who left with the group would be saved from this fate. Then an event brought everything to a head.

Dr. Courtney Brown, claiming to be adept at "remote viewing," or seeing things that occurred far away and out of his normal line of vision, told nighttime radio host Art Bell that he was in possession of photographs of the approaching Hale-Bopp comet. They clearly showed a ringed object in its wake that had all the appearances of an alien craft. In fact, Brown said he'd "looked" inside and had seen alien life forms. This claim drew many expectant listeners who wanted to see the photos, including members of Heaven's Gate.

The revelation seemed to Applewhite to be what he was waiting for. Hale-Bopp's last visit had been in 2200 B.C., and had been viewed then as a harbinger for the arrival of a great teacher, or Peace-maker, who would visit many different civilizations around the world to deliver a sacred doctrine and save true believers from the end-time tribulations. The comet supposedly signaled the final three years of Satan's reign on earth and ushered in a more enlightened age. Do told the group that Ti had communicated telepathically to him that Hale-Bopp was the sign. On their Web page, the members excitedly announced Hale-Bopp's approach.

Sensing the arrival of the most significant event in their brief history, the crew-minded group went together to watch *Star Wars*, playing in a nearby theater. They also attended a UFO conference, bought insurance against alien abductions and impregnation, and purchased a high-powered telescope. They were looking for the "companion" to Hale-Bopp, they told the store manager. That was their mother-ship. But when they failed to find it, they returned the telescope. The manager found their ideas puzzling.

Then in January 1997, the promised photographs were posted on

Art Bell's website and then were subsequently exposed as a hoax. Yet the Heaven's Gate crew was not deterred. On their website they wrote, "Whether Hale-Bopp has a companion or not is irrelevant from our perspective." The comet's approach alone was "the marker we've been waiting for." Visible or not, the spaceship would be there, ready to take them home. They were about to "graduate" from human to more-than-human. Anyone reading their message might want to get "boarding passes."

By the end of that month, on January 23, a remarkable celestial event occurred: The outer planets of the solar system of which Earth is a part aligned themselves in what many people said was a six-pointed star. That is the Jewish star, the symbol of Jesus. The last time this alignment occurred was just before the Renaissance. Many people believed that something of universal significance was about to occur. For Heaven's Gate, it was an end and a beginning. At this time, Rio DiAngelo moved out, with Applewhite's support, so someone would be left who could receive their final communication, ensure the cleanup, and keep their message in front of other souls not yet ready to go. The other thirty-nine prepared for the day they had long awaited. Several went to Mexico to purchase supplies of the drug phenobarbital, and others prepared the rest of what they would need. They kept an eye on Sirius, the star at the foot of Orion that was their destination, and videotaped their "exit interviews."

On Friday, March 21, 1997, they cleaned the house and polished the silver. That night Applewhite and his followers went to a chain restaurant, Marie Callender's, where they ordered thirty-nine identical meals of salad and pot pies, and finished off with cheesecake. This was to be their final earthly meal, because the next day the comet would be in its closest proximity to earth. It was time to begin their departure.

On Saturday they started the process. By some reports, they drank juice first to purify their bodies. Then they donned identical outfits and packed identical bags for the trip. It was time to say good-bye to earth. They put out the garbage and left one door unlocked. They made a videotape that instructed their surviving member about how to get inside.

The story was revealed in documentaries they had made to help practice their routine for parting. They worked in three teams. The first team of fifteen received the barbiturate phenobarbital mixed into pudding or applesauce. They then drank vodka to wash it down. A lethal dose was some 50 to 100 pills. It's surmised from reconstructions that after consuming this toxic mix, they lay on their beds with plastic bags over their heads until they passed out. Those who still lived removed the bags and covered the bodies with purple shrouds. Then they probably participated in some ceremony of departure. The following day, Sunday, the next team of fifteen followed. Finally there were seven on Monday, and then only two, who took their own lives alone. The plastic bags were still on their heads, and no shrouds covered them.

DiAngelo received the video two days after the last of them had died. He went to the house, let himself in, and took video recordings of the bodies. Then he called the police.

Some former members were rather unhappy with the news. Wayne Cooke, 56, appeared on *60 Minutes* with Lesley Stahl to talk about his experience with Heaven's Gate and his feelings about missing the "graduation." There were tears in his eyes as he described what the departure meant and how much he wished he'd gone, too. In fact, his wife had been one of the thirty-nine. Five weeks later, on May 6, he and another former member, Chuck Humphrey, 55, both dressed in dark clothes, packed a bag, pocketed five dollars and three quarters, and used the same drugs to take their lives in a hotel room in Encinitas. Cooke succeeded, but Humphrey survived. In a video-tape, Cooke told his daughter he had to follow his wife. "I'm just really happy," he said.

Humphrey decided that he'd been held back to continue to pros-elytize, so he created a website to dispense Heaven's Gate theology.

He did as much as he thought he could to get the word out, and then in February 1998, he ended his life in the Arizona desert. He placed a plastic bag over his head and used his car's exhaust to fill it with carbon monoxide. Dressed in black with the requisite "fare," he left a purple shroud on the seat next to him with a note that said, "Do not revive." He called his suicide "an opportunity for me to demonstrate my loyalty, commitment, love, trust and faith in Ti and Do and the Next Level."

In 2007, Rio DiAngelo did an interview with *LA Weekly*, which had run a 1994 story about the cult that had inspired him to join. He said that he still believed in Applewhite's ideas and that he was still around to help other souls learn the truth.

SOURCES

Bearman, Josh. "Heaven's Gate: The Sequel." *LA Weekly*, March 21, 2007.

Gardetta, Dave. "They Walk among Us." *LA Weekly*, January 21, 1994.

Henry, William. *The Keepers of Heaven's Gate: The Millennial Madness*. Anchorage, AK: Earthpulse Press, 1997.

Holliman, John. "Applewhite: From Young Overachiever to Cult Leader." CNN.com, 1998.

Krueger, Anne, and Susan Gembrowski. "Strange Odyssey of Heaven's Gate." *San Diego Union-Tribune*, April 13, 1997.

Moran, Sarah. *The Secret World of Cults*. Surrey, England: CLB International, 1999.

Thornton, Kelly, and Susan Gembrowski. "Cult Claims Two New Victims." *San Diego Union-Tribune*, May 7, 1997.

Wessinger, Catherine. *How the Millennium Comes Violently*. New York: Seven Bridges Press, 2000.

four

C.S.I.: "Double Cross": Two nuns find the body of another nun crucified on a cross in a church, and a priest is the primary suspect. Bruises on the victim's neck indicate that she was strangled with rosary beads.

TRUE STORY: The investigation of Father Gerald Robinson for the 1980 murder of Sister Margaret Ann Pahl in a hospital chapel.

In June 2003, a nun wrote to the Catholic diocese review board in Toledo, Ohio, to accuse several local priests of satanic ritual abuse, including locking people in coffins and killing children. The letter found its way to the state attorney general's office, and on the list of priests was Father Gerald Robinson. While police could not substantiate the ritual abuse allegations, a cold case squad was aware that Robinson had been the sole suspect in a murder that had occurred over Easter weekend in 1980. That murder remained unsolved, and at the time there had been no evidence with which to charge anyone, but things had changed since 1980. If there was DNA available for analysis, for example, they could now achieve results that could either identify or eliminate a suspect. They could also do more refined crime scene analyses on blood and trace evidence.

Less than a year later, despite Robinson denying that he was near the chapel at the time of the murder, on April 23, 2004, he was under arrest. In his home, police found more than one hundred photos of corpses in caskets and a book on the occult, in which passages about satanic rituals were underlined. It was the first time in history that a

Roman Catholic priest was charged with the murder of a Roman Catholic nun, and it brought national attention to the investigation of cold cases.

Around eight in the morning of April 5, 1980, a nun found Sister Margaret Ann Pahl strangled and stabbed thirty-one times. About to turn seventy-two the next day, the frail victim had been undressed and exposed directly in front of the Holy Sacrament.

It was Holy Saturday, and only an hour earlier Sister Margaret Ann had eaten breakfast and risen to go prepare the chapel as part of her regular duties. There was evidence that she had begun to empty the altar of its sacred items and place them out of the way. Hard of hearing, she apparently did not even sense the other person in the chapel with her, behind her. Whoever was there knew just what he wanted to do as he wrapped a cloth around her neck and pulled it tight enough to force her necklace to make an impression in her skin and break the hyoid bone in her throat. He apparently believed that no one else would come in to disturb them at that hour.

The elderly nun was left on the floor of the chapel sacristy at Mercy Hospital in Tiffin, Ohio. She lay straight, staring up, her arms positioned at her sides. By some accounts, the murder had a ritualistic element, because a series of stab wounds supposedly took the

COLD CASES

By the mid-1990s, murder rates nationwide had declined, freeing homicide detectives in many departments to open the files of past unsolved cases. Thanks to dramatic new developments in forensic science and technology, the solution to some of those cases seemed promising. In the past decade, cold case units around the country have cleared hundreds of backlogged cases, putting criminals behind bars who had believed they'd escaped detection. Science and improved methods of detection have addressed crimes several decades old to both exonerate innocent individuals and convict the guilty.

shape of a cross, perhaps placed on her body upside down to get the pattern right. Nine distinct puncture wounds—three times the Holy Trinity—crossed her chest over the heart. But she had also been stabbed twenty-two more times along her left side, including her neck and jaw. The weapon used, a blunt item with a sharp edge, had been pressed against the sister's dress and forehead, as if in a symbolic gesture of anointment.

In addition, in what seemed a calculated humiliation, the killer rolled her dress up to her chest and yanked down her girdle, underwear, and pantyhose until he'd pulled them to her ankles and off her left leg. It gave the appearance of sexual assault. The final act was to insert an object inside her vaginal cavity, violating her, and then remove it and take it with him. A white linen altar cloth was wrapped around her forearm, partially draping her body. It was stained with her blood and it did not take investigators long to realize the nun had been stabbed through it. She had no defensive wounds, and there was no sign of a struggle.

An alarm was raised, and medical personnel rushed in to resuscitate her, contaminating the crime scene irreparably, but she was already dead. The assistant chaplain, Father Jerome Swiatecki, was at the scene, but the hospital administrator had to summon the chaplain, Father Robinson, and he came right away, claiming to have been in the shower. The police had already heard his name mentioned as a potential suspect, and it seemed odd to some that from his quarters just down the hall he had not heard the screaming of the nun who had found the body.

The latent print examiner found smudged prints on a door where a nun had seen a black man walk through at 7:00 A.M., acting strangely, and a strand of hair was collected from that door as well. The nun's body was removed midmorning, and staff were urged to clean up the small pool of blood that had collected under her head. Black-and-white photos were taken of everything.

A few days later, a cleaning woman went into Father Robinson's quarters and came across his letter opener. It was shaped like a sword, nine inches long, with a slightly curving, four-sided blade. It had a ribbed metal handle, knuckle guard, and a medallion featuring the U.S. Capitol building, as if it were a D.C. souvenir. She left it alone.

By that time, police were collecting information about possible enemies that the victim might have had. They believed this overkill had been committed by someone who knew her or by a wandering mental patient or crack addict. The former seemed more likely, despite the black man spotted in the halls. The woman's dress had been neatly rolled, not flung up to her chest in a delusional frenzy. But there were a great many people to check out before closing in on clear suspects.

On April 9, Father Robinson presided at Sister Margaret Ann's funeral mass. Rumors began right away that high-ranking police officers were conspiring with the Toledo diocese to cover up the murder if the investigation pointed to a priest. A number of detectives were of that opinion during the earliest stages of the investigation, simply because protocol had suddenly changed, without explanation.

As one of the two priests assigned to the hospital, Father Robinson had worked closely with Sister Margaret Ann. She was the chapel caretaker and by many accounts had a strained relationship with Robinson, whom some associates viewed as aloof and cold. He was known to consider Sister Margaret Ann domineering, and he disliked taking orders from her.

Robinson was brought into the police department for an interrogation, and he reiterated that he had been taking a shower. He said he had no keys to the chapel, which the nuns owned and operated, and would have no reason to borrow one. After a while he offered a striking bit of information: Someone had confessed the murder to him. But when the detective expressed surprise at this violation of trust, Robinson quickly said he'd fabricated it to take the pressure off. When police searched his quarters, they found the letter opener and confiscated it. Although the coroner had determined that the wounds could have been made with scissors similar to a pair missing from the sacristy, she thought that something sharper had been used on the victim's face. Suspiciously, the letter opener proved to be devoid of fingerprints and had been freshly polished. With a test, it appeared that a tiny drop of blood was present beneath the medallion, but it was too small for further testing, and thus could not be used as evidence.

Robinson was not charged with any crime at the time, as the only evidence against him was the possession of a lethal-looking souvenir from a Boy Scout troop. All the evidence went into police storage, including the letter opener and stained altar cloth, which were never examined for bloodstain patterns. A few officers tried reopening the case so that Sister Margaret Ann would get justice, but nothing came of these attempts. After the accusatory letter arrived mentioning Robinson as part of a cult of satanic priests, the DA's office hired forensic experts to reexamine the evidence. Robinson was quickly charged as well, possibly to prevent media leaks from tipping him off. He pled not guilty to the charge of aggravated murder, later reduced to murder without premeditation.

On May 19, 2004, the remains of Sister Margaret Ann were exhumed from St. Bernadine Cemetery. Most of the stab wounds were still visible on the embalmed corpse. Not only that, the bone of her left jaw retained a shallow impression of the murder weapon, so the deputy coroner removed that section to show to local forensic anthropologists Frank and Julie Saul. They cleaned and examined it, along with the suspected weapon, and declared it consistent with the shape of the letter opener. Bone trauma expert and forensic anthropologist Doctor Steven Symes, from Mercyhurst College, came to a similar conclusion, saying the letter opener could not be ruled out. Because it had an unusual shape, it was easier to identify via the marks it made than would have been a generic knife or pair of scissors.

A number of experts on the occult described for investigators how the arrangement of items at the crime scene, the shape of the victim's wounds, specialized knowledge about Catholic ceremonies, and the date chosen for the crime all pointed toward the probability that the crime had been a satanic ritual. The DA's office did not yet know if they would emphasize this angle as a motive, since the stabbings had shown much more vigor than that. In addition, they risked losing credibility in the courtroom.

By this time the famed criminalist Dr. Henry C. Lee had examined the evidence. As a former chief criminalist and director of the Connecticut State Police Forensic Science Laboratory in Meriden, Connecticut, he had assisted law enforcement around the world in over six thousand cases. From the victim's wounds and the blood evidence, Lee surmised that the killer had attacked the nun from behind, strangling her into unconsciousness. She fell to the floor, still alive but dying, as he then stabbed her in the face, neck, and through the altar cloth covering her upper body. Her heart had probably stopped, which accounted for so little blood. Lee thought the assailant had cut a deliberate pattern in her chest with the stabbing instrument, but did not speculate about satanic rituals.

He also examined the letter opener, the shape of the stab wounds, and the size and shape of the holes pierced through the altar cloth, and accepted that the instrument could have been the murder weapon. However, he did not identify Robinson's letter opener as the definitive weapon, since he could not say how many others were in

From about 1982–95, a hysteria arose in which people were accused of performing satanic rituals with children. Therapists used repressed memory techniques on the alleged victims to draw out what they had supposedly experienced. Children told stories that ranged from the shocking to the absurd, but many adults (mostly white, middle-class females) reported that they had been molested years earlier by neighborhood satanic cults and by priests. For a time the courts accepted repressed memories as sufficient evidence, and many people were convicted, but an FBI investigation turned up no evidence of the allegations. Eventually a backlash succeeded in freeing some of the imprisoned and persuading courts to require better evidence.

existence. He dismissed the failure of the earlier investigation to note the way the weapon matched certain bloodstains on the cloth as the state of the art at the time: There was no DNA analysis, microscopy was not as advanced, and pattern comparisons were not routine.

The key item of evidence that went against the prosecutors was that trace DNA from under the nun's fingernails, the altar cloth, and her underwear, while foreign to her and distinguishable as male, eliminated Robinson as the source. However, more witnesses had turned up who offered information that undercut the priest's supposed alibi and proved that he had lied to investigators.

The trial opened on April 17, 2006, when prosecutors played the video-recorded police interrogation from Robinson's 2004 arrest. There was little content, but when left alone, Robinson mumbled, "Sister." (His attorney contended that he had said, "You know I didn't do this, Sister.") He also seemed to be praying and in deep distress.

Yet by the fourth day, reporters noticed that there had as yet been no direct evidence presented against Robinson. Assistant District Attorney Dean Mandros kept driving home Robinson's known dislike of the victim, and her annoyance with him. One story offered was that Robinson had shortened the Good Friday services that year and Sister Margaret Ann had been distressed to the point of tears. It was possible they'd had an argument sufficiently forceful to set him off. His behavior after the crime was telling, as he fabricated a confession from a fictitious suspect and lied about being in his quarters.

While there had been some anticipation of a case about satanic practices, for Mandros it boiled down to an angry man who wanted to humiliate and degrade a woman. Their religious robes were incidental. "He had had enough," Mandros said. "He had taken a lot from her, but he was not going to take any more."

As one witness after another took the stand, it grew clear that the case was largely circumstantial. In the age of DNA analysis and "the *C.S.I.* factor," as the attorneys dubbed it, the science was con-

Father Gerald Robinson at his trial for the brutal murder of Sister Margaret Ann Pahl.
AP/Wide World Photos

spicuously lacking. Mandros dismissed the DNA that excluded Robinson as an artifact, unrelated to the crime. Sister Margaret Ann had likely been in no position to scratch her killer, and many others had handled the altar cloth. The DNA on her underwear, a slight amount, could have been from an investigator or medical person. The strongest evidence, and the trial's centerpiece, was the infamous letter opener found in Robinson's quarters, which appeared to be the murder weapon.

Dr. Lee took the stand to describe the work of his team. The most telling point he made concerned an impression in blood left on the altar cloth that resembled the U.S. Capitol. Lee used enlarged photos to show jurors how the dime-size medallion and stain were similar, but he would not call it an exact match. The ten-foot cloth had other blood-stains as well, and one mirrored the ribbing on the letter opener's handle. Another looked like the slight curve of the long blade.

Paulette Sutton, a medical examiner who specialized in blood-stain analysis, agreed with Lee, but was just as hesitant to say they had a clear match.

The anthropologists for the prosecution reiterated their findings about the stab wound impression in Sister Margaret Ann's jaw, and medical experts estimated the time of the murder between 7:00 and 7:30 A.M. This was important, as three witnesses placed Robinson near the scene of the crime at just the right time.

Leslie Kerner, an EKG technician at Mercy Hospital at the time, said she spotted Robinson outside the chapel around seven in the morning. Medical personnel were summoned an hour later and one physician, Dr. Jack Baron, took a wrong turn down the corridor leading to Robinson's rooms and saw a priest of his description hurrying away from the chapel. He had looked over his shoulder as they passed, Baron testified, and "gave me a stare. I'll never forget that. It went right through me." A lab technician who was also near the scene at 8:00 A.M. remembered seeing Robinson carrying a duffel bag. These witnesses effectively contradicted Robinson's alibi.

Then came the most controversial testimony. Reverend Jeffrey Grob, an expert in the occult, testified that the murder had been committed in a way that mocked the church and defiled the nun, which indicated a satanic ritual. It could only have been committed by someone with advanced knowledge about the symbols, he stated, which narrowed down the pool of suspects to church officials.

Defense attorney John Thebes, who led the defense team of four, managed to get the coroner to admit that the wounds could have been made by a pair of scissors like those missing from the sacristy. He also pointed out inconsistencies in the accounts given by some of the witnesses, and dismissed the investigation as shoddy and politically contaminated.

He began with an officer from the county's cold case unit, Sgt. Steve Forrester. Thebes asked about inconsistencies and gaps that showed up when comparing the original investigation in 1980 to the one in 2004. Either the memories of witnesses had changed over time, he suggested, or evidence had not been appropriately collected in one or the other of the investigations. Witnesses who now said they had seen the priest near the scene at the approximate time of the killing had added more to their stories or changed the time frames. Forrester admitted this was all true.

The rest of the detectives received the same treatment, especially Arthur Marx, who had been in charge of the 1980 investigation. The notes he insisted he had taken during his two interrogation sessions with Robinson were now missing, and he was unable to explain it. He also remembered writing a report, but it could not be found.

On cross-examination, he described how Robinson had told him that someone had confessed to committing the murder but had then withdrawn it.

To counter the anthropological testimony, the defense also had a celebrity witness: best-selling mystery writer Kathy Reichs, who was also a forensic anthropologist. She was a consultant for the popular television series *Bones*, which was based on her writing, but she insisted she kept the fiction and the facts separate.

She described the "*C.S.I.* factor" in terms of how television shows like *C.S.I.* and *Bones* were having an impact on the way jurors listened to and understood evidence. The mass media has offered the public an education about forensic science, making potential jurors somewhat more savvy. As a result, they often expected certain procedures and even looked for better results than could actually be produced, or awaited testimony about techniques that did not exist. In addition, sometimes jurors confused experts who had poor credentials with board-certified experts, simply due to the aura that surrounds forensic expertise.

Not privy to the exhumation, Reichs had examined the case records, photos, and reports from 1980 and 2004. She said that from what she could tell, the coroner had conducted tests on the jawbone before it had been properly cleaned, which made precise measurements inaccurate and had possibly altered the shape of the wound impression. "There could be modifications of the edges of the defect," she stated. Such a procedure risked contaminating the evidence irreversibly, especially with bones of the fragility evident with the elderly nun's.

Prosecutor Chris Anderson asked Reichs how often she made such observations based only on photos, and she acknowledged that it was the first time she had done so. The implication was that her ideas could be less accurate than those who had handled the evidence directly, but her intent was that the evidence could have been altered to the point where even a direct examination would be pointless. Still, she admitted that she could not say with certainty that the test had adversely affected the puncture defect in the jawbone.

The case quickly drew to an end, and the two sides summed up their positions: An angry man had killed a woman, and there were too many coincidences for the killer to have been anyone other than Robinson, versus the cold case detectives had botched the investigation in the rush to arrest a man against whom they had no evidence and, as a result, did not consider alternative explanations.

The jury went to deliberate, and on May 12, 2006, they returned a guilty verdict. Robinson was sentenced to a mandatory term of fifteen years to life. He has many supporters who believe he is innocent, but others claim that justice was a long time in coming.

SOURCES

Ewinger, James. "Jurors Sort Out Two Accounts of Nun's Killing." *Cleveland Plain Dealer*, May 11, 2006.

———. "No Proof of Priest at Scene of Killing." *Cleveland Plain Dealer*, April 28, 2006.

———. "Priest's Trial in Death of Nun Will Include Talk of Rituals, Cults," *Cleveland Plain Dealer*, April 12, 2006.

———. "Three Witnesses Recall Seeing Priest at Murder Scene." *Cleveland Plain Dealer*, May 8, 2006.

McNally, Richard. *Remembering Trauma*. Cambridge, MA: Harvard University Press, 2003.

"Priest Convicted in Nun's Slaying." CBS News, May 12, 2006.

John Seewer. "Letter Opener, Bloodstains Key to Prosecutor's Case." Associated Press, May 1, 2006.

————. "Prosecutor Says Priest Wanted to Humiliate Nun in Her Death." Associated Press, May 11, 2006.

————. "Twenty-six Years Later, Jury Convicts Priest of Nun's Slaying." Associated Press, May 12, 2006.

Yonke, David. *Sin, Shame, Secrets*. New York: Continuum, 2006.

five

C.S.I.: "Blood Drops": The team investigates the murder of four members of a family—the parents and two boys—while two sisters survived. There are drawings in blood on a wall and mirror, and the bodies, all stabbed, are strewn about the house. Catherine notes that the scene is an imitation of a cult killing.

TRUE STORY: Four members of the Flores family were murdered in 2002 in California. The episode also has hints of the slaughters associated with Charles Manson in 1969 and Jeffrey MacDonald in 1970.

At first, this episode has striking similarities to the 1970 copycat slaughter that occurred at the home of Jeffrey MacDonald, because a reference is made that it's an imitation of a cult murder. MacDonald's wife and two young daughters were slaughtered, while he sustained minor injuries. He claimed that hippies had entered his home, high on drugs, but due to suspicious circumstances he was later convicted of the murders. On the table in the room where he claimed the intruders attacked him lay an open magazine featuring the 1969 massacres outside Los Angeles, California, by the hippie "family" led by Charles Manson.

On Saturday, August 9, at the home of film director Roman Polanski, five people were slaughtered in a blood-drenched spree, including Polanski's pregnant wife, Sharon Tate. On a door, the word *PIG* was written in blood. The next night, Leno and Rosemary La-Bianca were murdered by a band of hippies, who carved "war" into Leno's chest with a knife and used his blood to write *Death to Pigs*, *Rise*, and *Healter Skelter* [sic] on the walls. All were convicted.

In the *C.S.I.* episode, the killer wrote on the wall with blood, but

The body of actress Sharon Tate is taken from her house on Cleo Drive in Beverly Hills. Tate and four others were found there, murdered by members of the Manson Family cult.
AP/Wide World Photos

one of the show's first-year law enforcement consultants from Los Angeles said in an interview that the inspiration for this episode actually came from a more recent incident in Los Angeles—a family massacre in Pico Rivera. There was no writing on the wall, but there was plenty of blood.

A family of eight was asleep in their home in Pico Rivera, a largely Mexican-American area of East Los Angeles, when an intruder entered during the early hours of July 21, 2000, and stabbed five of them. An elder daughter, eighteen-year-old Esperanza, arose around 3:00 A.M. when she heard noise, and walked out of her bedroom to find her father in the hallway, bleeding from the throat.

"I've been stabbed," he gasped, "get us some help." Her mother yelled from the bedroom for her to call 911, but she could not get through, so she ran screaming out of the house to a neighbor's home, where they phoned the police.

When officers arrived, they found the hallway slippery with blood, and forty-two-year-old Richard Flores Sr. was dead. They found Sylvia Flores in her bed, bleeding from multiple wounds but alive. As they raced to get her emergency care, she said she had not recognized her attacker in the dark, but he was a smooth-shaven Latino, perhaps twenty, who had worn blue shorts, a white tank top, and a blue bandanna. In a shared bedroom, seventeen-year-old Richard Jr. and ten-year-old Matthew were slain, as was Sylvia, thirteen, in a separate room. Esperanza and her eighteen-year-old adopted sister, Laura, both in another room, had not been attacked.

The final survivor, sixteen-year-old Monica Diaz, had been sleeping in the same bed with her younger sister, Sylvia. She'd been saved by a timely visit to the restroom. Niece to Richard and Sylvia, she, too, had been adopted by them when her own mother died thirteen years earlier. When police questioned her, she said she'd heard someone in the house, so she'd stayed in the bathroom to hide until she heard her sisters' voices.

Investigators picked up a bloody knife outside the back door, which showed no signs of forced entry. They bagged it and hoped for fingerprints.

A motive for the attacks eluded them, since nothing was taken. It seemed to be simply an all-out attack against the family, although questions to neighbors who watched the police activity indicated that they were well regarded and very involved in sports programs with their children. They didn't have readily apparent enemies, and certainly not someone who wanted them dead. While Richard had strict rules, he was also affable and loving, and had even agreed to take in the daughters of his wife's nieces when their mother died. In fact, Richard was an imposing six-foot-nine, so whoever had planned this frontal assault with a knife had to be confident or stupid. He had certainly been lucky.

Investigators turned their attention to Monica's fortuitous escape, which seemed just a little too lucky, especially after they found three knives in the bathroom where Monica claimed she'd been hiding. She insisted they hadn't been there, but she was able to identify what type they were and said she had a knife similar to one of them from her ROTC training. Two knives were the type used in hand-to-hand combat, with locking blades, and one was a dagger. The handles of two had been wrapped with cord and tape for a better grip.

The next day the surviving girls were asked to come to the sheriff's office, so Monica took her seventeen-year-old boyfriend, Michael Naranjo. A detective noticed that Naranjo, with dark hair dyed red, was wearing a bandage on his forearm. When asked what had happened, he claimed he'd been hurt at school when some kids had broken glass. He took off the bandage to show them, but they remarked that the wound did not resemble a glass cut. Naranjo quickly recalled that it had actually been a razor cut—he'd cut himself. No one said anything to him then, but detectives began to follow him. He was now a suspect. So was Monica.

The entire neighborhood was alarmed, wondering at the chances of another such attack in the area, so detectives worked quickly to piece together a timeline for the fatal night. They learned that Monica and the younger Sylvia had played in a basketball game at their high school that evening, and most of the family, except for Esperanza, had come to watch. When the family arrived home, the children all went to bed. Then Esperanza came home, and she, too, went to bed after placing a call to a cousin. She said she had fallen asleep around 1:00 A.M. Laura was already in bed asleep. By that time, both parents had turned in. All in all, it had been an uneventful evening, with nothing to indicate what was to come.

It seemed that little Sylvia had been the first victim, knifed to death in her sleep. A piece of duct tape left on her cheek indicated how they had kept her quiet as she was stabbed several times from her throat to her abdomen. In the adjacent room, Richard's throat was slashed, and Matthew, only ten, had been partly disemboweled. The next target was the parents' bedroom, where both were sleeping. Sylvia was stabbed several times, and then Richard, who had jumped up to struggle with the assailant. The intruder was on the bed, so

Sylvia shoved him with her foot, surprising him, and he leapt off the bed, then left the room, closing the door behind him. Apparently he left the house as well, because Richard, badly wounded with a slashed throat, made his way out to the hallway before he collapsed from blood loss.

Esperanza had heard noises in her parents' room and then the sound of the back door shutting, which roused her from bed. As she left to get help, Monica appeared to assist Sylvia, who had been stabbed in the chin and chest. She applied pressure to keep the most serious wound from killing her aunt and adoptive mother. Laura was going from room to room, screaming over what she discovered.

Six days after the attack, Naranjo and Monica were both under arrest. Naranjo's fingerprints matched those found on the knife, the duct tape, and the battery of a military-style flashlight found inside the Flores home. Since it did not belong to the family, it appeared the intruder had left it behind. Monica's fingerprints were on the duct tape and on the knives in the bathroom.

Evidence was also found in Naranjo's home: fifteen knives, a manual for combat, a collection of books about serial killers, and a book entitled *Stalk to Kill*. In the garage was a spool of cord consistent with that wrapped on the knife handles, and blood was on Michael's bicycle. Detectives surmised that he'd made his getaway on it when he fled the house, riding two and a half miles back to his own home. But he had not done the deed alone, and the inside person for this crime was clearly Monica. It was evident they had planned the slaughter in advance, probably aiming to annihilate the entire family, but they had also committed errors typical of youthful and inexperienced criminals. Monica barely answered detectives' questions, and Naranjo refused to talk at all.

Both were slightly above-average students at El Rancho High School, had enrolled in ROTC courses for a time, and were about to enter their senior year. She wanted to go into biology, and he wanted to become a Marine. They had been dating throughout their junior year, despite Richard and Sylvia's concerns. One person said that Richard did not approve of Naranjo's style of dress, which was largely Goth—spiked hair, black clothing, and a black trench coat. However, by some accounts, Richard tried to hinder *any* relationship the girl started. While a dedicated family man, active in both the church and the community, he was known to be quite strict and protective. That did not sit well with Monica, who felt neglected in the large family and had found an abundance of adoring attention from Naranjo. Richard had been kind to the boy but had recently told Monica he thought Naranjo was sneaky.

The more inseparable the two kids became, even withdrawing from social circles to be alone together, the more the Flores family tried to intervene. Then Monica asked if she could go away with Naranjo for a weekend in July, and when Richard said no, they devised a plan to kill the family and stage it as an intruder attack. They knew quite a lot from their studies in combat and thought they could pull it off. Naranjo had a knife collection and manuals. If they could immobilize each person and cut their throat, it shouldn't take too long. So they prepared for it, and Monica made sure the back door was unlocked for Naranjo's entrance.

These kids had no record of violence, and neither had had any disciplinary problems, although Michael was known to have a fierce temper. There was nothing about their personalities that would have inspired a prediction of such extreme violence. There were no warning signs. Some of their friends were so surprised, they decided the charges could not possibly be true: The police had made a mistake.

On August 12, both teenagers pled not guilty to the charges, but Monica did not once look at her mother, sitting in the courtroom in a wheelchair, flanked by the two eighteen-year-old girls. The DA, Gil Garcetti, suggested that given the horrendous brutality involved, they should both be tried as adults.

Naranjo wrote a four-page confession a few months after the murders, in which he said that he'd considered committing the murders for a week and only needed the right opportunity. He'd even come with knives prior to July 20, prepared to go forward. He claimed to have devised the following plan: He would come over and tell Monica to go into the bathroom to wait for him. He would then kill Sylvia, show Monica the body, and gauge her reaction. If she was with him, then fine. If not, he would lock her in the bathroom and continue on his own.

Then Monica mentioned staging a robbery, to make the family cohere emotionally, because she feared that her adoptive father and mother might separate. She did not know he meant to kill them, but for him, this was the moment. They decided on a date when Naranjo would not have to attend summer school the following day. That was July 21. After Monica helped Naranjo cut duct tape, gave him a "good-luck kiss," and then went to hide, expecting (he says) no more than a robbery, he carried out the killings on his own, hoping he and his girl could soon live "happily ever after." He thought his plan was "pretty smart." He added that he'd intended to kill the older sisters before the parents, but he came to the parents' room first, so he entered. "That was the point where things started to go wrong." He was kicking himself for that mistake.

After he fled the parents' room, he ran to where Monica was hiding, handed her three knives, and then left the house. (He didn't explain how it was that Monica stayed in the bathroom after she saw his blood-covered clothing rather than immediately calling for help.) "If people still wonder why no one ever woke up," he wrote, "it's because my first attack to the victims was directed to the throat and lungs, thus enabling no sound from them other than deep grunts."

Clearly he was bragging, but without much substance. Two victims did awaken and one survived. Nevertheless, he went on to discuss his life, viewing himself as having a tragic destiny, like the monster from Mary Shelley's nineteenth-century novel *Frankenstein*.

He imagined he would experience "lengthy and well-deserved suffering in the afterlife" and suggested that if people wanted to punish him, they should pray for that. Yet his apparent despair was punctuated with smiley faces and a bit of self-congratulation. Clearly this note was an attempt to take the heat off Monica by explaining how the evidence could be construed another way.

However, he hadn't counted on authorities locating some of Monica's letters to him. Ten months before the crime, she had stated that her goal in life was to become a mass murderer and thought the best job would be a hit man, imagining how many victims she would have if she lived eight hundred years. "Hitler only lived for a few years," she wrote, "and killed lots, though he did it the cowardly way." She wanted to "bring terror to the earth" and make people suffer. She sought a partner who would desire the same things she did. She wanted them to be like the two killers in the gory team-killers movie *Natural Born Killers*.

In September 2003, Naranjo eventually changed his plea, receiving five terms of life in prison without the possibility of parole. Since he had been a minor during the attack, he was ineligible for the death penalty. Apparently he had just wanted to skip the ordeal of a trial. Sylvia Flores was in court for the plea, and she was allowed to address her family's killer. She wanted to know why he would do such a thing and stated that her life had become a nightmare since the crimes occurred. She had lost almost everyone. But no answers were forthcoming. She feared that her niece was guilty.

But Monica held out, claiming through her court-appointed attorney that she had killed no one; she had merely cut the duct tape. She'd not even known what Naranjo had planned until after he was there. The only thing that bothered her conscience, she said, was that she had not told anyone. She had said in several interviews with reporters that her family life had been difficult and she'd felt like Cinderella. In fact, that had been Naranjo's name for her.

Her letters to Naranjo were read in court as the trial began in January 2004, and the prosecutor insisted that Monica's participation in the planning and her assistance in letting Naranjo into the house made her equally culpable. He referred to them both as "narcissistic sociopaths."

Naranjo took the stand to reiterate that the plan had been his alone and Monica was not involved. Before he'd even met Diaz, he said, he'd thought about killing people. He offered no motive except that the idea of killing was "set" in his head. It was a "personal choice."

Monica testified on her own behalf, insisting that Naranjo was the mastermind and she had not known what he'd planned. Her letters, she said, had been mere fantasies, inspired by Naranjo's intense interest in serial killers. She'd been trying to keep him interested in her. "I expressed an interest in anything Michael was interested in to have a romantic relationship." She had loved her family, she insisted, and had never thought about killing them. But she could not easily explain a letter she had written about wanting to celebrate her marriage to Naranjo by killing people on that day. By then they were already involved, even obsessed with each other. Monica had written, "I just have to do something crazy real soon, because if I don't, I might have to hurt the people" she loved.

A psychiatrist indicated that Monica Diaz had a personality dis-

TEAM KILLERS

Oliver Stone's film *Natural Born Killers* features a couple who indulge in random violence to vent anger and exercise power. The film demonstrates how couples can develop a murderous drive together, blending their impulses through mutual encouragement into a spate of violence. Responsibility is spread between two or more people, relieving whatever guilt may exist and finding affirmation—and even more ideas—from another's actions. The brutality is typically guided by a dominant partner, with a weaker accomplice doing whatever it takes to remain together.

order that triggered an intense fear of abandonment. Thus, she had planned a staged burglary to keep her family together. The murder of her family would be inconsistent with her pathology.

The evidence, both physical and circumstantial, went against her, and the jury convicted her. She looked down when she heard the verdict but showed no visible reaction. Also ineligible for the death penalty, she received four life terms without the possibility of parole, and fifteen years for the attempted murder of her aunt and adoptive mother. Her attorney insisted that the sentence was overly harsh and vowed to appeal.

Eerily, a year and a half after the episode aired, the LAPD investigated another family massacre in South Whittier, just east of Pico Rivera, that bore several similarities. Miguel "Mike" Ruiz, 37, worked two jobs to support his family and take care of his grandmother, Ana Martinez, who'd suffered a stroke and needed assistance. He had a wife, Maritza Trejo; an eight-year-old daughter, Jasmin; and an adult daughter who lived nearby.

A neighbor caught a glimpse of Ana on Friday morning, July 13, but that was the last time anyone saw a member of the family alive. On Friday evening, Trejo's twenty-one-year-old daughter knocked on the door, but no one answered, so she went to the home of her aunt and spent the night. They returned the next morning and entered.

Bloody trails throughout the house led to Mike, his wife, his grandmother, and his daughter, all stabbed to death. It was clear to police, who arrived at once, that they had been tortured and dragged into other rooms. There were blood spatters all over the walls as well. While there was no evidence of forced entry, the house had been ransacked and vandalized throughout, with furniture overturned and drawers emptied. The three adults had been left in a bedroom, while Jasmin's blood-covered corpse lay in the bathtub, drowned. She had been sexually assaulted before she was slain. The throats of Mike and his grandmother had been slit, while his wife was stabbed some thirty times. A bloody mop in a bucket of water suggested the perpetrators had made some attempt to clean up.

According to family members, computer equipment was missing from a home office, and police located a computer dumped in the yard of a neighboring home. Neighbors said they'd heard nothing on Friday afternoon and night, not even the family's two dogs barking. That suggested that whoever had entered had known the victims.

The crime scene technicians collected blood samples from every room for both blood typing and DNA analysis. What made the scene more difficult to process is that some of what initially appeared to be blood was in fact a mix of food items: maple syrup, barbecue sauce, Italian dressing, and other products. It was apparently an attempt to hinder investigators. It was the age of *C.S.I.*, after all, and plenty of people were aware of how crime scenes were processed.

On a chair that had been moved from one room to another, technicians used an electrostatic dust lifter and collected the outline of a shoe print. A detective went out to search the neighborhood for a shoe that would match. As they questioned people in the neighborhood, they learned about a serious falling out between Mike and another man who had worked for him, and quickly made an arrest. On July 14, Alfonso Ignacio Morales, 23, was apprehended in his home, around the corner from the Ruiz family's residence. He had visited the Ruiz family daily and had even sold them one of their beloved dogs.

He claimed that he had entered the home to find two men dressed in black already at work and that he'd been tied up and forced to watch, but there was no evidence that anyone but him had been there. Apparently Morales had done some work for Mike, but they had argued over money that Morales owed, so he'd been fired. That accounted for the anger that motivated the viciousness of the attack, but there was more. Just over a week before the massacre, he'd asked out Maritza Trejo's older daughter, and she had turned him down. On the day of the killings, Morales was seen wearing a T-shirt with "Slayer" on it, in reference to a heavy metal band that sang about violence and death.

The shoe print from the chair matched a shoe from Morales's home, a palm print from the mop was his, and some computer parts in his garbage can had belonged to Mike. Police also found a knife with blood on it, and Morales's stepfather brought in several items that Morales had given him that contained items belonging to Mike. Most damning was DNA found inside Jasmin's body that was matched to Morales. The case came to trial in 2005, and some thirty different forensic experts reconstructed the crime. On April 20, 2005, Morales was convicted, and four months later he received a death sentence.

SOURCES

Cardenas, Jose. "Daughter Says She Spurned Suspect." *Los Angeles Times*, May 9, 2003.

———. "Jury Finds Woman Guilty of 4 Murders." *Los Angeles Times*, February 4, 2004.

———. "Woman Accused in Four Slayings Wrote of a Desire to Murder, Prosecutor Says." *Los Angeles Times*, January 22, 2004.

Chavez, Stephanie, and Anna Gorman. "Four Family Members Found Stabbed to Death in Home." *Los Angeles Times*, July 14, 2002.

"Details in California Family Slaying." Associated Press, July 15, 2002.

Hall, Carla. "Letter from a Mass Murder." *Los Angeles Times*, October 25, 2003.

———. "Murder in the Family," *Los Angeles Times*. November 16, 2002.

Hall, Carla, and Jose Cardenas. "Man Takes Blame for Murders." *Los Angeles Times*, January 28, 2004.

"Investigators: LA Homicide." CBS News, July 25, 2003.

"Judge Sentences Man for Slaying Four Members of Family." Associated Press, October 23, 2003.

Liu, Caitlin. "Neighbor Is Convicted of 4 Slayings." *Los Angeles Times*, April 20, 2005.

Mathews, Joe. "Four in Pico Rivera Fatally Stabbed in Rampage." *Los Angeles Times*, July 22, 2000.

"Murderer of Four Family Members Gets Death." *Los Angeles Times*, August 24, 2005.

Olivio, Antonio. "Communities Struggle to Cope with Brutal Slayings." *Los Angeles Times*, July 30, 2000.

Schuster, Beth. "Daughter, Boyfriend Held in Family Killings." *Los Angeles Times*, July 28, 2000.

———. "Details Emerge in Pico Rivera Slayings." *Los Angeles Times*, July 23, 2000.

"Woman Gets Life in California Family Killing." Associated Press, April 22, 2004.

six

C.S.I.: "Anatomy of a Lye": A dead body with two broken legs, found in a park, shows signs of a slow death by bleeding, and it's learned that the man was the victim of a bizarre accident that turned into murder.

TRUE STORY: A nurse's aide in Texas hit a man with her car and left him to die over the course of several hours, stuck in her windshield.

It was a story few people would forget, not only for the shocking treatment of a human being but also because the person who perpetrated this crime could have mitigated it. She chose not to.

Chante Mallard drove her Chevrolet Cavalier home in the early morning hours of October 26, 2001. She had been drinking and indulging in drug use that evening, smoking pot and dropping ecstasy with a girlfriend, Titilisee Fry. They then went to Joe's Bamboo Club to drink more before returning to Fry's apartment.

Mallard, twenty-five, probably shouldn't have been behind the wheel, but she seemed to believe she could make it home without incident. She drove onto the six-lane Highway 287, about five miles south of Fort Worth, Texas, and picked up speed. As she approached the Village Creek exit, several miles from her home, and turned onto it, a man suddenly appeared in front of her and she was unable to control her car. She ran right into him. There came a loud crunch of metal against a human body and then the explosion of glass as the body slammed into her windshield and came through. Mallard felt wind and glass shards smacking her, and she shrieked and stomped on the brake, but it was too late. She had hit him, hard. He'd flown right into her windshield and was halfway into her car, his head against the floorboards and his torso lodged between the dashboard and the passenger seat. His legs were on the car's hood, with one sticking through the jagged glass.

She panicked. She had no idea what to do. To her horror, the man was moaning; he was still alive and badly injured, but she had some notion that if she called the police to report the accident, they would realize she was high. She couldn't have that happen. She might go to jail.

She sat in her car for a few minutes to try to clear her head. No one else was out there on the road; no one had seen anything. Afraid to touch the man, she pushed gingerly at him, hoping to dislodge him, but he was stuck and his weight prevented him from being moved. She got out to try to pull him. She pushed on the glass to break it so she could get the man out, but after touching his leg, which was clearly broken, she grew frightened and got back into the car. The man remained stuck, mumbling and groaning in pain.

Mallard put the car into gear and drove with him lodged in the glass, impeding her view. She tried not to look at him, but couldn't help but notice that part of his leg had been severed and was lying along the hood. As she drove, she screamed and yelled to drown out his moans. She did not have far to go, and within a few minutes, she

ECSTASY EFFECT

This psychoactive illegal street drug works on the neurotransmitter serotonin, with the idea of producing and mimicking emotional transport. Users report an enormous sense of peace and connection to others as well as a transcendent state and an abundance of energy. Taken with other substances, especially alcohol, it can affect one's judgment.

pulled into her driveway and opened the garage door. Driving all the way inside, she knew she had to hide her car and the victim. She was so far into this now, there was no way to call the police or go to a hospital. He moaned a little as she parked, and she apologized over and over. Still afraid to touch him, she closed the garage door, got out, and went into her house.

Weeping profusely, she walked around praying and wondering what she should do, then lay down on the floor. She wasn't good about making decisions for herself, especially not one like this and not after she'd been drinking and doping. She had never done anything like this before. After a few minutes, she returned to the garage to check and found the victim still breathing. She apologized again and closed the door.

Mallard knew she had to get help, so she called Fry and begged her to come and pick her up. As they drove around, Mallard described what had happened. Fry returned with her to look inside the garage. She demanded that Mallard call 911, but Mallard refused.

Mallard had already made nearly two dozen calls to her former boyfriend, Clete Deneal Jackson, but he had not answered the phone. She left messages begging him to call her. He finally did, and she asked him to come over. He arrived around nine o'clock in the morning. Mallard asked him to go into her garage and look at her car. He saw a broken windshield, but then he opened the car door and saw a dead man wearing a suit jacket and sweatshirt; his pants and underwear had been knocked down to one of his ankles. Jackson panicked. He realized that they had to do something, and quickly, but saw that the job was too big for him, so he called his cousin, Herbert Tyrone Cleveland. They arranged to meet at Mallard's house later that evening. Jackson wasn't keen about being involved, since he had just emerged from prison on a two-year sentence for burglary. He was persuaded to help cover for the incident only because he was certain it had been an accident.

Mallard then took him back to Fry's apartment, and they discussed what to do. Mallard wanted to commit suicide, but the others assured her the situation could be managed. Fry mentioned burning the body, and Jackson later said that he had resisted that option. He wanted to place the body where it could be found so that the victim's family would know what had happened to him. Because the whole thing had been an accident in the first place, it wasn't far-fetched to stage it thus. They agreed together that, after dark, Jackson and Cleveland would dump the body in a park where people were likely to find it quickly.

The two men arrived at Mallard's home that evening, taking a blanket into the garage. The air was thick with the odor of blood and death. Gingerly, they opened the car door. By now the body had stiffened with rigor mortis into a crumpled position, and its weight against the door made it fall out onto the blanket. The trio was loath to touch him, so Jackson used a shovel to position the legs on the blanket. The two men tied the ends and hauled the heavy corpse into the car they had borrowed.

With Mallard accompanying them, they dumped the dead man in Cobb Park, not far away, placing him on his back and putting the blanket back into the car. They hoped it would look like a hit-and-run. In effect, that's what it was. Mallard was relieved, although she still felt terrible over what she had done and had trouble controlling her fits of crying.

The next day, October 27, two men in the park saw the dead man and reported it to a firefighter. He went to the location where a white adult male lay on his back on the ground. Checking for a pulse, he found none and called 911. He could see that the victim had broken legs and other damage and had been dead for several hours. The police arrived to collect the man, and a detective was assigned to the case. He awaited the results of the autopsy.

Dr. Nizam Peerwani, the Tarrant County medical examiner, performed the autopsy, finding that both of the man's legs were broken. The lower part of his left leg was nearly severed, and his right shinbone and thighbone were broken, as was his right arm. He had scratches and lacerations to his upper torso and contusions on his scalp. Dr. Peerwani believed the man had bled to death over the course of about two hours. Yet with no damage to the internal organs or brain, he could have survived had he received quick assistance.

With fingerprints, the police were able to identify the victim as Greg Glenn Biggs, age thirty-seven, a resident of a homeless shelter in downtown Fort Worth. The investigation concentrated on the area where he was found.

An accident scene had occurred not far from the park, but the driver of the wrecker pulling a car from the ditch had seen no body, so detectives surmised that Biggs had been struck there and carried to the place where he was found. In other words, someone had definitely moved him and left him. The ME confirmed that the victim's injuries were consistent with being hit by a car while upright and being dragged. However, an officer from the Traffic Investigation Unit (TIU) observed that lividity—where the blood runs to and settles at the point of lowest gravity in a corpse—indicated that he'd been on his face for a long time. Someone had hit him elsewhere and brought him here, positioning him in a way different from the position he was in when he died. He had lain elsewhere for several hours. Another factor was that the speed at which the car had been traveling, according to the man's injuries, exceeded the speed possible on Cobb Park Drive. Under these circumstances, the TIU took over the investigation. However, further examination failed to provide leads, so the case went cold.

Near the end of February 2002, the Tarrant County Sheriff's Office received a call from an acquaintance of Mallard's who had overheard Mallard describe the incident at a party. They had been drinking and trying to decide who should drive so they could go out. Mallard said she did not drive. She then explained that she had "killed a white man" on Highway 287 and drove home with him stuck in her windshield. She giggled as she said it, according to the arrest affidavit, and added that after parking in her garage, she went inside and had sex with her boyfriend before checking the man again with the boyfriend in tow. He had asked for help, but they returned to the house. She stated to the other women that it had taken the man several days to die, and then they had dumped him in the nearby park. The caller said that another friend had seen the car in the garage, still with blood and hair inside. She offered Mallard's address and warned that Mallard planned to burn the car after she received her income tax refund to purchase another.

The police went to the home with a driver's license photo and a search warrant, anticipating that any evidence of the incident would have been wiped away by this time. They were wrong.

Mallard came to the door at their knock and acknowledged her identity. Inside the garage, which stank, they found the dented two-door gold Cavalier, missing its front passenger seat and windshield. There were bloodstains inside, especially in a side pocket on the passenger side door and on the floor of that side of the car. The crime scene unit was called to take the car for processing, and a hammer was collected from the backseat for analysis. On the backyard lawn they found the missing car seat, burned.

Mallard was arrested and charged with failure to stop and render aid. She offered a self-protective statement in which she planted several lies. She claimed she had only had two drinks on the night of the accident but had felt funny, as if someone had slipped something into her drink. She described the incident occurring on the loop of the exit and said that the victim had tried talking to her, but she could not understand him. She went into her house and cried. She checked the victim several times and heard him moaning. After calling a friend named Vaughn, she did not know what happened to the body. Vaughn had taken care of it for her. She remained away from her home for several days. When she found the dead man gone, she removed the car seat and burned it.

Trace analysis indicated that the hammer left in the backseat had been used against glass, an indication of evidence tampering. Mallard was charged with this and released on bond. However, the case soon took a more serious turn when the lead investigator discussed the victim's injuries with Dr. Peerwani. The evidence indicated that the victim had died slowly and might have been saved. Mallard, a nurse's aide, had sufficient expertise to have saved him or could at least have called for help. She had admitted that, although stuck, Biggs had been moaning and moving around, so she had known he was alive. On March 6 they arrested Mallard again, and this time charged her with murder.

"I'm going to have to come up with a new word," said Tarrant County DA Richard Alpert. "Indifferent isn't enough. Cruel isn't enough. Heartless? Inhuman? Maybe we've just redefined inhumanity here."

On April 25 a grand jury indicted Mallard on more charges: murder and tampering with evidence. She faced five years to life and a fine of up to ten thousand dollars. She changed her story, admitting to taking ecstasy and saying that Biggs had pleaded with her to get help. She also named her accomplices, and Jackson and Cleveland were both arrested as well. Mallard's attorney was Mike Heiskell, who quickly stated that the police and prosecutor were "overreaching" and believed that charges should be reduced to a failure to render aid. She had yet to give a satisfactory reason for why she had failed to call for help.

Biggs's mother had been contacted by reporters, and she said that around the time of his death, she had begun looking for him. She could not understand how Mallard could have been so callous.

The crime reconstruction, sorted out after several conflicting statements, indicated that as Mallard hit Biggs, he came through her windshield headfirst and lodged there, his arms pinned to his sides. She then drove to her house and parked in her garage, leaving Biggs struggling and bleeding in the windshield. By early reports he had suffered for two days before dying, but it was later judged to be closer to two or three hours. As he slowly expired, Mallard checked him. When she found him dead, she and two male friends dumped him in the park. She then destroyed the car's windshield and burned the seat. The lack of any attempt to get help and the obvious effort to conceal the crime seemed to make it far more serious than a mere failure to render assistance. But that would be for a Texas jury to decide.

On September 12, 2002, Cleveland accepted a plea deal. For a nine-year sentence, he agreed to plead guilty to evidence tampering and to testify at Mallard's trial. It took Jackson a few more months, but in January he also pled guilty to tampering with evidence. He agreed to testify as well and received ten years in prison for his part in the crime.

Mallard's trial for murder was scheduled for June 2003. Just before it began, she pled guilty to evidence tampering, but that was all she would agree to, so the trial proceeded. The jury saw parts of the car where Biggs had made contact, where he had landed, and where his blood had spattered in various places. They also saw photos of his injuries from the autopsy, and some could not look. Forensic analyst Max Courtney described the scene and discussed the crime re-creation.

Titilisee Fry told what she knew of the events leading up to the accident and Mallard's behavior afterward. Jackson was then called to testify, as he had agreed, but the prosecutor never called Cleveland. Jackson stated that he had seen Mallard at the nightclub just before the incident and she had been high from alcohol and drugs. He had smoked pot with her. After the incident, she had called him nearly two dozen times, leaving messages on his answering machine to come and help her, although she was not specific about what she needed. He came and she showed him the car. He saw that she had hit something large and opened the door. It was then that she admitted through hysterical tears that she had run into a white man. Seeing "the dude," Jackson said, he panicked, too.

The prosecutor used Jackson to show that Mallard had ignored many opportunities to get help for Biggs. It came out that her brother was a firefighter in the Fort Worth department. She could have called him, but did not.

To indicate how Biggs had suffered, Tarrant County medical examiner Nizam Peerwani said that the victim had taken about two hours to die and was probably in excruciating pain. He had several breaks in his legs, and the lower part of his left leg had been nearly severed off altogether. Mallard's driving had exacerbated his injuries, and he could have been saved had she gotten him medical attention. The crash had not caused any injuries to his spine, brain, or internal organs.

A crime scene processor added that the amount of blood in the pocket of the passenger side door indicated that Biggs had managed to grip it and had possibly coughed into it.

Brandon Biggs, son of the deceased, was the last person to testify for the prosecution. He told the jury that his father was a self-employed bricklayer with bipolar disorder and a mild case of schizophrenia. He had been on medication for both. He had divorced Brandon's mother many years earlier and had become homeless when he'd loaned money to a girlfriend who did not pay him back. He then moved into a homeless shelter in Fort Worth and continued to work. Brandon, age twenty, had seen him many times but lost touch with him the summer before he was killed.

To attempt to mitigate the matter, the defense called several key witnesses. Vincent Di Maio, chief medical examiner for Bexar County, had reviewed the autopsy report and said that Biggs had bled to death. He had problems breathing because his head was in the floorboard and he could not move. Di Maio thought that Biggs had lost consciousness upon impact, never regaining it, so he had not suffered. He also thought that it was conceivable that Mallard would not have known what to do, since she was only a nurse's aide, which meant she had no medical training.

A toxicologist, Gary Wimbish, testified that the drugs Mallard had taken had impaired her ability to make an appropriate judgment, although he could not say if she was unable to distinguish right from wrong.

In closing, the prosecutor argued that by hitting Biggs and

driving home with him rather than rendering aid, Mallard knowingly caused his death. "She stole his life," said Alpert. "She stole his hope of anyone else saving his life. That's murder."

Defense attorney Jeff Kearney tried to press home the point that a murder charge was too serious for what had occurred: an accident in which a motorist had failed to render aid. "Murder has to be an act; it can't be an omission," he said. It was Jackson who had talked her into dumping the body in the park and concealing the crime, and Mallard's drug use that night had prevented her from thinking clearly enough to make the appropriate decisions. Thus, the incident was an accident, not murder.

After the three-day trial, the jury deliberated less than an hour before they found Mallard guilty of murder.

During the sentencing phase, Mallard took the stand, admitting she had a drug problem and claiming that if she had been sober that night, she would have made the right decision: "There wouldn't have been any doubt in my mind what to do." She described the noise and the glass flying at her. She talked about her fear of the man as he lay contorted and halfway inside her car, his leg sticking through the glass. Her only reaction was to scream and drive home. "I didn't know what to do," she stated, believing she ought to serve some prison time.

She also apologized to Biggs's family. "I have ruined the lives of other people," she said, through tears. "I have ruined my family's life. I have put people through pain. And I am so truly sorry. I'm so sorry, Brandon. I am so sorry for what I have caused your family, and I am sorry for the pain that I have put my family through."

Brandon read a statement saying he accepted her apology and forgave her. Mallard cried throughout.

Facing anywhere from five years to life, Mallard received a sentence of fifty years in prison, along with ten years for tampering with evidence, with eligibility for parole after serving twenty-five. She burst into tears, aware that she would be in her fifties before she could have a life again.

Chante Mallard testifies during the penalty phase of her trial after having been found guilty of murder for hitting a homeless man with her car, driving home with his bloody body jammed in the windshield, and leaving him to die in her garage. *AP/Wide World Photos*

Mallard's attorney appealed on the grounds that the evidence was insufficient to convict her of murder. In March 2005, the Second Court of Appeals in Fort Worth, Texas, upheld Mallard's murder conviction, stating that while the impact did not kill Biggs, Mallard's actions afterward ensured that he would not survive. Her appellate attorney, Robert Ford, vowed to take the case to the Texas Court of Criminal Appeals. The case is still pending.

SOURCES

Arrest warrant affidavit, Tarrant County, PC-9929.

Bean, Matt. "Mallard Hit Hard with 50 Years." CourtTV.com, July 1, 2003.

Brown, Angela K. "Medical Examiner: Homeless Man Died in about Two Hours." Associated Press, June 25, 2006.

———. "State, Defense Rest in Trial of Woman Who Left Man to Die in Windshield." Associated Press, June 25, 2003.

Douglas, Jim. "Grand Jury Indicts Woman in Windshield Death." *Dallas Morning News*, April 25, 2002.

Steinhaus, Rochelle. "Ex-boyfriend of Driver Describes Disposing of Accident Victim's Body." CourtTV.com, June 25, 2003.

"Timeline of Events in Chante Mallard Windshield Death Case." Associated Press, June 26, 2003.

"Woman Panicked after Touching Man in Windshield." CNN.com, June 27, 2003.

seven

C.S.I.: "Post Mortem": This episode introduces the "Miniatures Killer," who re-creates crime scenes with dollhouses that replicate the crimes—in advance. The killer's work shows up in several episodes, including "Loco Motives," "Monster in a Box," and "Living Doll."

TRUE STORY: Frances Glessner Lee's crime scene miniature dollhouses were created from actual incidents during the 1940s for teaching purposes.

On display at the medical examiner's office at the Baltimore city morgue is a series of dollhouses. However, they're not your mother's dollhouses. Inside, you'll find blood-spattered walls and tiny dolls faceup on kitchen floors, sprawled in bathtubs, or hanging from nooses. They are the work of an unusual philanthropist who had a keen interest in crime, Frances Glessner Lee. Constructed during the 1940s to teach inexperienced police officers about different types of death scenes, Lee's unique structures encouraged them to use careful observation before drawing a hypothesis.

In "Burned Cabin," for example, the model shows a meticulously built cabin after a destructive fire had incinerated it. To achieve a sense of authenticity from the 1943 crime, this model was built and then burned with a blowtorch. Lee's description indicates that two men had resided there, a man and his nephew; the older man was dead in the bed, and the nephew gave a statement to the police that he'd woken up, smelled smoke, and run from the burning building. However, he was fully dressed, which undermined his story and cast suspicion on him for murder and arson.

Lee's motto was "convict the guilty, clear the innocent, and find the truth in a nutshell." She had once heard this sentiment from a detective, and it had stayed with her. Thus, she dubbed her series the "nutshell studies of unexplained death." How she came to this life venture is a story unto itself. It's not a crime story like the others in this volume, but it certainly involves crime.

Born into a wealthy family on March 25, 1878, in Chicago (their fortune came from International Harvester), "Fanny" was raised in an austere, castle-like home. She was exposed to many great minds but coddled and tutored in private. Hers was a life of privilege; she was surrounded by servants and the most exquisite handcrafted furnishings. Her father, industrialist John Jacob Glessner, even wrote a book about the house, now a museum. Young Frances was bright, with an eye for detail, and she hoped to study law or medicine, but to her disappointment her father forbade her from attending a university. She had to watch as her older brother, George, went off to Harvard while she was doomed to the domestic scene.

When she was twenty, Frances married Blewett Lee, an attorney and law professor at Northwestern University. They had three children before the marriage failed, and they eventually divorced. But Frances was soon caught up with a new interest. She had met a friend of her brother's named George Burgess Magrath, who was just getting his MD from Harvard Medical School and aiming for a career in pathology. Since the Glessners had a summer mansion in New Hampshire's White Mountains, called "the Rocks," Magrath would often visit. He talked with Frances about legal medicine, especially death investigation, and his tales inspired her.

After Magrath became the medical examiner for Suffolk County (Boston), he confided to Lee the need for better training for death investigators, especially since coroners were not required to have medical degrees. He thought it was important that medicine be included in their backgrounds, because to make accurate assessments, they had to be familiar with the nuances of wounds and the different types of poisonings.

A Medico-Legal Society was formed in Massachusetts to advance the science, and a few cities emulated it, but the groups were splintered and largely inactive, so it was left to passionate physicians like Magrath to pick up the torch. He taught Lee about legal medicine, which inspired her, as did Conan Doyle's stories about Sherlock Holmes. Lee was fascinated with the "surprise factor"—the way small clues could offer different directions than an initial examination of a crime scene indicated.

She set out to become an expert in the field of crime investigation and was eventually considered sufficiently knowledgeable to be viewed as an authoritative consultant. She was convinced that this was her chance to make the contribution about which she had dreamed since childhood. She asked Magrath what she could do to assist in medico-legal education. He told her, "Make it possible for Harvard to teach legal medicine and spread its use."

Lee took up the cause. At the Rocks, she created a home for herself not far from Boston, so she could keep track of what happened at Harvard. In 1931, Lee helped establish a department for the teaching of legal medicine, and she paid the salary of its first professor. In Magrath's name in 1934, she donated a library of more than one thousand books and manuscripts that she had collected from around the world—many of them rare. She also endowed the department with a sizable grant, and Magrath became its first chair.

Many officers saw the value in being forced to think carefully about a crime scene, which gratified Magrath. However, he did not have long to enjoy the fruits of his collaboration with Lee, as he died in 1938. Lee was heartbroken, but she continued to support Magrath's vision. She was just picking up steam.

In 1943, Frances Glessner Lee received an honorary appointment as a captain of the New Hampshire State Police, which made her the first woman to hold such a position, and in 1949, she was also the first woman to be invited to the initial meetings of the American Academy of Forensic Sciences. In addition, she became the first female invited to join the International Association for the Chiefs of Police.

Thanks to Magrath, Lee noticed that police officers often made mistakes when trying to determine whether a death was the result of an accident, a natural event, a suicide, or a homicide. Too often they simply missed clues. She thought that something concrete and practical should be done to mitigate this, and she envisioned a series of crime tableaux as teaching devices. They could be made to scale, she believed, and include all the items found in actual crime scenes. From her domestic upper-class training, she knew just what to do: She would replicate crime scenes in miniature.

To put herself fully into the project, she set aside the second floor of her four-story mansion at the Rocks for a workshop, filling one room entirely with miniature furniture from which she could select whatever she needed. To create each diorama, she blended several stories, sometimes going with police officers to crime scenes or the morgue, sometimes reading reports in the newspapers, sometimes interviewing witnesses, and often utilizing fiction. She apparently even attended autopsies. She preferred enigmatic scenarios, where the answer was not obvious; one had to examine all the clues, including items that did not initially appear significant. Always changing the names, she kept real scenes confidential. At times, for her own delight, she included items or wallpaper patterns from her own household.

It wasn't long before Lee had everything she needed to put together some grisly scenes. For her, these were not dollhouses or miniatures, but teaching tools. She spent an enormous amount of time on each diorama, collecting deluxe miniature furniture from all over the world when she went on her travels or commissioning a carpenter to make what she wanted. The little buildings—from cabins to three-room apartments to garages—were also fashioned from her design, built on a scale of one inch to one foot. Her carpenters were instructed to make doors and windows that actually worked, with shades that rolled up and locks with minikeys that opened them. In some rooms, Lee even placed scaled-down dollhouses that the tiny doll children might play with—miniatures inside miniatures.

Carpenter Ralph Mosher worked with her for eight years, and when he died, his son, Alton, took over. They lived at the Rocks, in a house that Lee provided, and managed to turn out an average of three Nutshells per year, although some years were slower than others. Each one cost about the same as an average house at that time. And it was no surprise, for the amount of detail Lee demanded involved many hours of painstaking work. She made each doll herself by hand, using a cloth body stuffed with cotton BB gun pellets and bisque heads. She painted the faces, ensuring authenticity for different stages of decomposition. Lee added sweaters and socks that she'd knitted with great difficulty on straight pins, and items of clothing that were meticulously hand-sewn.

Once the dolls were ready, Lee would decide just how each should "die," and proceed to stick knives in them, paint signs of decomposition on their pale skin, or tie nooses around their necks and hang them up. By far the majority of victims were female, and some were children—even a baby. All of the dolls were Caucasian and many lived in economically deprived circumstances, a long way from Lee's safe and privileged world.

In the rooms or yards she placed tiny cigarettes she'd rolled, clothespins she'd whittled, books or newspapers she had prepared, and prescription bottle labels she had printed by hand. A trash bag would contain open cans and boxes; a sink, half-peeled potatoes; and an ashtray, too many stubbed-out butts. Sometimes Lee used items from charm bracelets or Cracker Jack boxes, and a "mouse" caught in a trap was actually a pussy willow bud. And there were always subtle clues—an open beer bottle, bullet casings, or a pile of letters—that would become instrumental in the seminars. Lee labeled the dioramas with titles like "Unpapered Bedroom," "Kitchen," or

"Burned Cabin," and each of the nineteen scenarios told a complicated story.

While Lee generally based the dioramas on a combination of
items, one can only speculate on how much certain sensational news
reports at the time had influenced her. The famous "Brides in the
Bath" case occurred in the early 1900s in England as a potential
inspiration, at least in part, for the Nutshell labeled "Dark Bathroom." Lee was certainly familiar with it.

In Highgate, Margaret Lloyd had died in her bath. It seemed an
unusual albeit accidental drowning, and the case might have been
closed had not a relative of a victim of a similar drowning spotted
Lloyd's obituary and gone to the police. That victim's husband had
been one George Joseph Smith, who also turned out to be the husband of the unfortunate Lloyd, under an assumed name. Detectives
then turned up the fact that Smith had been married three times, and
all three wives had died mysteriously in their baths. Coincidence
seemed unlikely, though the police were hard pressed to explain how
a person could be drowned in a bathtub without evidence of a
struggle. Truthfully, there had been no mark of violence on any of the
three bodies.

Pathologist Bernard Spilsbury experimented with young women
in bathing outfits who agreed to sit in water-filled bathtubs and allow
him and a detective to try to drown them. After repeated failures, it
seemed to investigators impossible to make a person drown in this
context, and they were about to let Smith go. But then they figured
it out: Smith had killed each woman by grabbing her by the feet and
pulling her torso and head into the water. The quick action and rush
of water had made her helpless. When the team tried this with the
experiment participants, one of them went instantly unconscious.
It was evidence enough to believe that Smith had figured out what
to do to kill these women without much effort and enrich himself
on their money or life insurance. He was convicted and, in 1915,
executed.

The scenario that Lee depicted was somewhat different, but it

Death in the miniature kitchen—one of the miniature crime scenes created by
Frances Glessner Lee for teaching purposes.
Corinne Botz

---

involved a woman lying faceup in her tub, with the water running
on her face. Rather than being the victim of outright murder, however, she might have been the accidental victim of friends' attempt to
revive her after some hard partying. One had to read the clues.

By 1949, some 2,000 doctors and 4,000 lawyers had been educated at
the Harvard Department of Legal Medicine. In addition, several thousand state troopers, detectives, coroners, district attorneys, insurance
agents, and reporters had attended the weeklong seminars Lee put on
twice a year. She would be the only woman in attendance, and once
the Nutshells became part of the seminars, one day of each week was
set aside to showcase them. They were placed in a temperature-
controlled room, and officers were given a limited amount of time to
take notes of what they observed and report back to the others. The
point was not to "solve" the crimes but to notice the important evidence that could affect investigative decisions.

In a written instruction, Lee urged those preparing to observe a scene to imagine themselves as less than half a foot tall. She also advised that they adopt a geometric search pattern, such as a clockwise spiral, to accomplish a methodical examination. They must look at the entire scene, searching for clues that might not be obvious, such as a bullet caught in a ceiling, a pattern of blood that undermined an obvious theory, a weapon in an odd position, or evidence of behaviors that would point away from a determination of suicide. Lee would pen a few spare descriptions to assist, such as one referring to a crime that "occurred" on April 12, 1944: "Mrs. Fred Barnes, housewife, dead." Lee might also provide a bit of background and assure observers that all the clues were evident. They were then on their own to attempt a reconstruction.

In each scene, she had included items that weren't clear at a glance, such as an item under the bed or a smudge of lipstick on a pillow slip, but when these were revealed, they would help alert detectives and police officers to the need to look for subtle clues. What appears to be a suicide, for example, might change when a key item is noted—a fresh-baked cake, a load of freshly laundered clothing, an ice cube tray beside the body (who does all this before ending her life?). Other scenarios included a bound prostitute with a sliced throat, a man hanging in a wooden cabin, a boy dead on a street, and an apparent murder/suicide. Detectives were forced to look at these models as carefully as they would an actual crime scene.

In "Parsonage Parlor," a young girl named Dorothy Dennison lies dead on the floor. This crime was "reported" on Friday, August 23, 1946. As the story goes, Dorothy had gone out to purchase meat for dinner four days before, and although witnesses saw her at the market, she did not return home. Her mother, Mrs. James Dennison, called the police late that afternoon and Detective Robert Peal responded. The police searched empty buildings in the area and finally found the body, faceup, in the parsonage, seemingly posed.

Temperatures in the mid-80s and high humidity readings had influenced the degree of decomposition, and there were bite marks evident on the girl's chest and legs. A knife stuck out from her left side, beneath the ribs. Except for the body and a few items, including a package of maggoty meat, everything in the room was paired. A church rector who resided in the house had been absent for several months, indicated by a pile of tiny pieces of mail by the door. Clearly, the perpetrator realized the place was both furnished and devoid of potential witnesses. Yet the body's condition does not square with the package of meat, which has been there much longer. Certain kinds of knowledge, such as awareness of the stages of insect activity, is required to work this crime scene.

A state trooper told Lee that the Nutshell Studies had helped him learn how to handle difficult cases. If not for the challenge she had put to him, and the surprises that he'd experienced upon learning about clues he had missed, he might not have been as careful as he'd become. For her, such reports made the endeavor—and the $60,000-plus she spent on the projects—worthwhile.

Once these seminars proved a success, others were organized in other states. On the anniversary of the first one in 1946, graduates came back together to form the Harvard Associates in Police Science (HAPS), and each graduate thereafter became a member. Lee assured them that she intended to be involved until the day she died.

That was not long away. When her eyesight failed at one point, her doctors forbade her from working, so she had a radio installed in her room to listen to the police reports. But with the poor reception in the White Mountains, she was able to hear only the reports from the Virginia State Police. She wrote encouraging letters, so the chief invited her to Virginia. There, she pleaded for support for medico-legal education, and reform soon followed. At that time Lee estimated that it would take her until about 1960 to bring the rest of the country into line with medical examiner systems. She died in 1962 without realizing her vision, but nevertheless left a lasting legacy.

In 1966, the Nutshells were moved to the Office of the Medical

Examiner in Baltimore. In 1992, a grant made it possible to restore them. Yet Lee's creations do not all sit idle. The Harvard Associates in Police Science continues to use several of the models in its biannual teaching seminars.

SOURCES

Botz, Corinne May. *The Nutshell Studies of Unexplained Death*. Monacelli Press, 2004.

"Francis Glessner Lee." Biographies, Visible Proofs, nlm.nih.gov. Retrieved June 17, 2006.

Hanzlick, R., and D. Combs. "Medical Examiner and Coroner Systems: History and Trends." ncbi.nlm.gov. Retrieved June 23, 2006.

Kahn, Eve. "Murder Downsized." *New York Times*, October 7, 2004.

Maxwell, Douglas. "Oh, You Beautiful Doll." *New York Arts Magazine*, May–June 2006.

Miller, Laura. "Frances Glessner Lee: Brief Life of a Forensic Miniaturist." *Harvard Magazine*, harvardmagazine.com. Retrieved June 18, 2006.

Oswald, George. "Grandma Knows Her Murders." *Coronet* (1949), reprinted at www.sameshield.com. Retrieved June 18, 2006.

Sachs, Jessica Snyder. "Welcome to the Dollhouses of Death." *Popular Science*, 2005.

eight

C.S.I.: "Justice Served": A jogger found mauled to death by dogs is traced to a female nutritionist who uses her dogs to attack people so she can harvest their fresh organs to treat her blood disorder.

TRUE STORY: In 1978, "the Vampire of Sacramento," Richard Trenton Chase, killed pets and people to drink their blood and take their organs for his imagined blood disorder.

Ambrose Griffin opened the trunk of his car to retrieve some packages he and his wife had purchased that day. It was between the December holidays in 1977, and they were loading back up. He picked up two sacks of groceries and followed his wife into the house, then came back for more. But he didn't return.

Mrs. Griffin heard her husband yell something, followed by two loud pops, but thought nothing of it. Then from inside she saw him drop to the ground and believed he had just suffered a heart attack. She ran to the phone to call for an ambulance. When she went to him, she saw that he was bleeding and realized that he had been shot.

At the emergency room, Mrs. Griffin gave her husband's information: he was fifty-one, an engineer, the father of two grown sons. When Griffin died at the hospital, the investigation was now for murder.

The following day, a news crew found two spent shell casings on the pavement near the Griffin residence. Detectives followed up on reports of a suspicious car driving around the neighborhood, but no one offered a clear description. Then a twelve-year-old boy riding a bike reported that a twentyish-looking man with brown hair had shot at him from a brown Pontiac Trans Am. Put under hypnosis, he recalled a license plate number, 219EEP, but this tip produced no other leads.

A check on recent records turned up a report from a woman who said that a shot had been fired into her home on December 27, two days before Griffin was shot, and she lived only a few blocks away. A search of her kitchen produced a .22-caliber slug, and tests showed it had been fired from the gun that had killed Griffin.

The new year arrived but without any promising leads. Detectives feared the shooting incident had been random, without motive—one of the most difficult crimes to solve. But three weeks later another murder occurred that would be associated with it and send them in a new direction—one much more gruesome and frightening.

David Wallin came home on January 23, 1978, to 2360 Tioga Way. The dark house was quiet except for a stereo playing, and he could tell that something was wrong. His German shepherd was there but appeared to be nervous. He called to his wife, three months pregnant, but received no answer. He wondered if she was sleeping.

A bag of trash lay on the floor, surrounded by dark stains. In the kitchen Wallin saw what appeared to be a pool of blood, with a trail leading to the bedroom. Alarmed, he ran in and found Teresa, murdered and disemboweled. He screamed.

The police were quick on the scene, and even seasoned officers were stunned. Teresa had been shot in the head, and she lay on her back. Her sweater was pulled up to expose her breasts, her pants and underwear were around her ankles, and her knees were splayed in a position of a sexual assault. Worse, her left nipple had been carved off, her torso cut open below the sternum, and her spleen and intestines pulled out. She had been stabbed repeatedly in the lung, liver, diaphragm, and left breast. An autopsy would later determine that her killer had cut out her kidneys and severed her pancreas in two. Inexplicably, he then placed the kidneys together back inside her. It was as if he'd simply been curious. David Wallin did not realize this, but it was later learned that Teresa's mouth was stuffed with animal feces. She still had all of her jewelry.

Blood in the bathroom revealed the killer's movements, and a discarded, bloodstained yogurt container lay near the body. In addition, odd rings of blood around the body looked as if someone had placed a cup or small bucket there.

The Wallins had no enemies, and thus detectives had no leads. Bizarre and rare as such an incident was, it seemed to have been a random home invasion for the sheer purpose of murder. Three neighborhood residents reported seeing a thin white male with stringy brown hair, twentyish, walking around in black tennis shoes and an orange parka, going onto porches and crossing lawns. They all reported that he was a stranger and quite creepy. One person saw him near the Wallin residence.

Three shell casings were found in the home, and the bullets removed from the victim were analyzed and found to be similar to those shot at Ambrose Griffin. The autopsy failed to determine if she had been raped but indicated that the knife used had been about six inches long.

On the same day, a burglary nearby revealed that the intruder had defecated and urinated in the home and had tried to steal a decorative sword before the homeowner arrived and scared him away. But the crime spree did not end there. In fact, it got worse, as if this person were growing bolder.

On January 27, Evelyn Miroth, 38, was babysitting her twenty-month-old nephew in her home on Merrywood Drive, a mile from the Wallin residence. Her fifty-one-year-old friend, Dan Meredith, was over to the house. Evelyn was supposed to send her son Jason, six, to a female neighbor's home, and when he failed to arrive, the woman sent her daughter to check. Looking through a window, the little girl saw movement inside Evelyn's house, and went home to report that no one had answered the door. Evelyn also did not answer the phone, so the woman went over and entered the house, then immediately called the police. The entire homicide bureau was instructed to report to the scene. They had multiple bodies.

Dan Meredith lay in the hallway in a pool of blood. The deputy who checked him saw a close-range gunshot wound on his head and blood in the bathroom, including bloody water in the tub. Then he found Evelyn lying naked on a bed, her legs splayed open. She had a gunshot wound to the head, and her abdomen had been cut open and the intestines pulled out. Two carving knives, stained red, lay nearby. It appeared that she had been taking a bath when she was surprised by her killer and then dragged to the bed. He sodomized her, stabbed her through the anus into her uterus at least six times, made several slices across her neck, and tried to cut out an eye. Bloody ringlets on the carpet indicated that he had used a container to collect blood. He stabbed several internal organs as well. Inside Evelyn's rectum was a large amount of semen.

On the other side of the bed, police officers discovered the body of a boy, who turned out to be Jason. He had been shot twice in the head at close range.

The intruder had left bloody footprints behind that resembled the shoe marks found at the Wallin murder scene. He had also ransacked the kitchen, perhaps in search of a knife. Meredith's red station wagon was missing from the front of the house, where neighbors had seen it parked that morning, so a bulletin was sent out to look for it. They assumed the intruder had taken it to get away.

Detectives located an eleven-year-old girl in the neighborhood who described a man near the victims' residence around eleven o'clock. He fit the description of the man seen in the Wallin neighborhood. In fact, residents in the Merrywood Drive neighborhood had seen him walking around as well, knocking on doors.

Then Karen Ferreira arrived, seeking the whereabouts of her infant son, David, left with Evelyn that morning. No one had seen him, but a bullet hole was discovered in the pillow in a crib, along with a lot of blood. They feared the worst.

Soon, Meredith's station wagon was found not far from the

Richard Trenton Chase, who killed pets—and people—to drink their blood.

house, with the keys still in it. Latent print examiners processed it for fingerprints. Whoever this man was, they had to find him fast, as he clearly had escalated and would likely kill again.

On January 28, a woman called to tell them about a disturbing encounter she'd had with a disheveled Richard Chase, whom she had known from high school several years earlier. A background check turned up a history of mental illness, including an escape from a hospital, a concealed-weapons charge, a series of minor drug busts, and an arrest in Nevada. There was also the registration of a .22-caliber semiautomatic handgun, sold in December 1977 to a Richard Chase on Watt Avenue—not far from the murder scenes—and on January 10 he had purchased ammunition. Motor vehicles provided more: He was five-foot-eleven and weighed 140 pounds—just like the description of the strange man walking around. The day after the triple homicide, investigators went out to question him.

They knocked repeatedly, but Chase would not open the door, so they walked a short distance away and waited. A brown-haired, skinny man wearing an orange parka emerged with a box in his arms and made his way toward his car, where officers apprehended him.

They took a .22 semiautomatic handgun from him, which proved to be bloodstained. In his back pocket was Dan Meredith's wallet. The contents of the box also proved interesting: pieces of bloodstained paper and rags.

They took Chase to the police station and tried to get him to confess. He admitted to killing several dogs but refused to say anything about the murders.

While he was in custody, detectives searched his apartment, which was dirty and smelled awful. Nearly everything was bloodstained, including food and drinking glasses. In the kitchen they found several small pieces of bone as well as dishes in the refrigerator on which body parts lay. One container, analyzed later, held human brain tissue, and an electric blender was badly stained and smelled of rot. Photographic overlays of human organs from a science book lay on a table, along with newspapers of which ads selling dogs were circled—and there were three dog collars in the apartment but no dogs. They grimaced over what that indicated. A calendar showed the inscription "Today" on the dates of the Wallin and Miroth murders, and chillingly, the same word was written on forty-four more dates yet to come. But there was no sign of the missing baby.

Evidence was gathered from Chase's clothing and apartment to compare to samples already being analyzed in the crime lab from the victims. However, when technicians attempted to take a blood sample, Chase had to be restrained. He seemed panicked over losing any blood, even a minute amount, and as detectives learned more about his background, they began to understand why. They also realized his bizarre motive for murder.

Richard Trenton Chase had a thing for blood. He also had a fear of disintegrating. Born May 23, 1950, he liked to set fires as a child and to torment animals. By the time Richard was ten, he was killing cats. As a teenager, he drank, smoked dope, and took hallucinogenic drugs.

He grew preoccupied with any sign that something was wrong with him, and he once entered an emergency room looking for the person who had stolen his pulmonary artery. He also complained that the bones were coming out through the back of his head, that his stomach was backward, and that his heart often stopped beating. A psychiatrist diagnosed him with paranoid schizophrenia but thought he might actually be suffering from a drug-induced toxic psychosis.

His life grew increasingly slovenly and he submersed into more drug abuse. At five-foot-eleven, he weighed only 145 pounds. Although he had tried living with his parents, his mother was afraid of him, so his father had rented an apartment for him.

At some point Chase began to kill and disembowel rabbits that he either caught or bought, and to eat their entrails raw. Sometimes he would put the intestines with the animal's blood into a blender, liquefy them, and drink this concoction in an effort to keep his heart from shrinking. He once injected rabbit blood into his veins and got very ill. He believed this rabbit had ingested battery acid that had seeped into his stomach.

Finally he was committed to a psychiatric hospital for somatic delusions. Antipsychotic medications failed to work, and in 1976 he escaped. He was returned to the hospital, earning the nickname "Dracula," because he often spoke about killing rabbits, and because one day he was found with blood around his mouth. Two dead birds, their necks broken, lay outside his window.

Eventually he was released, with a conservatorship granted to his parents. His mother paid his rent and shopped for his groceries. Still on his own, Chase began to catch and torture cats, dogs, and rabbits, which he killed for their blood. He also purchased guns and started to practice with them.

During this time, Chase's mother weaned him from the antipsychotic medications, deciding that he did not really need them, and declined to renew the conservatorship. But Chase did need help. That same year, police officers encountered him in Nevada. Two rifles lay on the seat of a truck stuck in mud, along with a pile of men's clothing. A blood-filled white plastic bucket containing a liver raised their suspicions. When they spotted Chase through binoculars, he was nude and covered in blood. He saw them and ran, but they caught up with him. He claimed the blood was his: It had "seeped out" of him. The liver, it turned out, was from a cow, so they let him go.

On March 24, the missing baby was found. A church janitor came upon a box containing its mummified remains. The child had been decapitated and the head, with a bullet hole, lay underneath the torso. There were several stab wounds to the body and several ribs were broken. Beneath the body was a ring of keys that fit Meredith's car. Chase was now going to trial for six murders, and the lead prosecutor, Ronald W. Tochterman, intended to seek the death penalty.

However, the court-appointed defense attorney, Ferris Salamy, entered an insanity plea, and they had a fairly good case, considering Chase's history of delusions. But Tochterman was determined to show that, despite psychosis, Chase had known the difference between right and wrong and had not been compelled by these delusions to kill anyone. Part of Tochterman's strategy included boning up on the legends of Dracula and blood rituals from various cultures. He also identified a history of voluntary substance abuse.

A number of psychiatrists for both sides examined Chase. He admitted to one that he was disturbed about killing his victims and afraid they might come for him from the dead. There was no evidence in his admissions that he had ever felt compelled; he'd simply thought the blood was therapeutic. One psychiatrist for the prosecution found him to be an antisocial personality, not delusional or psychotic, and all of the professionals thought he was competent to proceed.

On January 2, 1979, the trial began. Tochterman emphasized that Chase had prepared for the murders by bringing rubber gloves with him to the victims' homes. He also argued that, in each instance, Chase had been able to choose whether or not to commit the murders.

Thus, he had been sane. The real hurdle was that he had killed in the middle of the day, when he could have been seen, and had taken no pains to hide the evidence. In many cases, this kind of behavior indicated someone who was unaware that what he was doing was wrong.

After all the witnesses had had their say, including those who affirmed his psychosis, an emaciated Chase took the stand in his own defense. In a rambling narrative, he described a lifetime of mistreatment (uncorroborated) and drug abuse, and said he had been semiconscious during the Wallin murder. He admitted to drinking her blood. He did not recall much about the second series of murders, but knew that he had shot the baby in the head and decapitated it, leaving it in a bucket in the hope of getting more of its blood. He had consumed some of the organs. He thought that his problems stemmed from his inability to have sex with girls as a teenager and apologized for what he'd done.

On May 8, 1979, after five hours of deliberation, the jury decided that Chase was guilty of the six murders. During the sanity phase, he was found to have been legally sane at the time of each incident, so he was sentenced to die in the gas chamber at San Quentin Penitentiary.

The press had dubbed Chase "the Vampire of Sacramento." Since he was an interesting study and a good example of a disorganized criminal, FBI profilers took an interest in Chase and visited him in prison.

Special Agent Robert Ressler described the killer's strange notions. His behavior from the time Chase was arrested in Nevada in August 1977 until the murders began late that December revealed a deteriorating mind. Ressler asked Chase how he selected his victims, and he responded that he went down the streets testing doors. "If the door was locked," he said, "that means you're not welcome." Apparently he found the door at the Wallin home unlocked. Before entering, Chase deposited a .22-caliber bullet in the mailbox. He opened the door and saw Teresa taking out the garbage, so he shot her and then cut her up to examine her organs and drink her blood.

Among the many delusions that Chase described was one about "soap-dish poisoning." When he lifted the soap in the morning, he said, if it was dry underneath, he was all right. If wet, then he had the poison, which turned his blood to powder. The powder then depleted his energy and ate away his body, so he had to go out and drink blood. (This contradicted the marks on his calendar that indicated long-range planning.)

Although Chase was scheduled for execution, he came up with his own means of exit. On the day after Christmas in 1980, three days short of the third anniversary of the start of the killing spree, he overdosed on antidepressants he had been hoarding. Despite his lifelong obsession over his heart, the autopsy proved it was normal.

SOURCES

Biondi, Ray, and Walt Hecox. *The Dracula Killer: The True Story of California's Vampire Killer*. New York: Pocket, 1992.

Rasmussen, Cecelia. "Serial Killings Are a Darker Part of State's History." *Los Angeles Times*, October 29, 2004.

Ressler, Robert K. *Whoever Fights Monsters*. New York: St. Martin's Press, 1992.

Vorpagel, Russell. *Profiles in Murder: An FBI Legend Dissects Killers and Their Crimes*. New York: Plenum Publishing, 1998.

nine

C.S.I.: "Coming of Rage": A fifteen-year-old boy is found beaten to death, seemingly with a hammer, at a construction site where kids hang out, and a tracking dog leads investigators to a shopping bag with items purchased by a girl.

TRUE STORY: In 2003 in Philadelphia, a teenage boy was murdered by a gang of his friends, and they used his money to shop and buy drugs.

Jason Sweeney, 16, had a new girlfriend—his first. His parents thought he seemed quite pleased, and they smiled as he prepared on the afternoon of May 30, 2003, to go see her. He had been dating her for only two weeks, but he wanted to bring her over to meet them the following day at a family dinner. They knew only that this pretty and popular dark-haired girl's name was Justina, she was fifteen, and in a few weeks she would graduate from her eighth-grade class at Holy Name of Jesus Grammar School. Jason told them she was from a good family. They were pleased for him but hoped he wouldn't be distracted from his ambition to join the navy in a year to become a SEAL.

He was such a hard worker, having saved up from the part-time construction work he did for his father. He'd cashed a recent paycheck that day so he'd have money to spend on his date with Justina. Jason left home around four that afternoon, walking away from the blue-collar neighborhood of Philadelphia known as Fishtown. He was gone for hours, but by nine his parents began to worry. His mother, Dawn, called his cell phone, but there was no answer. They waited up, making more calls, but he didn't answer and didn't come home, so in the morning they started to call his friends. Among them was Eddie Batzig, a boy Jason had known for years and considered his best friend. But Eddie's mother did not know where Eddie was, either. He'd been out all night.

Paul Sweeney went to the police to report his son Jason missing. It was too soon to make a formal report, but the worried father could think of nothing else. This was so uncharacteristic of Jason. He was always a responsible kid, and he said he'd be home after his date. The Sweeneys did not know how to contact Justina or her parents, and they could only hope that both kids were all right.

Late that morning Eddie Batzig came over with Nicholas Coia, looking for Jason, and learned he was missing. Eddie was an honor student and had been friends with Jason since the fourth grade. Recently he and Jason had celebrated their sixteenth birthdays together in Florida, at Jason's grandparents' house. Yet Dawn had seen Eddie heading in the wrong direction and had asked Jason not to hang around him so much. He seemed to be growing sadistic, and two years earlier, when a pit bull had attacked Jason, Eddie had prevented him from getting away from the dog. As for the Coia brothers, Dawn had also asked her son not to associate with them because she had heard they were involved in petty theft and drugs. Now one of them was at her door.

Eddie listened to Dawn's concern and responded with sympathy. "I can't imagine who would do this," he said, seemingly incredulous. "Jason was my best friend." As if to help, he said that Jason and Justina had been at a party the evening before with him, Nicholas, and Domenic Coia. Yet he offered nothing that helped her find her son. As they left, she had the uneasy feeling that they knew more than they were saying. "I knew those boys knew something."

Around two that Saturday afternoon, a couple of boys on mountain bikes rode through a weedy industrial area off Beach Street known as "the Trails." It was a stone's throw from the Delaware River, near

I-95. Amid the litter, they came across a blood-soaked, bruised body in the weeds that looked fresh and called the police. Officers arrived to collect it, but found no ID. According to Deputy Medical Examiner Ian Hood, speaking to the *Philadelphia Inquirer*, the autopsy indicated that the victim's head had been crushed with multiple powerful blows, made with both sharp and blunt objects. Because every bone in the face, save the left cheek, was broken, the victim was unrecognizable. Pieces of bone were lodged deeply in his brain. His head was so chopped up, his skull was nearly split in two.

Since Paul Sweeney had reported a young man of this description missing, on Monday morning he was asked to come to the medical examiner's office to look at photos of a body—one of five murder victims that weekend. By now he was frantic, but hardly comprehending that his son might actually be the victim of violence, he agreed, unpleasant as it would be. He knew he had to eliminate the possibility.

Paul and Dawn were told that the body was too damaged to see, but photographs had been taken of several key areas. Paul recognized his son from a recent cut on his wrist, although the idea that Jason was dead seemed impossible. He had never been involved in drugs or gangs like other boys in Fishtown, Sweeney told the police. How could this happen? And where was the girl with whom he had been on a date? Why had Jason been found in that out-of-the-way area? He told them everything he knew about Jason's plans for the evening and then left them to find his son's killer. It did not take long.

The police learned Justina's address and went to her home. They also learned from witnesses that Eddie Batzig and the Coia brothers, ages seventeen and sixteen, knew Jason and had been seen with him recently. When officers requested that the boys come to the police station for questioning, Eddie and Domenic both talked, telling a shocking story. They admitted to their part in the murder of Jason Sweeney but expressed no remorse; they seemed interested only in when they could return home. As the story developed, officers also questioned Justina, but she refused to say anything. Nicholas Coia also provided little to no information. All four acquired legal counsel. Yet enough was now known to piece together what had allegedly happened.

Much of what follows was taken from published details of the confessions:

Justina, Eddie, and the two Coias were together all day on May 30. At least one of them knew that Jason would be flush with money that day from a paycheck, and they had been plotting for a week about how to get their hands on it so they could purchase drugs. Over and over, "about forty-two times," they listened to the Beatles' infamous song "Helter Skelter"—the one that had inspired Charles Manson to send his "family" on a murderous rampage one night in 1969 against actress Sharon Tate and her friends, following up with a double homicide the next night at the LaBianca residence. On a wall, in blood, they had written *Helter Skelter*.

According to the plan this lethal quartet finalized that afternoon, Justina would lure Jason into an isolated spot where the boys would be hiding, and they would then beat him up and take the money. As the hour approached, the boys donned latex gloves, and two of them grabbed weapons. Justina prepared for her part as well.

Jason was apparently eager to go wherever Justina invited him. They walked through the neighborhood and made small talk. Jason told her about cutting his hand at work that week. They stopped at a corner store, where Jason bought a bottle of juice. Justina called her cohorts to tell them her progress while Jason went to a drugstore to buy her a soft drink. When he returned, she suggested they go to the Trails. She hinted that it was time to get intimate and they needed a secluded spot. He was eager to go.

As they walked along a gravel path, her cell phone rang. She allegedly answered with an angry retort: "What did you do, bitch out?" Apparently the boys had missed their initial rendezvous.

It's surmised that once she reached a certain spot, Justina urged him to remove his clothes. A sixteen-year-old enamored of his first girlfriend, he wasn't about to say no. He removed his shoes and began to unzip and pull down his pants. She partially undressed as well. Once he was in a vulnerable position, he looked up to see Eddie running toward him with two other boys he knew—the Coias. He didn't know what they had in mind, but he struggled to pull up his pants.

Batzig reached him first, lifting a hatchet and striking Jason on the skull. He yelped in pain and asked what they were doing. Then he felt the blood on his head and tried to run. Domenic and Nicholas ran in with their own weapons, tackling him. Eddie was in a frenzy. He struck again as hard as he could, four or five times, before Domenic hit Jason with a hammer, slamming so hard that it stuck in Jason's skull. Nicholas reached in to beat Jason with a rock he'd picked up in the trash-strewn area.

"Blood was spurting," Domenic later recalled. "We just kept hitting and hitting him." Supposedly, Domenic did not believe they were really going to do it, thinking their plans had been part of a game, but once Eddie struck the first blow, he'd stepped in to do his part.

Even as Jason fended off blows and begged for his life, he apparently realized this had been a trap. His so-called girlfriend had played him for a fool. Through the blood that streamed into his eyes he saw that she looked on, doing nothing to intervene or get help. His last words were "I'm bleeding," and to Justina he said, "You set me up."

The boys kept beating Jason, ignoring his screams, until he finally choked on his own blood with a gurgling sound. One of them finished the job, using a boulder to crush Jason's skull. He fell to the ground and went still. They shook him and, getting no response, rifled his pockets for the money. To their delight, he had five hundred dollars in his pocket. Apparently he had planned a very nice date. Excited, they all joined together over the bloody form at their feet in a group hug. "It was like we were happy with what we did," Domenic told his interrogators. "We took Sweeney's wallet and we split up the money and partied beyond redemption."

They left Jason where he lay and went to the home of a friend to

The four teens charged with the beating death of fellow teen Jason Sweeney. Justina Morley lured Sweeney to an isolated area, where the boys attacked him. *AP/Wide World Photos*

wash up and change clothes. He would later tell the police that he had overheard their plans and had helped wash out their bloody clothing (as did an unnamed sixteen-year-old girl). They had gone out that evening, he said, and returned after failing to meet up with Justina as planned. They then called her and went out again. About twenty minutes later they were back, but now covered in blood spatter and gore, claiming they had killed Jason Sweeney.

"They were shaking," he would say in court. He'd had the impression they were exhilarated as they divided the money at the kitchen table, with each participant taking $125. Justina appeared to be happy. According to this witness, she called the incident "a rush." In fact, none of the perpetrators exhibited anxiety or remorse. "They seemed pretty fine." The ill-gotten gains were used to purchase marijuana, heroin, cocaine, and Xanax—and even toiletries such as deodorant. For the rest of the night, they got high. They probably gave no thought to the battered body that lay on the ground near the Trails.

When Eddie Batzig did not come home, his mother started making calls, including to Justina's home. The girl agreed to come over and help search for him, although she knew where he was. This woman would later say that Eddie had told her that Justina was not Jason's girlfriend but was involved in some manner with all the boys. Yet she had given Jason the impression she was his girl.

* * *

At the hearing in the Court of Common Pleas, the boys were all charged as adults with first-degree murder, conspiracy, and related charges. They were aware that they potentially faced the death penalty. Their party was now becoming a disturbing reality, and it wasn't fun.

Justina, too, was taken to court, where she shed a few tears, but during one sidebar she also snickered with her codefendants. Eddie kept his eyes on the floor while Domenic appeared agitated. While there was speculation that they had been high at the time of the murder, Domenic denied it. "I was as sober as I am now," he said, and added, "It is sick, isn't it?"

Judge Seamus McCaffery noted the barbaric nature of the violence, questioning any civilization that produces such callous depravity. "This is something out of the Dark Ages," he said. Philadelphia assistant district attorney Jude Conroy, who would try the case, echoed him: "The brutality involved in the case is really beyond the spoken word."

However, Justina's attorney, William J. Brennan, insisted that she should be decertified and tried as a juvenile, adding that she was not guilty of anything and her actions (or lack thereof) were attributable to depression. He stated that she'd had no knowledge about the planned attack. Even if she were tried as an adult, she was too young for the death penalty. Her mother went on CNN to defend her, saying, "I know my child. I know who she is. I know she's not capable of the things that they're saying. She's a sweet kid. She's a timid girl. She's a nice girl." She was certain Justina was innocent of the charges.

Jason's grieving mother told reporters that the killing could only have been about getting a thrill, because her son was generous. He would have just given them the money. (The police agreed, indicating that if all they wanted was money, they could have knocked him out and taken it. They did not have to kill him.) She recalled how Eddie and Domenic had come to her home on the day following the murder pretending to be concerned, when all along they had murdered her son. Eddie had in fact betrayed a boy who believed they had been best friends. She had been right not to trust him.

Common pleas judge Benjamin Lerner listened as a psychiatrist detailed Justina Morley's mental problems: two suicide attempts and the self-destructive act of cutting herself. She had been under psychiatric care for depression during the year prior to the crime. ADA Conroy argued that she was manipulative, and that allowing her to be sent to a juvenile facility, with release at age twenty-one, was risky.

Despite her sniffles through the hearing, Lerner denied her petition for decertification, and she was kept in the adult venue. Lerner said, "I can't recall a set of circumstances and facts more gruesome, more chilling, more destructive of one's belief in the inherent goodness of human nature."

Thus, Morley agreed to make a deal. She pled guilty to third-degree murder in exchange for her testimony against the boys. Under this deal, she would be free before her thirty-fifth birthday. Conroy admitted he had made the deal "with the devil," so he could learn what had occurred—at least, what she wanted to tell. "We had to pick our poison, and Justina was exactly that."

In our society, young females are routinely regarded as "less criminal" than young males and their crimes less serious. Gregg McCrary, a former FBI special agent, has observed this bias and its effect. "We have an overall sense that females are the nurturers in society and males the combatants. We carry that stereotype into our perceptions and fail to see that women are equally capable of aggression."

There is no evidence that female crime is somehow intrinsically different, but there is evidence that female crimes are increasing. The FBI's National Incident-Based Reporting System indicates that one in four juvenile arrests involves a female, and their arrest rate since 1987 has risen. In the past decade the population of incarcerated females has tripled. It turns out that aggressive behavior for both genders develops in similar ways.

The trial began in March 2005, and one reporter now indicated that at the time of the murder, Justina had had a heroin habit. She took the stand to testify against the others, indicating they had planned the murder for several weeks. Her part was to flirt with Jason and then lure him into the isolated spot. In a detached voice, she described their enthusiasm over the plan. They had actually devised more than one scheme, finally settling on the brutal beating. She then had sex with Eddie and Nicholas in exchange for heroin.

When she reenacted the beatings, showing how she had stood just eight feet away, she began to cry. Jason had tried to run, she said, but the boys tackled him. She then said that after they split the money, her own mother had driven them to South Street the next day so they could shop. After they were all arrested and placed in a prison van, she had stripped for the boys to entertain them. She claimed she now regretted it all.

However, her postcrime correspondence to her cohorts, turned over by them to their attorneys, undermined her schoolgirl façade. "I am guilty," she wrote to Domenic, "but I still don't feel bad for any of it. I still enjoy my flashbacks. They give me comfort. Pleasure." In another letter, she said, "I'm a cold-hearted, death-worshipping bitch who survives by feeding off the weak and lonely. I lure them and then I crush them." She wrote about how she liked the serial killer Hannibal Lecter and had "always wanted to live off human flesh." She wanted to be a vampire, with fangs. "I'm the worst person in the world," she wrote. Domenic also received a note that said, "I tried to take advantage of you while you were vulnerable . . . I just wanted you so bad." She suggested a suicide pact, but also wrote about being released one day so she could have his baby. At the same time, she was flirting with Batzig, praising his sexual prowess, and telling Nicholas she would have sex with him in a prison waiting room and asking him to name their future baby. As the trial approached, she told Domenic, "It would be hard to make myself cry—to make people think I was remorseful, or scared, or whatever."

Conroy asked her how she was able to write these letters. He referred to them as "evil."

One reporter thought Morley was suppressing a smile when she defended herself, claiming she wrote the letters because she wanted the boys to "accept" her and because she was afraid of them. They had threatened her. Yet when asked to produce these so-called threats, she said she had thrown them out. She also said in one letter that she had received no letters from Batzig. In that case, she had received no threats from him. The appearance is that she lied, played a role for the court, and ducked responsibility for the crime.

In court, Morley admitted to her tendency to manipulate: "I write what I think Nick, Dom, and Edward want to hear," and said she's "good" at choreographing "gullible humans." She also mentioned how easy it was "to persuade them into lies." Domenic's attorney, Lee Mandell, used these words as an indication that Morley had been the mastermind and had bent the boys to her will. He claimed she had a "passion for violence" and said to the jury that Domenic should be held no more responsible than Morley. Batzig's lawyer echoed this with a claim that Morley needed control and manipulated with sex. Nicholas's attorney said he was like a little puppy dog who followed along in order to be accepted by the group.

Ultimately, the trial ended with convictions, and the three boys who swung the hammer, hatchet, and rock that delivered the fatal blows were deemed guilty of first-degree murder. They were also found guilty of conspiracy, robbery, and possessing an instrument of crime. All received life sentences, without parole, plus 22 to 45 years for robbery. Only Domenic, the oldest of the boys, had faced a possible death sentence, because in January 2004 prosecutors had decided against that for the other two. But then the U.S. Supreme Court ruled on March 1, 2005, that it was unconstitutional to execute anyone under age eighteen, so a life sentence was the only option. (Domenic was two weeks shy of his eighteenth birthday when Jason was killed.) The Coia brothers showed no reaction, but Batzig dropped his head and appeared to be resisting tears.

"My son got justice today," said Paul Sweeney.

Judge Renee Cardwell Hughes said that she believed the incident had inspired at least one copycat, and reporters speculated that she was referring to the murder of a fifteen-year-old girl in April 2005. An adult woman had lured the girl with the promise of sex but, with three men, had killed her instead.

SOURCES

"Accused Teens Won't Face Death Penalty." Associated Press, January 11, 2004.

Conroy, Theresa. "Teen's Savage Killing Detailed in Court." *Philadelphia Inquirer*, June 18, 2003.

Dale, Maryclaire. "Judge Denies Juvenile Status for 15-Year-Old Murder Suspect." Associated Press, November 21, 2003.

"Interview with Mother of 'Helter-Skelter' Murder Defendant." CNN transcripts, June 24, 2003.

Moran, Rovert. "Lawyer Wants Girl Tried as Juvenile in Fatal Beating." *Philadelphia Inquirer*, June 10, 2003.

Nolan, Jim. "Suspect Had Turned on Sweeney before He Was Slain, Mom Says." *Philadelphia Inquirer*, July 1, 2003.

Nolan, Jim, Catherine Lucey, and Tremaine Lee. "The Plot to Kill a Pal." *Philadelphia Inquirer*, June 19, 2003.

Porter, Ira. "Police Identify Body in Fishtown." *Philadelphia Inquirer*, June 3, 2003.

Soteropoulos, Jacqueline. "Adult Trial in Fishtown Beating." *Philadelphia Inquirer*, November 21, 2003.

———. "Fishtown Defense Goes After Witness." *Philadelphia Inquirer*, March 2, 2005.

———. "Fishtown Teen Labeled 'Evil' by Prosecutor." *Philadelphia Inquirer*, March 3, 2005.

———. "Jailhouse Letters Are Described as Evil." *Philadelphia Inquirer*, March 4, 2005.

———. "Jailhouse Letters Heavy on Love, Gore." *Philadelphia Inquirer*, March 11, 2005.

————. "Morley's Descent Began at Tender Age." *Philadelphia Inquirer*, March 20, 2005.

————. "Tale of Teen's Betrayal: Music, Murder, Hugs." *Philadelphia Inquirer*, June 18, 2003.

"Teen's Brutal Beating Death Stuns Philly." Associated Press, June 19, 2003.

"Three Teens Get Life in Philadelphia Death Lure." Associated Press, May 6, 2005.

ten

C.S.I.: "Overload": An unlicensed therapist using a rebirthing treatment for reactive attachment disorder kills a boy and claims that he had a seizure and hit his head against the floor. Blanket fibers on her sweater and his underwear give her away.

TRUE STORY: Candace Newmaker, 10, was smothered as a result of "rebirthing therapy" in Colorado.

A series of broken attachments in the life and legacy of a troublesome child seemed to two therapists the perfect venue for an extreme form of therapy. But they didn't even know her and had never met her before the two-week treatment began. They never had the chance to find out if it would have worked.

Born in North Carolina in 1989, young Candace was an unfortunate product of the foster care system. Her maternal grandmother had been a foster child who grew up, gave birth, and quickly abandoned her own child, Angie, who was to become Candace's mother. Angie got married when she was seventeen to an abusive man who eventually left. By then Angie had three children and was unable to support them, so they were removed and placed in foster care. Thus, Candace was a third-generation foster child. In addition to losing her mother and her home, she was separated from her siblings as well. In time she developed a strong temper, making her difficult to place with foster families. Finally, Jeane Newmaker, a single woman and pediatric nurse, came along and adopted her. But Candace missed her family.

Jeane lavished gifts on the child and gave her as much as she could, but would later say that Candace was violent, destructive, and cruel. Jeane took the ten-year-old to one therapist after another in the hope that someone could help, and Candace received a variety of diagnoses. Among them was reactive attachment disorder (RAD), which bode ill for the child's future. It meant she might never develop a conscience and could be a budding psychopath. Medications were prescribed, but they had little effect.

A seminar conducted by an association that specialized in attachment disorders, ATTACh, seemed to offer direction. Jeane filled out a questionnaire, and from her responses Candace was diagnosed with a severe attachment disorder. Jeane was referred to an unlicensed therapist in Colorado, Connell Watkins, who practiced out of her home and a facility called the Evergreen Attachment Center. Jeane was willing to do anything to connect with her adopted daughter, so the sessions were scheduled to begin on April 10, 2000. A psychiatrist prescribed a strong dose of an antipsychotic drug, and Candace was then given over to the team of attachment therapists.

Watkins had prepared an intensive two-week, seven-thousand-dollar program in which Jeane would participate. Watkins worked

Attachment theory posits the implications of emotional relationships, stressing the attitudes and behaviors of children as they grow up and bond (or don't) with their caregivers. How well a child attaches to parents or others motivates his or her subsequent behavior in, perceptions of, attitudes about, and development into adult relationships. Therapists who utilize this theory generally focus on issues from early attachment, with the goal of healing damaged children and restoring their ability to bond in a balanced manner. It is the dominant theory today in the study of infants and young children, with four basic attachment styles identified: secure, avoidant, ambivalent, and disorganized. The style affects such things as anxiety levels, willingness to explore, need for attention, and ability to manage anger and stress.

with another therapist, Julie Ponder, and together they began the session with what they called "rough love" and "rage reduction therapy." In this stage, they would hold Candace and only restrain her with force if she got out of control. But they would yell at her and force her to make eye contact. When the sessions were done for the day, Candace lived with a foster couple so that Jeane's presence after hours would not distract her from the treatment. This was an immersion-type program, at the end of which Candace was supposed to be a whole new girl.

Jeane watched from the sidelines as the therapists yelled at Candace, cut her hair, forced her to sit still for long periods, and threatened her. They insulted her birth mother, so that Candace could detach more easily, and encouraged the girl to put that life behind her. But Candace resisted; she missed her mother and siblings and did not wish to replace them with Jeane. This attitude indicated to Watkins and Ponder that she was holding on to her anger. They decided to subject her to more intense treatment.

For one session, Candace had to lie on a blanket on the floor while Jeane (weighing 195 pounds) lay on top of her for nearly two hours, threatening to leave her and licking her face twenty-one times. The idea was to make the girl mad, then have her come to her adoptive mother and sit in her lap to receive affection.

Candace obeyed every move, albeit without enthusiasm, which indicated she was ready for the next step, "rebirthing." She was to reenact her actual birth via being wrapped tightly in flannel blankets and fighting her way out. To get free, she would have to struggle, and at the end of the fight she would be a new person, hopefully less angry. Many attachment therapists who used this process proclaimed it nearly miraculous in its results.

It was April 18, a week after the therapy had started. Candace was anxious and tired. She had not slept well the night before and had even dreamed of being murdered. The therapists ignored her anxiety.

The process was explained to her, and Ponder assured her that no one would hurt her.

The idea was that she would reexperience the trauma of her birth, get in touch with repressed memories of going through the birth canal, and be reduced to an accepting infantile state that needed a mother. In a sense, she would start over, with Jeane as her mother, and after the session she should be much happier. The two of them would get along much better, and Candace would not feel so badly about her birth mother. So Candace got down on the floor, as she was instructed, and curled up in a fetal position. Ponder wrapped her in the flannel blanket to simulate the womb.

Four people entered the room. Jeane was one, along with Watkins, an office manager named Brita St. Clair, and her fiancé, Jack McDaniel. These latter two had served as Candace's foster parents at the facility, but neither had any medical training. They placed eight pillows on top of the child, in various angles, and applied their weight to simulate the contractions of a uterus trying to expel a fetus. Jeane stood aside to "catch" Candace as she wriggled out, with the hope that the difficulty of her journey would seal their bond. But the theory fell far short of what actually happened.

From within the blanket, Candace quickly complained of too much pressure and asked to be let out. They would not allow it. Either she had to "decide" to be born or she would die, just like a baby in a womb. Watkins added that if Candace didn't make it, Jeane, her mother, would die, too. Thus, she added a bit of guilt to the process.

The four adults continued to press down on Candace, but Candace struggled and said she couldn't do it. She started to cry, but even this did not persuade the therapists that perhaps she was not ready for so drastic a treatment. She then began to scream and say she could not breathe. She said she was about to die. The therapists encouraged her to fight to be born. Jeane did nothing to stop the session. In fact, they all ignored thirty-four separate pleas from the girl for release or assistance.

Candace kept asking for air and stated, "You mean you want me to die for real?"

Ponder told Candace to go ahead and die, meaning it metaphorically. Candace insisted she was sick and they had to get off her, but they didn't. They had heard children make this request before and no one had been harmed. It was just manipulation. They encouraged her to vomit if she wanted to, and defecate, as she threatened to do. She was not getting out until she fought on her own to get out.

Over half an hour had gone by and the child stopped talking. She stopped moving, so Ponder placed a pillow over her head to make her fight harder. She and Watkins started to insult Candace for quitting too easily. One of them asked, "Do you want to be reborn?" They heard her quiet response, "No."

Fifty minutes had passed, and she'd been unable to do more than kick a hole into the sheet by her feet. She said nothing more, no matter how they prodded or insulted her. Jeane allowed them to continue, although she could see that Candace was not fighting as she should be. Jeane grew upset, so she was asked to leave the room and watch from a monitor. It was crucial, they said, that she not interrupt the session.

Then after twenty minutes of no activity, the therapists unwrapped the "twerp," whom they believed was being defiant. Candace did not move. In fact, her skin was a bluish color, so Jeane ran back in to administer CPR to get her breathing again. Watkins called a paramedic, and they managed to get a weak heartbeat before they rushed Candace to a hospital. However, she had really gone into an extreme state while encased in the blanket, just as she'd told them. The therapists, who had made a video of the entire session, were concerned about how their technique could be interpreted. Candace died the next day in the hospital from cerebral edema—swelling of the brain.

The four people who had participated in the killing of Candace Newmaker were arrested and charged with a class 2 felony, reckless child abuse resulting in death. Jeane Newmaker was charged with negligent child abuse resulting in death. The therapists, freed on bail, were ordered to stop practicing.

Brita St. Clair and Jack McDaniel entered a plea deal, admitting their guilt in exchange for a ten-year probation and one thousand hours of community service. Newmaker agreed to be a witness for the prosecution, receiving the minimum sentence of four years, which the judge deferred because she had not really understood what she was doing. She was sentenced to four hundred hours of community service. The judge believed she had been the victim of unprofessional therapists offering a risky treatment. She was allowed to retain her nurse's license in Georgia and ordered to undergo mental health and grief counseling.

Watkins and Ponder went to trial together in a case that made headlines around the country and did some damage to the image of Attachment Therapy. Steve Jensen and Laura Dunbar prosecuted the case. They called Candace's regular physician to the witness stand to describe how the lack of oxygen had caused heart failure, which in turn had caused Candace's brain to swell. "She was in a position," he stated, "where the airway couldn't be checked and couldn't be cleared." She had also vomited, and gastric content was found in her lungs, which suggested she had asphyxiated on her vomit. As her doctor, he knew of no heart problems or respiratory issues in her medical history. In his opinion, her heart had seized due to suffocation.

Two psychologists and a psychotherapist, all familiar with Attachment Therapy and "holding" sessions of this nature, testified for the prosecution. They said that there was no evidence that the procedures used with Candace were effective for getting the behavioral results they claimed to achieve. In fact, this therapy, from all appearances, was unethical by professional codes of conduct. Jeane Newmaker also testified, describing Candace's difficult behavior as the reason she had been in the Evergreen program, yet there were no witnesses to corroborate the child's bad behavior.

Julie Ponder, Connell Watkins, and Watkins's daughter Teka (from left to right) arrive at court.
AP/Wide World Photos

The entire seventy-minute videotape of the rebirthing session was played, along with tapes of the earlier sessions and of other rebirthing sessions done at the facility. When jurors were forced to listen to Candace's pleas and the therapists' seemingly harsh and sarcastic responses, many were horrified and had a difficult time remaining in their seats. Most were in tears. Some said afterward that they just wanted to rescue the little girl and did not understand why the treatment had to be so harsh.

Even worse, in terms of impact, was Ponder and Watkins taking the stand to explain their theories, treatment, and behavior regarding Candace. They seemed defensive and unemotional, talking to the prosecutor as if she just did not understand. They were unwilling to "take responsibility for their error" because they did not believe they had done anything wrong. To them, Candace's behavior had been manipulative, so they thought they had been justified in their approach.

When asked why tapes of other sessions—the longest of which was under six minutes—had been so comparatively gentle, Watkins said that Candace was more difficult than the other children who had endured rebirthing. However, on the tape it appeared that Candace had done everything they had told her and had not come across as difficult. When Watkins was asked why she hadn't responded to the child's request for help, she said, "We did respond. We just didn't respond in the way you think we should."

Ponder, who had participated in at least twenty rebirthing session, described her own rebirthing experience (something Watkins had never endured) and said it had been like being held by a lot of loving people. She, too, defended everything they had done with Candace and insisted they had checked her breathing and did not think she was genuinely having the problems she claimed to be having. However, the video showed that while a full half hour went by with no word from the child before they finally unwrapped her, and twenty minutes had passed with no sound of her labored breathing, they had only checked her breathing once during that time. Ponder replied that she believed the child had fallen asleep.

The defense attorneys, Gregg Lawler and Craig Truman (for Watkins) and Joan Heller (for Ponder), pointed out that the therapists had sought only to help, not harm, the child. The rebirthing therapy had worked wonders for some people, and some of these former patients came in to testify. A number of colleagues and acquaintances spoke on the defendants' behalf to build the impression that Watkins and Ponder were responsible, reliable, and experienced therapists providing a tested treatment. In addition, a pathologist offered other reasons why Candace might have expired that were not related to the therapy. Yet nothing the defense presented outweighed the impact of the videotape of the fatal session.

In closing arguments, Steve Jensen had the jurors hold to their faces a flannel blanket similar to the one used on Candace to experience how difficult it was to breathe through it. Then he told them to add thick, nonbreathable pillows and the weight of four adults, to the tune of 673 total pounds against the child's 75. No other rebirthing session at Evergreen had lasted as long, so these therapists had no experience to judge what Candace might be enduring. The proof was that she had repeatedly told them she could not breathe and that she was dying, and then she did die. They had been negligent to the point of being abusive, and for that there was no excuse.

The defense for both therapists involved suggesting other factors in the child's death, such as an undiagnosed heart condition (her brother had died from one) or the effects of the medication she was taking. The attorneys even mentioned that the treatment center was over seven thousand feet above sea level, which could have affected Candace's ability to breathe. In short, they reached for anything and everything that might provide reasonable doubt.

It took only five hours at the conclusion of the three-week trial for the jury to find both therapists guilty of reckless child abuse resulting in death. They faced as much as forty-eight years behind bars, but at their sentencing, Judge Jane Tidball gave them the minimum time—sixteen years. Even so, they both broke into tears, and Ponder made a statement: "I have to live the rest of my life knowing that Candace was dying next to me and I wasn't aware of it." Watkins, who was practicing without a license, was also found guilty of criminal impersonation, obtaining a signature by deception, and the unlawful practice of psychotherapy. As she heard the sentence, she said that she accepted full responsibility.

Colorado passed a law banning the rebirthing therapy, and it has been criticized as both limited and patently ineffective.

Watkins and Ponder both launched appeals, Watkins on the basis that she had not received a fair trial because the judge did not allow parents with problem children to testify. Ponder said that her case should not have been attached to Watkins's. In 2005 the Colorado Supreme Court refused to consider Ponder's appeal, depleting her legal options in that state. Their cases are pending.

SOURCES

"Colorado Supreme Court Refuses to Hear Therapist's Appeal in Rebirthing Death." Associated Press, February 14, 2005.

Crowder, Carla, and Peggy Lowe. "Her Name Was Candace." *Rocky Mountain News*, October 29, 2000.

King, Patricia, and Sharon Begley. "A 'Rebirth' Brings Death." *Newsweek*, June 5, 2000.

Kohler, Judith. "Suffocating Girl's Pleas Went Unanswered, Prosecutor Says." Associated Press, April 20, 2001.

———. "Therapist Says She Learned Technique from New Age People." Associated Press, April 18, 2001.

Lowe, Peggy. "No Prison for Candace's Adoptive Mom." *Rocky Mountain News*, October 12, 2001.

———. "Video a Key Piece in Abuse Trial." *Rocky Mountain News*, March 25, 2001.

Mercer, Jean. *Understanding Attachment*. Westport, CT: Praeger, 2006.

Mercer, Jean, Larry Sarner, and Linda Rosa. *Attachment Theory on Trial: The Torture and Death of Candace Newmaker*. Westport, CT: Praeger, 2003.

Nicholson, Kieran. "Domino Effect Caused Girl's Death, Doctor Testifies in Rebirthing Case." *Denver Post*, April 10, 2001.

———. "Ponder Defends Rebirth Session." *Denver Post*, April 20, 2001.

———. "Therapists Guilty in Fatal 'Rebirth.'" *Denver Post*, April 22, 2001.

Robinson, Marilyn. "Three Jailed in Child's Therapy Death." *Denver Post*, May 19, 2000.

Rouse, Karen, and Kieran Nicholson. "Therapy Video Moved Jurors." *Denver Post*, April 22, 2001.

Tsai, Catherine. "Four Face Trial in Therapy Death." Associated Press, August 18, 2000.

eleven

C.S.I.: "I Like to Watch": A rapist gains access to a woman's apartment by posing as a fireman.

TRUE STORY: In 2005 in New York City, Peter Braunstein impersonated a fireman to gain access to a woman's apartment, where he molested her.

It was Halloween in Manhattan, and as parades of costumed people flooded the streets, few noticed the middle-aged man with a bag of items enter a Chelsea-area apartment building: Peter Braunstein, forty-one, had a plan. He waited and watched for the thirty-four-year-old woman to arrive home, and once he was certain she was there, he set down Dixie cups filled with chemicals of his own concoction. He slipped on a firefighter's outfit, purchased via his Internet moniker "Gulagmeister," and crouched down to light the Dixie cups. Smoke soon filled the hallway.

Braunstein readied his police badge, also purchased online, and pounded on the woman's door, shouting, "Fire!" He announced he was from the fire department and awaited her response. When she opened the door, he showed his credentials, then pounced with a BB gun and chloroform-soaked cloth, pushing his way inside.

It was easy to get the stunned woman under his control. Braunstein gagged her, tied her arms behind her, and used duct tape to bind her to her bed. He also produced shackles to use on her and donned a ski mask, so that if she revived, she would not recognize him or be able to identify him later. As real firefighters arrived to extinguish the tiny blazes in the hall, over the next thirteen hours Braunstein kept his victim captive, undressing and repeatedly groping her. He video-taped her ordeal, forcing her to put on various pairs of her stiletto shoes. He then gave her a sleeping pill and took one himself, lying down beside her to take a nap. For some reason he told her his birth date. When he awoke around 7:00 A.M., he grabbed money and sev-eral items from her apartment and left.

Still bound, the victim managed to free herself. She noticed an odd note on the mirror that said, "Bye—Hope things turn around for U soon." After phoning the police, she called a friend and waited. When another knock came, with an official announcing himself, she was so scared she could not let even the police inside. The 911 dis-patcher talked her through it. The police sent her right to the hospi-tal, but not before she gave a brief description of her ordeal and said she did not know her attacker's identity. She had burns on her face and neck from the chemical used to subdue her, and she underwent an examination to learn how far the assault was carried out while she had been unconscious.

When newspapers published a report on the incident, a woman who read it thought the behavior sounded suspiciously familiar. She even knew the victim, because they worked at the same publishing company, Fairchild, so she called the police to name a possible sus-pect: former fashion writer Peter Braunstein. He too had worked at Fairchild and had once been the caller's boyfriend. She knew that he fixated on certain types of women and was controlling and obsessive. After she broke up with him, he harassed her.

The police tried to contact Braunstein but could not find him. A search of his apartment and storage space in Queens turned up items taken from the victim's apartment: a fur coat, shoes, luggage, and her driver's license and résumé. As investigators pieced the story together, they learned that Braunstein had seen the victim on a regular basis at Fairchild and had apparently grown obsessed with the stiletto-heeled shoes she wore. And the suspect was nowhere to be found.

The police distributed posters throughout the city that featured Braunstein's photo, with his unruly mop of curly brown hair, and indicated that he was wanted for questioning. It listed facts about him supplied by friends and associates: He liked Guinness beer and beef curry with extra mustard. He rolled his own cigarettes, spoke French, and had a sarcastic wit. He was five-foot-eleven, weighed 150 pounds, and had been born in January 1964. In the past he had used aliases such as "Peter Grant," "Peter Bronson," and "Peter Brown."

Aside from his job at *Women's Wear Daily*, where he had commented on current fashions, this son of immigrants used to write about popular culture for publications such as the *Village Voice*, specializing in the 1960s and 1970s; he was also an aspiring playwright. But over the past year or so, Braunstein's life had taken a turn for the worse. Things began to decline for Braunstein in 2002, after he quit his job when his boss warned him not to bully people for comp tickets. Employed since 2000 at Fairchild, Braunstein was a long way from his previous status as a student at the Sorbonne and a Ph.D. candidate at New York University. His female idols were strong women, such as Faye Dunaway, Jackie Onassis, and Jane Fonda, and journalists digging for facts learned that he was both insecure and grandiose. Reportedly he possessed a sadistic streak and talked in rigidly moral terms. He'd once been hospitalized for an overdose of pills and was said to be taking Prozac. Model Kate Moss, scheduled for a New York visit in November, had been warned to be careful because Braunstein had once written an article entitled "Stalking Kate," about his decade-long obsession with her.

After he left Fairchild, his girlfriend had declined to quit her job as he requested, to show her support, and when she broke up with him, he harassed her with nonstop phone calls. He also sent threatening e-mails to her family and posted nude pictures of her on the Internet. Braunstein was sentenced to Bellevue for a brief psychiatric confinement, but he pled guilty to a misdemeanor and got probation. Then he apparently learned that the woman whose shoes he had admired from afar had resigned over a disagreement about shoes. That apparently got his attention.

For six weeks after the Halloween-night incident, Braunstein was a wanted fugitive with a twelve-thousand-dollar reward posted. His seventy-two-year-old father, Alberto, pleaded with him on television to give himself up and get the help he needed. From security camera videos at a Midtown motel, the police learned where Braunstein had been for a while. He had purchased a subway fare card with his credit card, but in late November he was reported at a bus station in Columbus, Ohio.

Braunstein settled for a few days in Cleveland, where he booked a room in the Town House Motel and placed an ad in the *Cleveland Plain Dealer* for a driver. As he was being chauffeured around, he posed as a television producer scouting locations and asked to be taken to a strip joint that featured lap dancing. He was also spotted drinking vodka at Moriarty's Pub. In one place, he was said to have flashed a U.S. marshal's badge—another eBay souvenir.

Next Braunstein turned up in Memphis, Tennessee. There he sold

Stalkers tend to be unemployed or underemployed, but are generally smarter than other criminals. They often have a history of failed intimate relationships and tend to devalue and sexualize their victims. They also idealize certain people, project onto other people motives and actions that have no basis in truth, dismiss what those people do to resist or discourage them, and rationalize that the target person deserves to be harassed and violated.

Some experts think narcissism is instrumental in delusions about a love object. It's the idea that one is so important or grand that no one is unattainable for him, and he will prove it. He can even persuade himself that the person he desires wants him back and will therefore welcome an advance. This delusion becomes a way to stabilize the grandiose self; it replaces something lost. But decompensation can occur, in which the obsessed person's inner stability erodes, and he will blame others and might decide they must be punished.

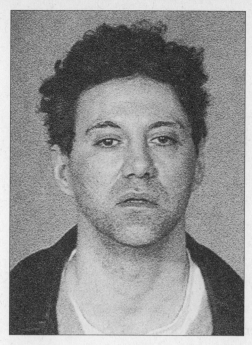

Peter Braunstein, who fled the state to elude NYPD efforts to question him about a bizarre Halloween attack on an ex-colleague, and was at large for over six weeks.
AP/Wide World Photos

blood on November 29 to make twenty dollars, using his real name and passport to register. He told the receptionist he was a journalist on his way to Kansas, but instead found a room at the local YMCA and sought ways to get money, such as looking for a lost dog for the posted reward.

On December 16, Braunstein wandered onto the University of Memphis campus. He'd been watching the New York tabloids and was aware he'd been featured on *America's Most Wanted*, but what he did not know was that an avid viewer of that program was standing not twenty feet from him, talking on the phone. She looked up and recognized him. Thinking quickly, she flagged down a campus police officer.

He called for assistance, and as they approached Braunstein, he supposedly said, "I'm the one they're looking for from New York," and proceeded to slash or stab himself three times in the neck with a double-bladed, three-inch knife. The officers hit him with pepper spray, but he didn't flinch. Finally they managed to handcuff him and rush him to a local emergency room, where he received approximately fifteen stitches. In his coat pocket they found the BB gun he had used on the victim in Chelsea, and in his knapsack was a journal about his flight, a videotape, and shackles.

When he was stable two days later, Braunstein was taken to a cell at the Shelby County jail, and the NYPD prepared to go get him. Tennessee authorities dropped charges so he could be extradited to New York. Police indicated that Braunstein seemed to enjoy the media attention he was getting. He was held at Bellevue on suicide watch, where his mother visited him for fifteen minutes and told reporters that he was not himself.

On December 23, 2005, Assistant District Attorney Maxine Rosenthal announced Braunstein's thirteen-count indictment for sexual molestation. He was also charged with arson, burglary, and robbery. At a hearing, he pleaded not guilty. The attorney Braunstein's father hired, Robert Gottlieb, requested a psychiatric examination to determine Braunstein's fitness to stand trial. He was found competent, so the legal proceedings moved forward, and in May 2007, Braunstein went to trial. Gottlieb announced his intention to mount an insanity defense.

Rosenthal argued that Braunstein's behavior as early as ten months before the incident indicated that he was aware of the criminal nature of his act; so did his six-week flight afterward. Gottlieb protested that someone as mentally ill as Braunstein could not be held responsible for forming criminal intent. There was also an issue as to whether Braunstein's actions constituted kidnapping, since the legal definition required that he hold his victim for over twelve hours.

The victim described how Braunstein had used a gun and a knife to force her to the floor and placed a chloroform-soaked rag over her nose and mouth. She had passed out for two hours and awoke to find herself tied up and mostly naked, except for stiletto shoes. The intruder, now wearing a ski mask and a badge, was groping her breasts and genitals. She tried to keep him talking in the hope it would prevent him from being too aggressive. When he finally left, taking her Louis Vuitton bag and fur coat, she waited half an hour, called a friend, and then dialed 911 to report the incident. The jury listened to the tape of her hysterical call. She also testified that when police took her to the hospital, the ligature marks on her wrist were bleeding, and she had burn marks on her face and neck from the chloroform.

With a neater appearance than on the day of his arrest, the defendant seemed to go in and out of consciousness, showing no evidence of the self-inflicted stab wounds to his neck from the previous December. He grew attentive when the jury learned from different merchants how he had accumulated the supplies he needed for the assault, beginning with eBay transactions dating back to January 2005. He'd used various screen names to buy chloroform, an FDNY coat and pants, a Detroit police badge, and a supply of potassium nitrate for his smoke bombs. There appeared to be a clear method to what he collected. Indeed, he purchased a ski mask to conceal his identity and a gun and a knife to ensure his victim's compliance. He also bought a pair of handcuffs and a gas mask.

Gottlieb wanted the jury to believe that his client had slowly devolved from a man once capable of holding a job and having relationships into one with a faulty neurological condition who could no longer take the pressure. There was no evidence that Braunstein had raped or even attempted to rape the victim, Gottlieb pointed out, so it had not been a sexually motivated assault.

Still, Braunstein's DNA and fingerprints had been found in the victim's apartment, and a shaft of her hair, identified via DNA analysis, was on his ski mask.

A week into the trial, Braunstein's former girlfriend took the stand. As the person who had originally identified him as the fake fireman, she described their difficult relationship and Braunstein's self-destructive threats. At first he'd been intelligent and funny, she said, but then he'd grown increasingly morose. After she asked him to move out, she received threatening phone calls and e-mails, for which he received a charge of harassment. Gottlieb was quick to frame this as proof of Braunstein's escalating illness.

The most provocative evidence to surface was Braunstein's manifesto and the journal he had penned while on the run. Justice Thomas Farber decided which parts the jury would be able to hear. He excluded Braunstein's entries about Hannibal Lecter, David "Son of Sam" Berkowitz, Andrew Cunanan, and the 1999 Columbine massacre, but decided that Braunstein's stated desire to attack a certain fashion celebrity was relevant. It seems that the accused had pondered killing the editor in chief of *Vogue* magazine, Anna Wintour. When he had worked as a fashion writer, he apparently resented the way she declined to accept his calls.

In the excerpts published in several news sources, Braunstein mentioned that God talked to him, but denied he heard voices, and said that during the course of the alleged incident, he had known what he was doing. Psychiatric experts who read these pieces for reporters failed to see evidence of psychosis; they viewed Braunstein as insecure, narcissistic, and angry.

To support the claim of insanity, Gottlieb hired both a psychologist and a psychiatrist to give professional assessments. Dr. Barbara Kirwin, a clinical psychologist, described Braunstein as a textbook case of paranoid schizophrenia. He was also suicidal. She explained that such a person can be functional in many contexts but still not be aware of the nature of some of his actions. She had learned from the defendant that upon his detention, he had banged his head against the bars of his cell and expressed his intent to kill himself. Kirwin went on to say that Braunstein's attack had been symbolic: The victim was just a stand-in for the fashion industry.

"He saw himself as a hit man for God," she stated. "He's an avenging angel, a special person who has been chosen to right hypocrisies." Anger and hurt over a romantic breakup had triggered his illness, and it had grown into a large-scale revenge fantasy, wherein Braunstein wanted to punish a corrupt arena of society—the fashion industry. Braunstein had told her, she testified, that the incident with the victim had merely been a game. They were both "synthetic people," and he was surprised that she had reported it. He admitted that he knew it was a crime but did not think it was wrong.

ADA Rosenthal dismissed all this as Braunstein's attempt to gain notoriety by committing a crime that would get him attention: He'd researched killers who had done so, including the man who had shot fashion mogul Gianni Versace, in order to form his own plan. He might be disturbed, Rosenthal added, but that did not preclude planning or awareness of the criminal nature of his act.

Another defense expert, psychiatrist Monte S. Buchsbaum, had also hoped to prove that Braunstein was unable to make a clear-headed choice, but his approach failed to undermine the possibility of planning. He had subjected the defendant to a PET scan and used diagrams to demonstrate that Braunstein's brain was defective in a way that was consistent with a diagnosis of schizophrenia. However, the scan had occurred six months after the incident, and the psychiatrist had to admit that a brain scan was not sufficient for diagnosing a mental illness. In fact, he had not looked at Braunstein's past psychiatric records or tested his ability to plan. Thus, while he could show the differences between Braunstein's brain and a normal brain, he was unable to prove anything about the defendant's mental state at the time of the offense.

The prosecution had an expert, too, who disagreed that Braunstein was so disengaged from reality that he was unable to appreciate what he was doing. Neuropsychologist William Barr stated that the Halloween attack on the victim was the first step in an elaborate plan to eventually kill the *Vogue* editor, Anna Wintour. He was angry that this woman, along with the girlfriend who'd broken up with him, had repeatedly spurned him. Via media accounts, he'd seen Andrew Cunanan do the same thing in 1997 when he killed former lovers and ended his spree with the death of designer Gianni Versace. Evidence of long-term planning on Braunstein's part seemed clear.

The accused might be a depressed narcissist with a substance abuse problem, said psychiatrist Li-Wen Lee, who observed him several times, but he did not have schizophrenia. There was no evidence of hallucinations or disorganized speech, she added, but he certainly had a need for attention and admiration.

Jurors also heard that when Braunstein was in Tennessee, he had posed as a Hurricane Katrina victim, three months after the devastating weather incident, apparently in the belief it would get him free meals and shelter. But he also stated that he'd intended to go to New Orleans to lead a group of survivors in a protest, because he viewed them, like himself, as having an "end-of-the-world" philosophy. Dr. Barr believed this arose from grandiose notions about himself rather than from a psychotic delusion.

It was Justice Farber who, outside the jury's hearing, raised the issue that schizophrenia did not preclude the ability to plan and form criminal intent. Prosecutor Maxine Rosenthal picked up on this idea in her closing argument, while Robert Gottlieb continued to hammer home the notion that Braunstein had a broken brain, particularly in the area where planning occurs.

The jury decided that Braunstein had indeed formed criminal intent. On Wednesday, May 23, 2007, after four hours of deliberations, they convicted Braunstein of kidnapping, sex abuse, robbery, and burglary, but acquitted him of second-degree arson.

While awaiting his sentencing hearing, Braunstein composed a lengthy letter to Judge Farber. He faced twenty-five years to life, and he hoped he could get that reduced to a minimum of fifteen years.

The crudely handwritten note, which Braunstein dictated to a fellow inmate because his hands shook from medication, maintained the theme argued by his forensic experts that he had suffered from untreated paranoid schizophrenia. He discussed the antiquated legal system in America as well as the lack of consensus on mental illness and criminal intent in the psychiatric community. Flattering the judge with his perception that Farber was "fair and circumspect," Braunstein promised to be a model prisoner. He asked the judge not to be influenced by "sensationalist" media coverage.

Braunstein admitted that he had indeed planned the crime but had not intended harm and had not really planned what to do once he'd entered the victim's apartment. To his mind, it was "more like an improvised pantomime of a crime," except that it had an effect on the victim that he now found deplorable.

On June 18, 2007, Justice Farber sentenced Braunstein to twenty years to life. He believed that Braunstein, consumed with narcissistic rage, had intended the crime. No sentence, he added, could undo the negative impact on the victim.

SOURCES

Baird, Woody. "Memphis Cops Nab Suspected Sex Fiend." Associated Press, December 17, 2005.

"Capture File for Peter Braunstein." *America's Most Wanted*, December 16, 2005.

Grinberg, Emmanuella. "Braunstein Sentenced to 18 Years to Life." CourtTV .com, June 19, 2007.

———. "Braunstein's Defense Highlights Lack of Rape Evidence in Halloween Attack." CourtTV.com, May 7, 2007.

"In Diaries, Peter Braunstein Writes about Life on the Run and His Impatience to Die." CourtTV.com, May 10, 2007.

"Kate Sex Stalker Is on the Run." *The Mirror*, November 14, 2005.

Maull, Samuel. "Peter Braunstein Indicted, Appears in Court on Assault Charges." *Newsday*, December 23, 2005.

"Peter Braunstein's Ex-girlfriend Takes the Stand." abclocal.go.com, May 9, 2007.

"Peter Braunstein's Plea for Leniency." CourtTV.com, June 15, 2007.

Ross, Barbara, and Corky Siemaszko. "Braunstein Wrote about Killing *Vogue* Editor. *New York Daily News*, May 14, 2007.

———. "He's Not Psycho, Say Pros Reading Fiend's Tale." *New York Daily News*, May 13, 2007.

twelve

C.S.I.: "Face Lift": Nadine Weston is burned to ash in her home, with only a foot remaining, yet her chair and the surrounding furniture have barely been damaged. In the ceiling overhead, the fire made a sizable hole.

TRUE STORY: The FBI investigated an apparent case of spontaneous human combustion in Florida.

Mary Hardy Reeser lived alone in an apartment on Cherry Street in northeast St. Petersburg, Florida. The sixty-seven-year-old widow had moved there from Pennsylvania after her husband died, to be closer to her only child, Richard, who was a doctor. It was a hot night on Sunday, July 1, 1951, and Reeser had just enjoyed dinner with her son and his wife, and her landlady, Pansy Carpenter, who lived in the apartment next door. Richard would later say that she told him she had taken two Seconals to help her sleep and planned to take two more, as was her habit. They bid her goodnight around 9:00 P.M., and sometime during the night or early morning hours she rose from bed and went to sit in her chair. The windows were partially open, and apparently she lit up a cigarette.

Pansy Carpenter came knocking around 8:00 A.M. to give Reeser a telegram that had just arrived. No one answered, but she believed her elderly tenant, who was overweight and not very mobile, was inside, so she tried the doorknob to see if it was locked. She found it quite hot to the touch, as was the door itself, so she summoned

All that was found of sixty-seven-year-old widow Mary Reeser, who had apparently died of spontaneous human combustion.
The Fortean Picture Library

painters from across the street and they helped her enter the apartment. As they opened the door, they felt a sharp blast of hot air.

They all saw black soot on the ceiling and upper parts of the walls that had a greasy odor, and then a chair in the living room that had been reduced to ash, with only the springs intact. Mrs. Carpenter called the fire department, and when they arrived, they used a hand pump to put out the still-smoldering fire. Reeser was nowhere to be found, but they soon realized that she had been sitting in the chair when it burned, and she'd been entirely incinerated.

Only a pile of ashes lay in that spot. A table next to the chair had also burned, except for two of its legs, and a carpet beneath Reeser's feet had burned for about three feet. While it was clear that a fire had killed her, the fact that many items around her had not burned, including a newspaper, seemed a mystery. The ceiling showed signs of extreme heat in the area over her head.

The police arrived to process the scene and in the ash found some teeth, bone fragments from a spinal column, and a clump of soot that, cleaned up, turned out to be her left ankle and foot, hollowed out and still encased in an undamaged suede slipper. The slipper was saturated with a thick, greasy substance, as was an uncharred part of the rug. Reeser's skull, or what seemed to be a skull, was also located, but it had shrunk considerably, to about the size of a grapefruit. None of her facial features remained intact.

To consume a human body, the fire had to have burned quite hot, and in fact several plastic light switches had softened and melted, but

SPONTANEOUS HUMAN COMBUSTION (SHC)

Also known as self-cremation, SHC is the alleged burning of someone's body without an identifiable source of ignition. Typically, but not always, the person dies. Combustion may produce burns or blisters, or consume a body entirely. It allegedly starts inside the body and reduces a person to ash in less time than the hottest fires of a crematorium. The first recorded case occurred in 1613 in England, when John Hitchen went to bed and apparently combusted, killing his children and burning his wife in the process (all were in the same bed). He burned for three hours as others tried unsuccessfully to douse the flames.

The theory most often used to explain this phenomenon is the "wick effect," in which human body fat, which leaks out and acts like a candle-wick, burns a body inwardly with enough heat to dissolve it but not enough to incinerate other parts of the room. Most scientists insist that there is always an external source of ignition—a fireplace, a candle, a cigarette. Another theory posits a flash fire from a buildup of static energy, and a third cites ball lightning as the source.

People who cremate bodies as part of their profession have stated that the remains they have seen of supposed cases of SHC do not resemble bodies burned in an ordinary fire. No human body, they say, could generate the amount of heat required to be reduced to ash in the manner of these cases.

nothing else had been incinerated, including floor plugs lower down. Two candles had melted, but their wicks were intact and unburned. An electric clock had stopped at 4:20, presumably from the intense heat, but when plugged in to an unaffected baseboard, it ran again.

Officers tested for an accelerant, thinking perhaps someone had knocked Reeser out and set her afire, but the tests were negative. The investigators were stymied, as the scene looked like nothing they had ever experienced, and rumors of spontaneous human combustion turned up in the media. Because it was such a peculiar and puzzling case, on July 7 investigators called in the FBI.

The St. Petersburg police chief, J. R. Reichert, sent a box of evidence to FBI director J. Edgar Hoover, which contained glass fragments found in the ashes, six objects that resembled teeth, part of the carpet (burned and unburned), the intact shoe, fibers thought to be from a nightgown, a small piece of metal found near the body, charred legs from the table, cotton weave thought to be from the chair, and several other items. He also sent photographs of what they had found when they first entered the apartment, and a diagram of the layout.

What they knew, he stated, was that Mary Reeser had last been seen in her home the night before, at which time she was wearing a rayon acetate nightdress and a rayon housecoat, which could not be found during the investigation. She had taken a heavy dose of sleeping pills. At the end of his note, Reichert added, "We request any information or theories that could explain how a human body could be so destroyed and the fire confined to such a small area and so little damage done to the structure of the building and the furniture in the room not even scorched or damaged by smoke." The last line of his letter was a bit cryptic: "This evidence has not been examined by any other Examiner, nor will it be."

The results of the three-week FBI analysis indicated that there had been no accelerant present in the items sent, although the report's author added that the absence of such a fluid did not preclude the possibility that one had been used; it would have been consumed early in the fire. The greasy substance saturating several items was human fat, and it was possible for a body to incinerate to this point without the use of gasoline or other accelerants: "It is not generally realized the extent to which the human body can burn once it becomes ignited." The FBI, in fact, had numerous such cases on record, the report said, and was aware of preternatural explanations of human combustion, but in all cases an external source of ignition had been identified. The report noted that the unusual nature of such cases was the fact that there was little damage to items around the incinerated body, and cited one case of a woman seated on a staircase wearing "voluminous garments." Nothing was left of the clothing when her combusted remains were found, but "no extensive damage was done to the stairs."

For Reeser's case, the FBI offered an explanation. The agents who analyzed it theorized that Reeser had died from what they and others called "the wick effect." They started with the fact that Reeser relied on sleeping pills and had told her son the previous evening that she had taken two Seconals and planned to take more. While they could not prove it with a toxicology analysis, they assumed she had taken enough to be groggy. It appeared from the photos that she had in fact gone to bed but had arisen later, possibly to get some air. Then she'd sat in her chair and started to smoke (there were remains from a cigarette lighter in the ashes), but had fallen asleep before she finished. She had probably dropped the lit cigarette onto her synthetic nightgown and robe. A small spark, fueled by body fat, grew into intense heat.

"Once a body starts to burn," the report states, "there is enough fat and other flammable substances to permit varying amounts of destruction to take place. Sometimes the destruction by burning will proceed to a degree which results in almost complete combustion of the body." With the increasing heat, the fat seeps out into whatever the victim is wearing and feeds the fire. Thus, the person burns like a candlewick. The heat goes straight up, according to the theory, so items near the person may fail to catch fire. Reeser had been obese, at

175 pounds, so she'd had enough fat to achieve this effect. The cause of the fire, the FBI ultimately decided, was the cigarette. "The absence of any scorching or damage to furniture in the room," the report stated, "can only be explained by the fact that heat liberated by the burning body had a tendency to rise and form a layer of hot air which never came in contact with the furnishings on a lower level. This situation would have occurred particularly if the fire had smoldered rather than burned freely."

Not everyone accepted this idea, finding it difficult to believe that the "cinder woman," as she came to be called, could burn so hot but not start a fire that would destroy everything around her. One man sent a tediously detailed letter to a magazine, *True Police Cases*, which the editor forwarded to the FBI. The author, whose name was redacted, insisted that the only appropriate explanation for this case was that Reeser had been murdered. The fact that no one had smelled the odor of burnt human fat indicated that she had not burned in that room, because it would have permeated the place. Since the crime scene had been badly compromised, his theory could not be proven, but he felt certain about his idea, and his letter was retained in the files (perhaps his obsession with the incident as a homicide made him a potential suspect). He was a retired doctor, he said, who enjoyed reading detective stories.

This man believed he even knew what the motive was. First he launched into what he knew about shrunken skulls and the process of cremation, then declared that Reeser had not burned. Instead, while in a groggy state, she had been led from the apartment by someone who had carefully planned her execution. After eliminating her, he planted ashes, bone fragments, and the foot (perhaps hers, cut off and brought back) to make investigators think she had burned. He had acquired a shrunken skull from Africa and placed it in the ashes, for a more authentic presentation.

The letter writer was aware from case details printed in the magazine that Mary Reeser had been despondent, and he stated that her killer would have been someone who profited from her death either financially or emotionally. Her son, a doctor, was financially well off, but he might have found her to be irritating, as she was seeking to move closer to where he lived and expected him for dinner every Sunday, without fail. But she might also have confided to someone she knew that she had cash stashed somewhere in the house, as elderly people tend to do, and that person exploited it.

While the letter writer was adamant about his hypothesis, no homicide investigation was launched.

Chief Reichert did invite anthropologist and renowned "bone detective" Wilton M. Krogman, from the University of Pennsylvania, to examine the scene and the remains. Krogman was a specialist in the effects of fire on bodies. He examined everything available and read the FBI report, but did not accept the wick effect theory. He'd burned bones in all sorts of conditions, including "green" bones (stripped of flesh but not dried), and from his various experiments he had extrapolated a principle: "The destruction of animal or human tissue is a function of the conditions of combustion rather than of the type of combustible used."

In Krogman's experience, he later wrote, in conditions of intense heat, the human skull does not shrink, as it seemed to do in the Reeser case; it explodes. He would have expected to find portions of the cranium blown apart, but such was not evident at this scene. He said that he also had expected much more damage to the room in which Reeser had burned, and the lack of it puzzled him. He stated in a magazine article in 1952, "I regard [the case] as the most amazing thing I have ever seen. As I review it, the short hairs on my neck bristle with vague fear." His conclusion: "It couldn't happen but it did." He would say in another venue that he believed Reeser had been murdered elsewhere and then dumped back in her chair, already burned. Her killer had then used a heated device to melt the plastic items to make it appear that she had burned in her chair.

In August 1951, Chief Reichert officially declared the case to be a tragic accident. Nevertheless, he added that it was not yet closed, as it was the most unusual incident of his twenty-five-year career. He thought perhaps it would never be solved to anyone's satisfaction. He had received hundreds of letters suggesting what had occurred, yet no one had completely explained it. A reporter who published Reichert's statement, along with the gist of the FBI report, pointed out that there were still three loose ends that needed attention: (1) no odor of burnt flesh was ever detected, (2) no time of death had been established to determine how rapidly the blaze had burned, and (3) no smoke had been detected by neighbors (including the landlady next door) or workmen in the area.

As the FBI noted, there are numerous cases of supposed SHC on record. In April 1990 in China, for example, smoke had reportedly poured forth from four-year-old Tong Tang-Jiang, and his parents discovered that his underwear had ignited for no apparent reason. They rushed him to the hospital, and over the course of two hours he erupted again several times, causing burns on different parts of his body and on the bed mattress. The doctors thought he was generating electrical current in amounts high enough to kindle his clothing, and they diagnosed him as being "fire-prone." It's difficult to learn what happened to him.

A man in England in 1985 who survived the experience had supposedly been the victim of a fire bursting forth in his stomach. He got to a hospital in time to be extinguished and said he'd felt like he'd been plunged into a furnace. No one could explain how it had happened. He did not smoke and said he had not been near any flames. Another man whose arm burst into flames said he'd smelled it and felt hot before he felt pain. Yet most victims are elderly and don't survive. There are several cases in which the torso, arms, and head were incinerated entirely but the legs remained intact.

So many rumors about SHC persisted in the Reeser case and others that in 1998, Dr. John De Haan of the California Criminalistics Institute decided to test the wick effect hypothesis. For a British television program, he wrapped a dead pig in cotton, placed it in a furnished room, and used a little gasoline to set it on fire. As expected, the pig's body fat eventually boiled from the heat and leeched into the material, causing the fire to burn hot and then simmer long enough to reduce the corpse to ashes. The fat apparently rose to the temperature of a cremation, and thus had a greater effect on the body than would fire from an external source. A television set in the room was damaged but nothing else. So it seemed that the wick effect was at least a possibility in the Reeser case, if not in others, although even after the experiment, proponents of SHC continue to argue that it's a mysterious occurrence not yet explained by science.

SOURCES

Blizen, Jerry. "Reeser Death Accident—Body Furnished Own Fuel." *St. Petersburg Times*, August 9, 1951.

George, Leonard. *Alternative Realities*. New York: Facts on File, 1995.

http://foia.fbi.gov/reeser_mary_hardy, parts 1-5, 1951, File 95-HQ-41192.

Krogman, Wilton Marion. "The Strange Case of the Cinder Lady." *Pageant Magazine*, October 1952.

"New Light on Human Torch Mystery." BBC News, August 31, 1998.

Randles, Jenny, and Peter Hough. *Encyclopedia of the Unexplained*. New York: Barnes & Noble, 1995.

thirteen

C.S.I.: "Crash and Burn": An angry female driver crashes into a restaurant to kill as many employees of an insurance company who dine there as she can, as payback for the company's poor treatment of her.

TRUE STORY: Priscilla Joyce Ford crashed through two blocks of streets in Reno, Nevada, in 1980, killing seven and injuring two dozen more, as payback for the city's treatment of her.

It was midafternoon on Thanksgiving Day in Reno, Nevada. Ronald Reagan was about to step into the presidency as the decade of the 1980s began. People strolled along Casino Row of North Virginia Avenue, looking for a place to eat or just enjoying the weather, but never imagining what was about to occur. Without warning, a black woman driving a 1974 blue Lincoln Continental stepped on the accelerator and plowed into the nearest pedestrians. Then she kept going. The sun was behind the car, so people who heard the engine's roar had a difficult time seeing just how fast the car was coming until it was on them. Someone screamed, and a man was mown down in front of a couple from Idaho, who were struck next. The woman was caught on the hood, dangling between the headlight and radiator, and to her husband's horror, the driver kept moving as his wife fell to the sidewalk. Then another couple across the street suffered a similar fate.

The driver stared straight ahead as she accelerated to about 40 miles per hour, driving onto the sidewalk and striking several people without stopping. She twisted the car through side streets, knocked down newspaper boxes, and slammed into people, continuing on, even though one woman was still on the hood of her car. Bodies seemed to be everywhere, and people were screaming or crying out in pain, begging for help. Many pedestrians who could not believe what was happening ran into stores for protection.

The driver raced 100 feet down a sidewalk, moving straight toward a crowd in front of a club. She hit several people, and then drove more than 300 feet down another sidewalk. She might well have continued except that another motorist who saw what she was doing raced to get around and in front of her, and at Fifth Street he forced her to a halt. A patrol officer took her from her car and arrested her. She was angry that she'd been stopped and kept talking about her daughter. She referred to her victims, who littered the street from Second Avenue to the railroad tracks, as "beasts" and "pigs." The place looked like the aftermath of an explosion.

As she was taken to the station, rescue workers arrived, and the numbers of dead and injured rolled into area hospitals and morgues from the five-block massacre. Five people were dead, and a few others were injured so badly, the odds were against them surviving. (Two more would die.) Two dozen more people had suffered a variety of injuries. Several human limbs remained on the streets, along with

FEMALE MASS MURDERERS

According to the typical definition, a mass murderer is a person who kills four or more people in a single location (or loosely related locations) in a single incident. Mass killers are generally envisioned as white, middle-aged males who've lost their jobs or have some other anger issue or revenge fantasy. Disgruntled postal workers, bankrupt day traders, fired plant employees, and the like have typically dominated media headlines. Since female mass murderers are so few, they have not been studied as a group. Their weapons have ranged from guns to drowning to poison, but Ford is the only one who used a car.

knocked-over signs, upset trash containers, and items that people had been carrying. Survivors described the scene to reporters as similar to a battlefield. "She came right at us," one witness said, "she came at us with a body still on the hood of the car, and she looked like she was looking for someone else to hit."

Under interrogation, the driver told authorities that her name was Priscilla Joyce Ford, but added that some people called her Jesus Christ. She also claimed to be Adam, of Adam and Eve, and a prophetess. She said that she was tired of life and had deliberately planned to kill as many people with her car as she could, as a way to get attention. "A Lincoln Continental can do a lot of damage, can't it?" she reportedly said. Then she stated that a voice had urged her to do the same deed when she'd been in Boston six months earlier, but another voice (Joan Kennedy's, she said) had stopped her. She asked the officers how many she managed to kill, hoping the number was at least as high as seventy-five. They told her she had killed five, and she seemed to accept that. She admitted that she'd been drinking that day, and her blood alcohol level confirmed that she was intoxicated.

A native of Michigan with an IQ of 140—well above average— she had been a schoolteacher in Maine (she said New York) before moving to Reno, where she had briefly resided in 1973. She had returned to the town only three weeks before her rampage. People who knew her in Maine said she had told them she was going to Nevada to look for her missing daughter, Wynter Scott, who had been placed in foster care seven years earlier when Ford was arrested for trespassing. Apparently she had decided to make the people of Reno pay for taking her child, so the deaths she caused were largely symbolic. She had told a U.S. attorney in Maine the year before that if he did not help her get her daughter back, she would run down pedestrians. He apparently did not believe her.

It turned out that over the years Ford had been treated and released by seven different hospitals, diagnosed with paranoid schizophrenia. Some doctors believed she had violent tendencies. Found incompetent to stand trial, Ford was sent for drug therapy until such time as her competency could be restored. Then in 1981 she went to trial, pleading not guilty by reason of insanity on the charge of six counts of first-degree murder and twenty counts of attempted murder. (A seventh person had also died from injuries suffered, but it was reportedly too complicated to change the indictment.)

Despite how straightforward the case seemed, the proceedings lasted five months, the longest murder trial in Nevada's history to that point. Numerous witnesses attested to Ford's long history of mental instability, and mental health experts discussed her delusional religious beliefs. At one point Ford took the stand and insisted that the car had gone out of control. She did not recall hitting anyone, but there were plenty of eyewitnesses to contradict her. She offered other possibilities as well that she believed exonerated her, and said that she was incapable of sin because she was the incarnation of Jesus Christ. "I am in the state of mind that I am in heaven," she stated.

The prosecutor showed her pictures of the six people she had killed and asked her if she had been in a "heavenly state" when she ran them over. For each picture, she affirmed that, yes, she had been in a heavenly state. Looking at the crumpled bodies apparently did not disturb her or inspire remorse. She told jurors she kept her remorse private. She also described how in the past she had told her children that she hoped God would strike her husband dead, and the next day, he died. Apparently she had acquired the idea that she had supernatural power.

In closing, the prosecutor called her "evil personified" and reiterated that on that day, even with mental disorders and inebriation, she had known that what she was doing was wrong. Thus, she was legally sane. "She was angry that day," he said, "and what she did was what she intended to do." He had shown a videotape of her arrest in which she appeared calm and satisfied. Members of the jury apparently agreed with him, as they found Ford guilty on all counts and also sentenced her to death. She showed no emotion at the verdict or the sentence.

A year later, a reporter revisited her case. Confined to death row in the Southern Nevada Women's Correctional Center in Las Vegas, Ford was described by the warden as a quiet, introverted, and "unusual" inmate. The mass murderer spent most of her time with her nose in the Bible or watching television. She also appeared to be writing a book, but she guarded the manuscript zealously against prying eyes. Still filled with paranoia, she allowed no one close to her possessions. She had complained about hearing voices, and her conversation was usually filled with religious references. One day she had even fainted, and when she revived, she said she'd heard voices just before she passed out, but since they'd been friendly, she was fine. She was not afraid.

Ford initially waived all appeals and stated that she looked forward to dying, but the State Supreme Court nevertheless planned to perform the requisite automatic review. By the time the justices were ready to consider it, Ford had decided she had not received a fair trial, due to inadequate legal counsel, and asked to have her sentence commuted to life without parole. She lost. Ford then continued her appeals, exhausting them at the state level and moving on to the federal process.

But at the end of January 2005, Ford died in prison from respiratory failure. At the time she was the only woman on death row in Nevada, with eighty-three men awaiting execution. Seventy-five years old, she smoked heavily and suffered from emphysema. A flurry of papers carried the news, and when the DA heard it, his comment was, "She should have been executed long ago."

SOURCES

Cox, Don. "Idaho Rancher Recalls Deadly Thanksgiving When Car Drove Down Reno Sidewalk." *Reno Gazette-Journal*, November 24, 2005.

"Death Row Inmate Ford Dies." *Las Vegas Review-Journal*, January 30, 2005.

Lane, Brian, and Wilfred Gregg. *The Encyclopedia of Mass Murder*. New York: Carroll & Graf, 2004.

"Reno Woman Who Killed Six with Auto Sentenced to Die." *New York Times*, March 30, 1982.

"Sidewalk Killer Is Introvert in Prison." *Los Angeles Times*, November 26, 1983.

"Sole Woman on Death Row Dies at 75." Associated Press, January 30, 2005.

"Victims Still Suffer from Car Rampage." *Deseret News*, November 25, 2005.

fourteen

C.S.I.: "Meet Market": A burnt body on a shop floor opens up the gruesome world of illegal trade in cadaver parts when an autopsy reveals that the bones were removed and replaced with pipes, broomsticks, and other items. Skin tissue is missing as well, leading the investigators to a mortuary harvesting body parts without consent.

TRUE STORY: When the news came out in 2005 that the bones of Alistair Cooke had been plundered at a funeral home, the investigation turned up a partnership of funeral directors in the greater New York area who were illegally removing bones and tissue from dead bodies and selling them to tissue-processing companies.

While most families in New York were preparing for the winter holiday season in December 2005, Reverend Susan Cooke Kittredge was learning something horrific that would leave an impression well past Christmas. The Brooklyn District Attorney's Office had just informed her that before her father was cremated the year before, his remains had been vandalized.

Her father was Alistair Cooke, the British journalist who had taken up residence in Manhattan and broadcast a weekly program about his observations, *Letter from America*, on BBC radio. The show ran until he was ninety-five, at which point, ill and in pain from lung cancer that had metastasized to his bones, he retired. He was best known in the United States as the genteel host of the long-running PBS series *Masterpiece Theatre*.

Cooke died at midnight on March 30, 2004. His remains were taken to New York Mortuary Service, Inc., in Harlem, because they promised quick and inexpensive cremations. Little did his family realize that his death certificate was quickly altered and his arm, leg, and pelvic bones—unsuitable for transplant, due to cancer—were

The well-known British journalist Alistair Cooke, who was among those whose remains were vandalized by an unscrupulous funeral director.
AP/Wide World Photos

removed and sold to a tissue-processing corporation. A fictitious character had given her consent for this, and the business that received the parts believed the remains were extracted from a man ten years younger who had died at 6:45 A.M. from a heart attack. The spelling of his name was changed as well, and from the falsified paperwork he appeared to be a perfectly good—and legitimate—specimen for tissue harvesting. In the meantime, his daughter received a box of cremains and moved on. The story about what had occurred did not emerge until over a year later, when she learned that she had not received all of her father's remains. Other people had.

"It's so horrific on so many fronts," said Reverend Kittredge. Indeed, the news was painful not only for her but also for recipients of bone transplant products who might have received the diseased tissue. But the story was about to get much worse. It was not just one person's bones that were of concern, it was more than a thousand.

The *New York Daily News* first reported the potential for a problem in October 2005, and the investigation was already under way. Apparently a dispute involving a funeral home—the Daniel George & Son Funeral Home in Bensonhurst, New York—led to some shocking revelations. Funeral director and freelance embalmer Joseph Nicelli, fifty, had sold the home but had not cleaned up his business affairs. Late in 2004 the new owner contacted Detective Patricia O'Brien to report that Nicelli had allegedly cheated some customers out of their funeral deposits, and they were demanding restitution. O'Brien visited the funeral home to look around and spotted what appeared to be a hidden operating room, fitted out with surgical lights and a mechanical lift for hoisting bodies from the first floor to the second. In addition, the new owner suggested that corpses had been plundered for bone, and these items added up to the potential for shady business practices. Thus, Detective O'Brien opened up a broader investigation.

She examined the funeral home's previous records and found that Nicelli had associations with several companies that processed human tissue for transplants. That led to graves being opened and corpses examined to see if any had been criminally violated. It wasn't long before the Brooklyn DA's office realized they might have an illegal body-snatching ring right there in New York.

Nicelli had partnered in this enterprise with Biomedical Tissue Services (BTS), a corporation headquartered in Fort Lee, New Jersey, and owned by Michael Mastromarino. The forty-four-year-old businessman turned out to be a failed oral surgeon whose addiction to Demerol forced the forfeiture of his license in 2000. The following year, he and Nicelli set up the tissue procurement business. Paying a thousand dollars per body, they found funeral directors in New York, New Jersey, Pennsylvania, and even Canada willing to let them remove bones and tissue from "clients" before burial. Soon, business was booming well enough to take on associates, so Lee Cruceta and Chris Aldorasi were hired to do the grunt work. They were referred to as "cutters."

BTS supplied Regeneration Technologies, Inc., a Florida-based international company with profits in the millions of dollars; they also sold to four other large tissue-processing firms. While selling human tissue for profit was illegal in the United States, it applied only to the product and not the services. Thus, these businesses were alive and thriving, and the demand for transplants was increasing every year. Like the nineteenth-century surgeons and medical students who counted on body snatchers to procure cadavers from fresh graves, tissue-processing companies needed people willing to supply the goods. The assumption was that the families had given consent and the transactions were legal and aboveboard—unlike those of the nineteenth-century ghouls. But where profit calls, there are always people willing to cut corners and fudge the facts. The potential for that seemed evident in this case.

The standards called for harvesting a body within twenty-four hours after death, or fifteen hours if it had not been refrigerated. But it seems that no one was checking. In fact, no one was checking to see if families had actually given their consent for allowing their loved ones to be thus handled, or whether a corpse was accurately represented. In all but one case, investigators discovered, the removal of parts from 1,077 corpses was done without relatives being the wiser, and many of those parts had not been fresh or free of disease. The DA's office was faced with the prodigious task of informing the families that their deceased loved ones had been improperly "harvested." They also had to build an indictable case.

But the issues were worse than theft, corpse violation, and fraud. As many as ten thousand donor recipients in the United States and abroad could have received tissue that carried infectious diseases, such as AIDS and hepatitis C. Perhaps they now had cancer-ridden bone parts grafted to their own that could send the disease into their bodies. Thus, there was a chance that harm had been done to unsuspecting patients.

As the news broke, Regeneration Technologies ceased all association with BTS, instituted a recall, and assured customers that it had a patented procedure, BioCleanse, which considerably decreased the risk of contamination from bones and tissue received from cadavers. Other companies that purchased from BTS recalled some of their products as well. But the hysteria was already growing.

* * *

DA Charles Hynes questioned a number of people and finally alleged that the process worked as follows: Mastromarino would learn from one of his many associates in the funeral trade that a body had come in. Nicelli would pick it up and bring it back to his funeral home equipped with the surgical room, or the cutters would use a room at the other funeral parlor. If the deceased was slated for embalming and

TISSUE TRANSPLANT

This process began in the United States in the 1940s, at the Naval Medical Center in Maryland. A team of doctors kept bone pieces that were removed from living patients during surgery and froze them to use for the repair of bone fractures in other patients. Their success with this procedure encouraged other types of harvesting, including removing bones from cadavers or willing donors. Standards were instituted to ensure that the bones were fresh, disease-free, and unembalmed, and the products were offered at no charge. They also removed other items, such as corneas from eyes, tissue from veins, and pieces of skin.

The demand for tissue rose, so other hospitals set up tissue banks, and by the 1980s, independent agencies were being formed to harvest tissue for profit. This eventually encouraged the unscrupulous to get tissue from easier sources, such as bodies that did not meet the standards. Without careful government regulation, it was easy for profiteers at any point along the chain from body to recipient to market a poor product. Some companies cut corners and failed to observe safety regulations. Some suppliers misrepresented their products. Although the Food and Drug Administration required tissue banks to screen donors for disease or bacteria from decomposition, no one ensured that it was done.

Many tissue brokers cut funeral directors in for profit. The deal was for the funeral director to persuade the grieving family of a deceased loved one to allow the removal of these bones for the tissue company. The payment per body was a considerable incentive. While not illegal, it proved difficult to achieve in large numbers. Thus, someone decided to increase the donor pool by cutting out the families.

viewing, they removed only the bones from the waist down, replacing the missing parts with plumbers' PVC pipe to fill out the clothing and prevent anyone from suspecting that something was gone. (X rays of exhumed bodies also found surgical gloves and aprons.) They would screw the feet to the pipes and put some shoes on. They might even fill some hollow areas with socks. If a body was going to be cremated, with no viewing, they were free to pick the body clean, taking heart valves, fatty tissue, tendons, ligaments, veins, and skin.

If the families consented, there was no problem, but it turned out that most of the signatures on the consent forms in this operation had been forged. Relatives were shown the consent forms and most were stunned, claiming they had not signed any such documents. In the case of Alistair Cooke, his daughter's name had even been changed. In addition, it was alleged that death certificates were altered to make some bodies younger, fresher, and free of drugs or disease, thus avoiding automatic rejection as donors.

Early in 2006, New York papers were reporting on the body-snatching "ghouls." A grand jury probe, which included the results of many exhumations, resulted in indictments on February 23 for Mastromarino, Nicelli, and the two cutters. By that time the investigation had turned up 1,077 corpses whose parts had been harvested, allegedly without the consent of relatives. One officer on the Racket Squad dubbed it medical terrorism. The men were charged with 122 counts of stealing bodies, illegal dissection, enterprise corruption, grand larceny, and forgery, among other crimes. Supposedly the "body-snatching ring" made as much as $4.7 million in the course of four years, as they had associations with 30 to 40 different funeral homes. DA Hynes told reporters there was an "utter disregard for human decency" along with the outright crimes. "Their callousness is incalculable."

William Sherman from the *Daily News* said that the "ghouls sat stone-faced and silent during their arraignment," as prosecutors talked about "corpse stuffing" and fraud. Plenty of distressed relatives were on hand to ensure that the defendants understood the grief they had caused. All defendants pled not guilty to the charges, and two gave interviews to media sources insisting that they had done nothing wrong. New York City police commissioner Raymond Kelly held a news conference to announce the indictments and said that more arrests were possible. The investigation was still ongoing. But no licenses were suspended, and reports surfaced later that year that Nicelli was still soliciting.

The public was informed about a billion-dollar business that thrived behind closed doors, but given how many benefits there were to patients, it was difficult to know how to respond. The recipients were burn survivors who needed skin, heart patients who needed stronger valves, people with bone injuries or in need of hip replacements, dental patients requiring implants, and even people receiving cosmetic procedures. The going rate to the funeral directors was $1,000 per corpse, but the parts themselves paid off more grandly—anywhere from $5,000 for leg bones to $20,000 or more per corpse. By the time the tissue processors were paid for their services, they could receive as much as $200,000 per body (one source said $250,000).

Through his attorney, Mastromarino rightly insisted that it had not been his responsibility to acquire the families' permission but that of the funeral home personnel who dealt with them. He denied altering documents in order to make his raw material more valuable. His attorney claimed that the death certificates that listed medical conditions and cause and time of death were given to him by the funeral directors.

The Food and Drug Administration closed down BTS for failure to properly screen human tissues for contamination. A warning was issued to transplant patients in hospitals that dealt with the tissue-processing corporations associated with BTS that there could be risk of infection or disease. They recommended that such patients be tested, because by their calculations up to ten thousand people could have been affected.

By one report, Nicelli told investigators that he had overheard Mastromarino describe how he altered the paperwork for such things as age, cause of death, and time of death. Nicelli said he had questioned Mastromarino about this practice and was told not to worry about it. Mastromarino's attorney denied all the allegations.

That summer seven funeral directors were indicted, and that August a pair of snatchers became snitchers. Timothy O'Brien and his wife Susan, owners of the funeral home that had handled Alistair Cooke, agreed to cooperate with the Brooklyn DA. The deal came to light during a hearing for one of the cutters. It suggested that the case was getting more solid.

Information surfaced that in the course of expanding his business, Mastromarino had traveled to Russia to make a deal on behalf of Regeneration Technologies for access to deceased prisoners. All parties concerned decided the conditions were too unsanitary, despite the BioCleanse technology, so the deal did not go through. Reportedly, this was proof of the ethical side of the business.

Then in October, seven funeral home directors pled guilty to undisclosed charges and agreed to cooperate as witnesses against BTS. They surrendered their licenses and accepted the possibility of jail time. More charges were forthcoming against the original four, the results of an investigation involving fourteen more bodies. Again all four men pled not guilty. Cutter Lee Cruceta gave a detailed interview to *New York* magazine, describing his role and claiming there was nothing wrong with the business. He actually found it fascinating. It took about forty-five minutes to remove the bones, he said, and fifteen for skin from specific areas. They had performed as many as six or seven extractions a day, and while he had personally balked at the condition of some of the bodies, he said he'd always received orders to continue.

The case proceeded until Nicelli fell off a roof at a construction site and hit his head, sustaining severe brain damage. His attorney said he would be unable to cooperate in his defense for at least a year. The attorney recommended separating Nicelli's case from that of the other three. Proceedings were delayed, but the investigation continued.

In May 2007, three funeral home directors in Rochester and four former employees of the Rochester branch of BTS were indicted for mishandling the remains of three dozen corpses. They were charged with body stealing and unlawful dissection. A trial date has not yet been set for any of the defendants. Attorneys for the cutters claim that their clients were in no position to know that the consent forms had been fabricated, and they expect that no evidence will be found against them. The case would have come down to whether prosecutors could prove that either Nicelli or Mastromarino, or both, forged signatures and fraudulently misrepresented their products as well as violated corpses in a criminal manner, but on March 19, 2008, Mastromarino pled guilty. At this writing, he had not been sentenced.

SOURCES

Bone, James. "Undertaker Admits Stealing and Selling Alistair Cooke Body Parts." *London Times*, October 20, 2006.

Brick, Michael. "Alistair Cooke's Bones Were Plundered, His Daughter Says. *New York Times*, December 23, 2005.

———. "Seven Enter Guilty Pleas in Corpse Case." *New York Times*, October 19, 2006.

Cheney, Annie. *Body Brokers: Inside America's Underground Trade in Human Remains*. New York: Broadway, 2006.

Dobbin, Ben. "Seven Accused of Illegal Procurement of Body Parts." *Bergen Record*, May 18, 2007.

Hays, Tom. "Court Papers Describe Crude Attempts to Cover New York Body Parts Scam." Associated Press, September 29, 2006.

———. "Four Indicted in New York Human Tissue Theft." Associated Press, February 24, 2006.

———. "Lawyer: Defendant in NYC Body Parts Scandal Is Badly Injured." Associated Press, January 11, 2007.

Katz, Nancie, and William Sherman. "Ghoulish Trip: Body Snatch Suspect Sought Dead Cons' Bones in Russia." *New York Daily News*, October 19, 2006.

Patterson, Randall. "The Organ Grinder." *New York Magazine*, September 2006.

Ryle, Gerard. "The Body Harvesters." *Sydney Morning Herald*, June 24, 2006.

Sampson, Peter. "Body Snatchers Case Awaits Key Ruling." *Bergen Record*, March 26, 2007.

Sherman, William. "Dismantling the Bodies." *New York Daily News*, October 15, 2006.

———. "Ghoul a Body Snatcher." *New York Daily News*, August 8, 2006.

———. "Ghouls Can't Cut and Run." *New York Daily News*, February 19, 2006.

———. "Meet the Ghoul Suspects." *New York Daily News*, October 16, 2005.

———. "X (Rays) Mark Spot for Ghouls." *New York Daily News*, February 24, 2006.

Sneiderman, Phil. "Couple Blames Son in Funeral Home Scandal Trial." *Los Angeles Times*, April 17, 1992.

Yang, Lucy. "New Allegations in Body Parts Scandal." abcnews.com, June 5, 2006.

fifteen

C.S.I.: "The I-15 Murders": A trucker driving along Interstate 15 murders several women, and after each one someone leaves messages on the doors of restrooms. The team uses handwriting analysis to pin down the suspect.

TRUE STORY: Keith Jesperson, the "Happy Face Killer" from the Pacific Northwest, left messages in restrooms about committing several murders along his truck routes.

Cross-country trucker Keith Jesperson had strangled and dumped Taunja Bennett along the road, but to his surprise someone else took credit. Bemused, he read the papers to watch the case unfold.

On January 22, 1990, a bicyclist riding along a highway north of Portland, Oregon, discovered a female corpse along the side of the road. She notified police, who learned that the victim had been strangled with a rope and sexually assaulted. There was no identification on her, so a sketch was published in newspapers, asking for assistance. The victim was soon identified as Taunja Bennett, twenty-three years old and mildly retarded. She'd hung out in certain restaurant bars and truck stops, so some of the employees were aware of when they'd last seen her. A waitress in one of these bars told the police that a regular customer, John Sosnovske, had bragged one evening while drunk that he had killed a woman he'd recently met.

The police were already aware of him from numerous drunk driving charges and several domestic abuse reports made by his girl-friend, Laverne Pavlinac, who was twenty years older than he was. She had even called the FBI the year before to accuse Sosnovske of bank robbery, and she now turned him in as the killer of Taunja Bennett. He denied it, but Pavlinac insisted he had boasted about it. A search of Pavlinac's home offered an envelope on which had been written, "T. Bennett—a Good Piece." While the envelope was addressed to Sosnovske, he said he had not penned the vulgar notation.

Pavlinac now said that Sosnovske had done more than brag; he had raped and killed the girl in front of her. She produced a patch of denim that was consistent with a torn area of the victim's jeans, where the buttons had been removed, and even rode with the police to show them where she and Sosnovske had dumped the body on the night of January 21. She got it right, providing sufficient evidence to arrest Sosnovske. Pavlinac was arrested as well, as an accomplice.

However, witnesses claimed to have seen Taunja the night she died half an hour away from where Sosnovske was, at another bar playing pool with two unidentified men.

Then when the case came to trial, Pavlinac recanted her confession, saying she had made it all up as a way to escape the abusive relationship she had with Sosnovske. She had known about the body dump site from police markings on the road. But it was too late, and she had known too much to just let her go. Convicted, she received ten years for her part. When he heard this, Sosnovske, who still denied having any role, pled no contest in exchange for life in prison with the possibility of parole.

Keith Jesperson was initially amused as he read about the confessions and convictions, but then decided he wanted credit for his murders. The trick was to recover his bragging rights without revealing himself and getting caught. He knew he had killed Taunja after meeting her at a Portland bar. He had raped, beaten, and strangled her before tossing her down the embankment where she was found. Then he drove many more miles to toss her purse out by a river. He wanted someone to know that the two people convicted had not done this deed; someone else had. He thought it would be fun to read in the papers about the "new suspect."

So-called "Happy Face Killer" Keith Jesperson, who murdered people along his truck route in the Pacific Northwest. *AP/Wide World Photos*

Jesperson began to leave messages in truck stop restrooms. The first one was jotted in Livingston, Montana: "I killed Tanya Bennett January 21, 1990 in Portland Oregon. I beat her to death, raped her, and loved it. Yes I'm sick, but I enjoyed myself too. People took the blame and I'm free." Jesperson signed it with a drawing of a happy face—the kind that adorned the "Have a nice day" posters. He felt pretty good about getting away with murder and viewed Pavlinac and Sosnovske as losers.

But when he saw no media reports, he was disappointed. In Oregon he wrote another restroom message, adding a bit more detail about the Bennett incident—that he had cut the buttons off her jeans. That's something the cops would know, he realized, so it should get their attention, but once again no paper reported this message. He knew he would have to do something more formal, and perhaps a little riskier. He was also killing more women.

*   *   *

Jesperson had been raised in a large family by an emotionally distant mother and a father who beat him and his siblings—even administering electric shocks. He would say in an autobiography he penned that his father had encouraged him to kill stray cats, so he'd comforted himself when others teased him by torturing things weaker than himself. (His father denied these allegations.) He did finally marry a woman and father three children, but he continued his father's legacy of setting a bad example. By 1990, when he was thirty-five, he had transferred his rage and fetish for torment to young women. He justified it by claiming to be a victim himself. He found these victims easily enough along his truck route. Because he was big and relatively clean, they flocked to him.

After he had killed at least five women, the six-foot-six, three-hundred-pound trucker decided he had a problem. Eventually he sent a Happy Face note to the Washington County courthouse. Again, he discussed his first victim, describing her and how he had killed her. He even added a description of the position in which he had left her. But sending a letter like this, anonymously, got no response.

He decided to play a game—see if he could spring the two false confessors, Pavlinac and Sosnovske, without getting himself in trouble. He was dying to know if the cops were even talking about his enigmatic notes. In April 1994, Jesperson took out a sheet of blue writing paper and composed a lengthy note. He had decided to go right to the best source of publicity, a newspaper, so he mailed it to the *Oregonian*.

"I would like to tell my story," he said. Whether or not anyone wanted to hear it, he launched right in, prefacing his murderous deeds with the fact that at times he was a good person. He admitted he'd always wanted to be noticed and had elected to gain notoriety and attention with murder. He launched into the details about Bennett again and said his conscience was bothering him.

When the newspaper did not respond, he sent another note,

describing his last victim, a woman in California. He even stated where he'd left the body off Highway 152, near some rocks, but insisted he would not turn himself in. "It all started," he said, "when I wondered what it felt like to kill someone." In a pensive statement, he admitted he thought he deserved to die. Then he told whoever was reading the note that the ball was now in their court, and warned them to look over their shoulder: "I may be closer than you think." He placed his Happy Face signature on the note and mailed it.

After that, Jesperson began to read true crime books and newspaper articles about other serial killers to try to understand what he was doing. When he spotted an article written about the possibility that Oregon had a serial killer, he wrote to the author, but saw no follow-up. It was as if none of the people he notified about his actions were taking him seriously. To keep himself from killing, he set a few fires, but finally that outlet no longer worked.

What Jesperson did not know was that someone had come across the messages he'd written in the Greyhound bus station and truck stop restrooms, and that person had notified authorities. At first the police believed they were penned by someone trying to get Sosnovske out of prison, but when the *Oregonian* received a letter with the same Happy Face signature and similar handwriting, it seemed possible that a serial killer was covertly confessing. The author of this letter claimed to have killed six women, but would not provide clues about how to find him. Investigators dubbed him the "Happy Face Killer" and awaited more communications. While not all serial killers write letters to the press or the police, those who do tend to keep going. They enjoy the cat-and-mouse aspect and like to keep proving to themselves that they're smarter than the police. But Jesperson was not.

•

In March 1995 the remains of Julia Ann Winningham, forty-one, were discovered along a highway near Washougal, Washington. Investigators turned up information that she had been seen with trucker Keith Jesperson, and in fact had dated him and even told some people she was engaged to him. Detectives picked him up for questioning and then released him, because there was no evidence that he had done anything.

But having the police aware of him had shaken Jesperson. He wrote a letter to his brother in which he admitted to eight murders and unsuccessfully attempted to commit suicide. Then he called a detective to confess to killing Winningham. In custody, he continued to send out letters to other jurisdictions, apparently to see who would give him the most favorable sentence. Among his admissions was a confession to the murder of Taunja Bennett, and once again the authorities did not believe him, so he led them to where he had tossed her purse. Finally they realized that they had arrested the killer who had been taking credit in cryptic ways all along. DNA tests confirmed what Jesperson told them, as did a comparison of his handwriting to the graffiti and the Happy Face letters.

Pleading guilty in November to three murders of women in Oregon, Jesperson set into motion the proceedings that freed Pavlinac and Sosnovske after four long years (although Pavlinac's conviction stood, since she had fabricated a story that had resulted in a serious violation of Sosnovske's rights and his false imprisonment). Reportedly, when they were released, Jesperson wept for joy (or self-pity).

He pled guilty to Winningham's murder and would go on to

FALSE CONFESSIONS

Admitting to a serious crime one did not commit defies logic, but among serial killers vying for the title as the most dangerous man in the world, it's fairly common. Henry Lee Lucas, who falsely confessed to over 350 murders in many different states, holds the title for how many law enforcement officers he duped, but there are lesser killers who simply learn the record and then add one or two more. Usually there's something in it for them, such as a book deal, a thrill, an appearance on television, or some other type of notoriety.

admit to as many as 160 more, including some attributed to the as-yet-unidentified Green River Killer in Seattle, but then he'd recant one after the other.

It was difficult for authorities to know what to believe. Jesperson also continued to fish for attention. In 1996 he wrote another letter, claiming that he had killed Angela Subrize in Cheyenne, Wyoming. He said that he'd strangled her and then dragged her body beneath his truck for many miles. "If they feel that a death penalty is in order," he wrote, "then OK. I will give them everything they want to convict me." Authorities told reporters that only the killer could have known the details Jesperson offered. From the information he provided, investigators found Subrize's skeletal remains in a Nebraska ditch off Interstate 80. But when the death penalty actually loomed for this murder, Jesperson quickly backpedaled. He'd only known her, he said; he had not killed her. But Wyoming investigators sought to extradite him.

To stay in Oregon, he accepted responsibility for a crime that he could not have done—the 1992 murder of a woman in Bend, Oregon, Bobbi Crescenzi, whose husband, Jack, had been convicted for it. The confession became the subject of a report for the news television show *Dateline*. Jesperson offered details only the killer could know, including discussing an unsigned letter that provided a description, which had come into the hands of the police. He even tried to duplicate some of the phrasing that the FBI had used to tie the letter to Jack. But just as quickly Jesperson recanted, claiming that a relative of Crescenzi's had offered him ten thousand dollars, to be paid in installments to his children, for a false confession. He got the attention of a national news program, but after it was all over, Jesperson said that he'd lied about killing Taunja Bennett. Her real killers had been released.

Wyoming extradited him in December 1997 and he once again confessed, but said he had killed Subrize in Nebraska. Thus, Wyoming had no jurisdiction. Finally, he negotiated with persistent Wyoming authorities for a life sentence.

Jesperson also wrote a letter to the Santa Clara County District Attorney's Office that offered details about the murders of two women in California, whose dump sites had been geographically close to each other in the southern part of the state. In the letter Jesperson described how he met one of them while transporting meat from Washington State to Fresno. He had stopped in a rest area and a blond prostitute accosted him. He turned her down, viewing her as the sort of predator he despised, but she came into the cab of his truck while he was trying to sleep. He killed her right away. He then dumped the body at another truck stop. After that, he said, he locked his doors.

No one found her for a week, although her remains lay near a café. This discovery solved the mystery of where Cynthia Lynn Rose, thirty-two, had gone. Since the pathologist had found drugs in her system at the time and there were no obvious marks of violence, her death was attributed to an accidental overdose.

Twenty-five miles away and eight months later, another body was found behind a rock off Highway 152. Jesperson said he had bought dinner for this woman and gave her a ride. When he stopped to rest, he said she "wanted to play." He was game. "We men think with our groins 80 percent of the time," he wrote. After they had sex, she asked for drug money, then threatened him, so he told her she was going to die and quickly strangled her. "When the threats came," he said, "she died." He drove for a few hours with her body in the cab before he finally dumped her along the road at Pacheco Pass. He thought her name might have been Carla, but he could not recall. In an interview, he admitted that he had targeted her the minute she came through the door. He knew she was hungry and that he could get leverage by buying her a meal.

Finally charged with this murder in 2006, although the victim remained unidentified, Jesperson agreed to plead guilty in exchange for a life sentence. By this time he was taking credit for murdering twelve women.

Jesperson continued to enjoy attention as he received letters from groupies and wannabe serial killers. He bragged that he had devised a serial killer start-up kit that would, if followed, allow a man to commit a number of murders without ever getting caught. He took credit for mentoring serial killer John Robinson, an Internet predator convicted of multiple murder. Jesperson also struck up a prison correspondence with convicted family killer Christian Longo. In addition, he took up art and began selling watercolors of wildlife via willing vendors.

Always willing to be in the spotlight, Jesperson willingly explained his method to a *Seattle Post-Intelligencer* reporter in 2003. The secret to killing and not getting caught, he said, is time and distance. "The longer it takes to find a body, the better." He would meet a potential victim in one place, take her for a ride—sometimes a long one—then kill her and dump her in a town where it would be difficult to identify her. She might be declared missing, but no one would look for her there. It was best to kill strangers, or as he called them, "lot lizards." But when he broke his own rules and killed a woman whom people knew had been dating him, he was nailed. (Even so, he's the one who went to the police.)

Since Jesperson could lie as easily as tell the truth, authorities settled on eight victims for him in five different states. He's serving multiple prison terms, but has never received a death sentence. If he were ever to get out on parole, other states could step forward with a case against him, including Florida. "The bottom line," said Assistant District Attorney David Tomkins in the *San Jose Mercury News*, "is that he's never getting out of prison."

SOURCES

Cain, Brad. "Real Killer Convicted: Two Freed after Four Years." *Chicago Sun-Times*, November 28, 1995.

"The Happy Face Killer." A&E.

Kamb, Lewis. "In Their Own Words." *Seattle Post-Intelligencer*, February 22, 2003.

"Killer Describes Slaying of Cheyenne Woman." *Rocky Mountain News*, January 13, 1996.

"Killer Writes Again, Slaying of Two Women Detailed in Letters." *Seattle Post-Intelligencer*, March 1, 1996.

"Man Accused of Giving Facts to Jesperson for Confession." *Columbian*, January 8, 1998.

Newton, Michael. *The Encyclopedia of Serial Killers*. 2d ed. New York: Checkmark Books, 2006.

Olsen, Jack. *"I": The Creation of a Serial Killer*. New York: St. Martin's Press, 2002.

See, Carolyn. "The Slow Torturer." *Washington Post*, August 16, 2002.

Skipitares, Connie. "'Happy Face' Killer Sentenced to Life Term." *San Jose Mercury News*, July 27, 2007.

"Trucker Gets Third Life Term for '93 Killing." United Press International, July 28, 2007.

sixteen

C.S.I.: "Unfriendly Skies": The entire team investigates the death of a passenger aboard a flight, which involved several of the other passengers ganging up on him.

TRUE STORY: In 2000, Jonathan Burton died aboard a flight after passengers subdued him and beat him up to keep him from bringing down the plane.

Around 8:30 in the evening, Jonathan Burton said good-bye to his mother and boarded Southwest Airlines Flight 1763, a Boeing 737, in Las Vegas. He took his seat in Row 15. It was August 11, 2000, and the fifty-minute flight was bound for Salt Lake City with 137 passengers and crew aboard. Burton had no idea what lay ahead, not in terms of his behavior or that of other passengers, all of them strangers to him. He was on his way to visit relatives, but when the flight landed, the plane became a crime scene because Burton was dying.

Airlines do get the occasional person who dies en route, and in one situation a flight crew even inadvertently received a body that was in a wheelchair and appeared to be a comatose elderly person. However, it's not often that someone is actually killed on a plane.

As the flight landed, the police were ready to board. An officer who entered was told that the unconscious man, faceup on the floor and being restrained by five others, was dangerous and would fight if he was revived. The officer was warned to be careful. Most of these men, he noted, were wearing shirts spattered with blood, and they appeared to be bruised. One had a badly cut lip. Yet the passenger they were holding down was not moving.

The officer asked the men to back away, which they did only gradually, and then he rolled over the supposedly dangerous individual to place handcuffs on him. The young man did not struggle; he didn't even move. A second officer moved the passengers out of the front of the plane, and several men who remained nearby tried to get the comatose passenger to his feet. He failed to revive when shaken, so one man hoisted him over his shoulders and carried him to the waiting paramedics outside. He dropped his burden onto the jet way, letting the young man's head hit the ground. Another passenger, walking by, approved.

This behavior seemed bizarre to the paramedics, who loaded the passenger onto a stretcher and into the ambulance, but they had not been on the flight. They had not witnessed what had happened.

The FBI arrived to assist the local police with taking statements, and at some point during this procedure, just after midnight, they learned that the young man, Jonathan Burton, had been pronounced dead. It seemed incongruous. Burton had been a healthy nineteen-year-old. But then the story emerged about the terrifying events aboard Flight 1763.

While many passengers simply left, enough submitted to interviews, both that night and later, for police and curious reporters to reconstruct what had occurred: During the flight, Burton had been rude and at times aggressive, and the attendant responsible for his seat thought he showed signs of serious mental instability—especially when he paced the aisles back and forth with a glassy-eyed expression. He grabbed a soda and some food without asking and bumped into attendants as they tried to maneuver down the narrow aisles with their drink carts. At six feet and nearly two hundred pounds, he frightened many of the people around him because he seemed so anxious. The other passengers kept their eyes on him, and an attendant asked if there was anything she could do for him.

"No, it's okay," he told her. "It's just the drugs." Worried passengers exchanged wary glances, especially after he walked to the front of the plane, turned, and said, "Everybody, just sit down."

This was a year before the terrorist attacks in 2001 made traveling a scary proposition, yet there had been enough past incidents of hijackings to alarm the passengers near him. In addition, the problem of air rage, in which passengers were attacked by someone apparently unable to control himself, had increased to such an extent over the past five years that some reporters described it as a growing epidemic.

Five months earlier on an Alaska Air flight, a thirty-nine-year-old man had broken into the cockpit and grabbed the controls. Afterward he could not recall the incident, and his doctors determined that he had suffered from a swelling of his brain caused by changes in cabin pressure.

AIR RAGE

Also known as sky rage, this is a label applied to any type of disruptive behavior on an aircraft in which the person initiating it cannot be quickly calmed down. Taken from the notion of road rage, it's generally caused by a buildup of stress within individuals who have poor stress-management skills. However, inside an aircraft, where changing air pressure inside the cabin can affect both physical and psychological states, particularly causing a rush of anxiety, air rage is a greater problem. The person cannot simply be stopped and ticketed or escorted off the plane, and it can be difficult for female flight attendants to restrain a large male who might be drunk or panic-stricken. (Alcohol has been a factor in a high percentage of such cases.) The flight crew has no place on the plane to isolate such a person, and other disturbed passengers often add to the pandemonium. Among the most serious cases are people who believe they must break into the pilot's cabin or kick open a door to interrupt the flight.

In 1999, U.S. airlines reported fully 318 incidents of air rage, and that seemed to be far less than actually occurred. Nevertheless, in the larger scheme of things, such incidents are rare, and most passengers do not anticipate them.

Passengers on a U.S. Airways cross-country flight in 1997 had watched a football player, Dean Trammel, wandering up and down the aisles. He told passengers he was Christ and they were all going to heaven; if they touched him they would live forever. The flight attendant believed he was having a psychotic break, so she attempted to get him to the rear galley. Once in the back, he knelt down and prayed. She tried to block him in, but he jumped up, raced past her, knocked a second attendant to the floor, and headed for the cockpit. The first attendant caught up to him, but he flung her across the seats, causing internal bleeding, and four male passengers had to wrestle him down. He bit them repeatedly as they wrapped him in restraints made of belts and ties. If not for their quick thinking, he might have breached the cockpit to struggle with the pilots.

Southwest Airlines did not supply its crews with physical restraints for unruly passengers. It provided conflict-resolution training, but no instructions for how to physically subdue a passenger.

On Flight 1763 it was time for people to be seated, as they were about twenty minutes out of Salt Lake City. But Burton remained highly agitated. He walked down the aisle again and yelled, "Someone's got to fly this plane!" It seemed as if he was poised to make a more dramatic move, and he did. Suddenly he ran up the aisle straight at the cockpit door, kicking it hard. Some passengers grabbed him and wrestled him away, but he broke free and kicked again. On his third attempt he made a hole in the door and yelled, "I can fly this plane!" He got close enough to grab each pilot in his arms, one passenger reported later, but they were quick to defend their area and managed to push him out. A flight attendant reportedly shook her finger in Burton's face and yelled at him.

By this time children were crying and women were screaming, "We're going to die!" Then a group of eight men surrounded Burton and moved him away from the cockpit. A couple of them tried to speak with him in a calm voice, and one man asked his name. He gave it, but seemed confused as he sat down. The others watched him carefully, ready to act again if necessary. The man in the seat next to him tried to reassure him that the pilots knew what they were doing.

Burton sat without a word until the plane began its descent. Then he started to sweat, muttering, "I've got to get out of here." At that point he exploded again and headed toward an exit row. Someone shouted that he was going to open the emergency door, and he did indeed reach for the handle. The chief flight attendant stood by, telling Burton she would have him arrested.

He began to hit people and to spit on them, so the men who had surrounded him earlier got out of their seats and wrestled him to the floor, pinning him onto his back with his arms outstretched. Burton continued to scream that he had to get out. Clearly he was experiencing a full-blown panic attack. The flight attendants were unable to control what was happening. Even a passenger who identified himself as a police officer tried to help, but Burton freed himself and lunged at the cop, butting his head against the man's face.

One passenger later reported that the flight attendants appeared to do little except to console a few frightened passengers, and that a male flight attendant seemed to have disappeared altogether. According to this passenger, the crew offered no direction and largely failed to help restrain the frenzied Burton. Supposedly, a pilot even said over the loudspeaker, in reference to Burton's behavior, "One of you will not have a good weekend." Passengers later complained about his flippant attitude.

In the chaos, with blood flying from blows given and received, a mob mentality seemed to take over. The men managed once again to get Burton to the floor. Other passengers, angry and afraid, urged them to beat Burton up. Some people began to hit him, and a large man in black boots repeatedly kicked Burton and jumped off a seat to stomp hard on his chest. Another man crushed his hand. Five men who had taken blows themselves as Burton struggled sat on him to keep him under control for the rest of the flight. He was told it was over and he wouldn't be allowed to get up. One man put his foot on Burton's neck to stifle the young man's screams.

A Canadian passenger, Dean Harvey, traveling with his wife and child, did a revealing interview later with the *Edmonton Journal*, describing how a large man had repeatedly jumped on Burton. Harvey apparently asked him to stop, fearing for the young passenger's life, but he was unable to prevent further violence. In his opinion this killing had been merciless, brutal, and unnecessary. In fact, it appeared to him to have been done out of vengeance, as an act of punishment for scaring people. He had watched, appalled, as Burton weakened and grew quiet.

As the plane landed, the police boarded and found the reportedly violent passenger beneath several bedraggled men, who had their feet on his head, throat, and arms. He was bleeding from the mouth. The officers asked all the passengers to stick around. Some gave written statements, but others just left the scene, including some of the crew members.

The first report after Burton's death stated that he had died from a heart attack, but that was soon revised. An autopsy had found traces of cocaine and THC, not enough to have been influential, and the cause of death was determined to be "compressional or positional asphyxiation"—or strangulation. Multiple abrasions and contusions on the body indicated that Burton had been beaten from head to toe.

When Burton's mother learned about the incident, she was horrified as well as confused. Jonathan had no history of violence, and such behavior was completely uncharacteristic of him. He liked to play video games and volunteer with children. He had a loving family and was well regarded by friends and neighbors. Most thought of him as a gentle young man, even mellow, with a good sense of humor. He worked at a nursing home as a janitor and had been on his way to work a construction job. Before he boarded the plane, he had hugged his mother and told her he loved her. He'd been in a good mood.

As the investigation concluded, the U.S. attorney for Utah, Paul Warner, decided that the homicide was justifiable, done in self-defense, so he declined to file charges against anyone on board the plane—even those who might have been unduly rough with Burton. Given the obvious fear engendered by a passenger going berserk and creating a situation that endangered everyone, and the potential that he could have brought the plane down, it was difficult to say what should have been done. Only those who were there would know, although Burton's family believed that he could have been restrained without life-endangering maneuvers. Some passengers agreed: It had not been necessary, they said, to stand on his throat. But the incident was closed.

SOURCES

Hester, Elliott Neal. "Flying in the Age of Air Rage." Salon.com, September 7, 1999.

Morrison, Blake. "Death on Jet Spotlights Lack of 'Air-rage' Training." *USA Today*, December 21, 2000.

Sharkey, Joe. "An Apparent Case of Air Rage on Southwest Airlines Ends in What Is Later Ruled Homicide." *New York Times*, September 20, 2000.

Thompson, Tony. "Air Rage Man 'Murdered' by Passengers." *The Observer*, September 24, 2000.

Usborne, David. "Murder Debate on Air-Rage Killing." *The Independent*, September 24, 2000.

Wise, Jeff. "Dead on Arrival." *Maxim*, February 2001.

"Witness to Killing Canuck Saw Air-Rage Retaliation." *Toronto Sun*, September 21, 2000.

seventeen

C.S.I.: "Who Are You?": A plumber finds skeletal remains in a crawlspace that turn out to be those of a twenty-year-old female murdered by a man working on a construction site. Her remains were sealed into the concrete, and forensic art revealed her.

TRUE STORY: The identity of a middle-aged woman, murdered and buried in a cement foundation, is revealed via a police sketch and a unique fingerprint analysis.

Less than a week remained before Christmas 1987. In Venice, California—a district of West Los Angeles originally named for Venice, Italy—construction workers were renovating a fifty-year-old bungalow. Located on Nowita Place, a narrow tree-lined walking street that led to the beach, the house had been purchased two years earlier by a young couple, both of them attorneys. While cleaning out the dense foliage in the back, the homeowners had found a large collection of rusting motorcycle parts, an indication that their house had once been a biker hangout. No one was surprised, since many of the homes in Venice a decade earlier had been flophouses for social misfits. The real problem was that the bungalow's foundation needed shoring up, so they hired a professional crew.

On December 19 the crew was digging holes in the backyard when they turned up soil that contained a dirt-encrusted whitish object about twenty inches long with a thick end. On closer inspection, they thought it looked like a human femur, so they ceased operations and notified the male homeowner. He was shocked to see it, and not quite believing what they had turned up in his yard, he held it up against his own thigh. Sure enough, it was the right length and shape for a femur, so he called the police.

Detective David Straky, a homicide investigator, was among the first officials to arrive. When others came from the Scientific Investigation Division (SID), he watched as more dirt was overturned and more bones came to the surface. They, too, stopped the digging and called in a coroner's team, to ensure that the remains were appropriately handled. Coroner's deputies arrived to excavate the site. With two detectives, they got down on their hands and knees and used spoons and small brushes to carefully push dirt from the bones. The larger bones were easy to handle, but bone fragments, tarsals, and metatarsals required greater care. Since they were so small, it was easy to lose them, especially because they had discolored from long exposure to the soil. At the end of the day the forensic team covered the site and roped it off to keep out reporters and nosy neighbors.

Early the next morning they discovered that concrete poured into the hole had partially encased the upper torso and head, hardening in such a way as to provide a good outline of the skull and some of the facial features of the deceased—clearly a woman. Even her hands had left a distinct impression.

Needless to say, work on the house halted, and the young couple was mystified. More items were collected that could assist with identification and with determining an approximate date for when the body had been deposited there. Fragments of a dirty, torn soft pack of L&M brand cigarettes, Menthol Longs, were removed from the grave, and a detective was assigned to learn more about them from the maker, Liggett & Meyers. At this point anything was a potential clue, and they didn't have a lot to go on. There was no ID with the victim.

The bones and concrete pieces were sent right away to a forensic anthropologist—Judy Suchey from California State University, Fullerton, who worked as a consultant to the coroner's office. She was one of only two forensic anthropologists at that time in the state. It was her job to determine the woman's stature, race, and approximate age, and to examine the bones for evidence of trauma. It seemed likely, from the concrete used, that this woman, whoever she was, had been the victim of a homicide.

Suchey took X rays to get readings on the various bone formations and to make comparisons against medical records, if located. Then she laid out the bones to form a complete human skeleton, lying faceup. Starting with the skull (cranium and facial bones), she placed it on her osteometric board, followed by the cervical vertebrae, the vertebral column, the sternum, and the ribs, placed on either side. Then came the shoulder and arm bones: the scapulae, clavicles, humeri, and ulnae. Next she laid out the tiny carpals, metacarpals, and phalanges—wrist bones, hands, and fingers. Finally she added the pelvis and long bones, along with the kneecaps, lower leg bones, and feet, then measured for height. The deceased had worn a back brace, buried with her, which could have affected her stature and suggested she might be older.

Developing a biological profile relies on statistical descriptions from different populations and assumes that most people will fit within the parameters. The size and shape of the victim's pelvic bone and skull indicated she was Caucasian. To determine her age, Suchey examined the fracture lines between the skull plates for predictable

FORENSIC ANTHROPOLOGY

According to the American Board of Forensic Anthropology, this discipline involves the application of the science of physical anthropology to the legal process. Forensic anthropologists apply standard techniques to identify human remains and assist in the detection of crime. The human body has 206 bones. To calculate factors about the deceased, the bones are laid out on an osteometric board, which allows measurements to be made with calipers, and examined for features that reveal age, race, stature, gender, body type, certain personal habits, and sometimes the cause of death.

stages of growth before uniting at maturity, and noted that the victim had a full set of dentures. Given these indicators, the buried woman appeared to have been in her fifties when she died.

Then Suchey looked at specific bones on which damage was evident to determine if it had occurred before death or from some factors in the grave. She found nicks from a knife on several bones, which indicated a homicide by stabbing. It appeared that this Jane Doe had been stabbed several times and tried to save herself. But who she was and how she got in the bungalow's backyard remained a mystery. Hopefully the items found with her could offer leads.

In the meantime, the police checked records to compile a list of homeowners over the past fifteen years. It turned out that there had been several. The police announced their intention to investigate every one of them, focusing on missing women associated with them.

Since the cement had formed an outline around part of the victim's face before hardening, the LAPD composite artist used it to make a plaster cast, from which he then made a sketch that was published in newspapers. Other details were published with it, such as the fact that the woman had been wearing a plaid flannel men's shirt and jeans when she died. A request was posted for information from anyone who might have known her. But even with the posting of a photo and address, no one stepped forward to give Jane Doe #9 (#70 in another source) a name.

Police tracked down one person after another who had lived in the bungalow and asked neighbors if they had ever seen the woman featured in the composite drawing. They also asked if anyone remembered any renovations to the building or work done on the grounds. One person recalled Hercules Butler, a black man who had lived there during the 1970s, pouring concrete in the backyard. In fact, Butler had been quite the character in that neighborhood, riding his rickety bike at all hours and forever dragging stray people up from the beach. One person described Butler as a "wasted, sweaty Chuck

Berry with marcelled hair, a thin face, and real interesting eyes." Another said he looked like a transplanted mountain man.

This information was significant, because the cigarette package found in the grave had proven to be a test package distributed during a one-year period in California, between March 1974 and March 1975. That was when Butler had owned the property. So now they had him pouring concrete and they had an item buried with the victim, both occurring around 1974. If this was accurate, the woman had been buried more than thirteen years.

But further examination showed just how difficult solving the case was going to be. It appeared that some eighty people—or more—had been in and out of Butler's home, and any one of these vagrants could have killed someone and left, with no one the wiser. In fact, just locating them all proved to be an insurmountable task, and no one could say if they had accounted for everyone who'd passed through.

To understand better what they were up against, detectives considered what Venice had been like in the 1970s. It was quite a contrast to the busy home renovations and vibrant beach scene of the 1980s. The decade of the seventies had seen plenty of experimentation with sex and drugs. Venice, with its deteriorating houses and low rents, had been a haven for derelicts, counterculture poets and artists, drug dealers, and bikers. While a few celebrities had resided there on and off, the small town bordering two miles of oceanfront had been overrun with outlaws and transients. For a while it was even dubbed the Slum of the Sea. Many considered Venice to be a very dangerous place.

Still, the facts of the case known thus far implicated Hercules Butler as the main suspect. They needed to find and question him. Yet when the police managed to locate Butler, living in a convalescent home at 6520 West Boulevard, they were in for a disheartening surprise. A few years back Butler had fallen from a three-story window during an argument and hit his head, sustaining such severe brain damage that he was paraplegic and unable to converse coherently.

"We really wanted to sit down and have a long talk with him," Detective Straky told reporters, "but he was in no shape."

Butler remained a person of interest, albeit of dubious value. Still, there were ways around this problem. Police located one of his relatives and showed him the drawing of the dead woman. He recognized her as Adrienne, a woman who had lived with Butler for a while, but did not know her full name. Another dead end.

Psychics offered tips, as did private investigators, but the case was going nowhere. Then in March, investigators landed an unexpected break. A woman, once a resident of the Venice neighborhood, saw a television broadcast that featured the composite drawing. She came to the police station the next day with a photo. Like others, she knew the name Adrienne but not the last name. Yet her photo confirmed the forensic artist's rendition; the cement impression had proven an accurate guide. The detectives were certain their murder victim was this Adrienne, so they published the photo itself in the newspapers.

A man who had adopted a boy from foster care back in the seventies saw the photograph and told the police about court records that listed his adopted son's name, along with the birth mother's. This woman, he knew, had given up two sons to foster care. The detectives got a warrant and soon had a name: Adrienne Piriano. With this information, they tracked down a job application that had required Adrienne to give her fingerprints, and the prints were still on record.

To confirm the identification, there was one more step in the process: They had the concrete mold of her hands from where her arms, crossed in front of her chest, had rested in the cement. While no one expected something as fine as fingerprint ridges and valleys to leave a clear impression in cement, in fact the cement in that area had been smooth. They decided to give it a try. The latent print personnel of SID poured rubber silicone into the concrete mold and allowed it to dry. When removed, the silicone revealed a clear ridge pattern, which enabled the police to make fingerprints they could compare to those from Piriano's job application. They got a match. They also clearly saw the cuts on the fingers and hands, identified as defensive wounds.

They now knew that she had lived in the bungalow with Butler during the 1970s, and had been thirty years old, overweight, and the mother of two children. Thus, in April 1988, four months after the bones were exhumed, the police announced that they finally knew who the victim was.

They also had a better case against Butler: Adrienne had lived with him, and at the time she disappeared, a neighbor had seen Butler pouring concrete in the backyard. Adrienne was buried in that same backyard, encased in concrete. Another witness who had lived with Butler at a later point during the seventies said they'd once had an altercation in which Butler had said, "If you don't quit arguing with me, I'll bury you in the backyard with Adrienne." Finally, the detectives had enough information for the district attorney's office to file charges.

Hercules Butler, now fifty-six, was arrested on June 28 for first-degree murder and held in lieu of a one-hundred-thousand-dollar bail. Although his mental condition was still pretty bad, the arresting officer said that he'd been able to comprehend why he was being arrested and to respond somewhat to questions. The police decided to let the courts make the determination about his competency. They had done what they needed to do to solve the case and identify the perpetrator.

Butler went to jail to await the results of a competency test, and in December the Los Angeles Superior Court posted a decision: He was not competent to stand trial. Judge Florence Bernstein stated that according to a psychiatric report, Butler was not able to understand the charges against him. He was also unable to assist with his defense. Thus, he was to be confined until such time as his competency was restored, but given his age and the severity of his brain damage, there was little hope for that.

In any event, Jane Doe #9 was given back her identity and properly buried.

SOURCES

Boyer, Edward. "Paraplegic Seized in '74 Killing of Woman." *Los Angeles Times*, June 28, 1988.

Citron, Alan. "Foul Play Suspected in Death of Woman Whose Skeleton Was Found." *Los Angeles Times*, January 8, 1988.

———. "Slain Woman's Identity Pulled from a Venice of Another Era." *Los Angeles Times*, April 23, 1988.

Fisher, Barry A. J. *Techniques of Crime Scene Investigation*, 6th ed. Boca Raton, FL: CRC Press, 2000.

Malnic, Eric. "Paraplegic Accused in '74 Slaying Found Not Competent for Trial." *Los Angeles Times*, December 23, 1988.

"Woman's Remains Found." *Los Angeles Times*, December 24, 1987.

eighteen

C.S.I.: "Burked": The son of a casino mogul lies dead on the floor of his home, the apparent victim of a drug overdose, but clues point to the possibility that he was murdered with a procedure known as "burking."

TRUE STORY: The death in 1998 of former Las Vegas gambling executive Ted Binion appeared to be a homicide by burking, and two people were tried for the crime.

Lonnie "Ted" Binion, a wealthy Las Vegas resident and former gambling executive, was found dead in his gated mansion on September 17, 1998. His body was on a sleeping mat on the floor, and a comforter partially covered him. He wore undershorts and a dress shirt that was pushed up to his chest. Near Binion's corpse was an empty prescription bottle for Xanax—a drug for treating anxiety, which had been filled just the day before—as well as a package of cigarettes, three lighters, and a remote control device. He'd been fifty-five years old, and his estimated worth was $50 million.

Binion was the son of the owner of the historic Binion's Horseshoe, casino magnate Lester Binion, and he'd long been a recognized face on the Vegas gambling scene. Once the successful manager of the Horseshoe, Binion's fortunes had declined due to an uncontrolled drug addiction. While it appeared that he'd committed suicide, as the case grew more complex, the cause of death was anything but obvious.

Binion's twenty-seven-year-old live-in lover, Sandra Murphy, had found him, placing a hysterical call to 911 around four in the afternoon. She referred to him as her husband and said he was not

Ted Binion, a former casino executive, whose death was originally thought to be a drug overdose.
AP/Wide World Photos

breathing. The paramedics who arrived determined that Binion was dead. They noted a reddish mark on his chest and a few slight abrasions, but there was no sign of a struggle.

The police arrived and looked around. In a bathroom they found paraphernalia to indicate that someone had been using heroin. That was no surprise, given what was well known about the man. Binion had a reputation as a party guy and womanizer, and allegedly had connections with organized crime. Eventually he lost his gaming license and was temporarily banned from the casino, and his family sold off a considerable piece of property in Montana. Estranged from his siblings, Binion's substance abuse worsened. Seemingly he had reason to be depressed. Before he died, in March 1998 the Nevada Gaming Commission had made its ban permanent, which severed him from the family business altogether.

Yet Binion had a fortune in silver, so in July he commissioned Rick Tabish, whom he knew from Montana, to build a twelve-foot-deep vault on property he owned in Pahrump, Nevada, an hour west of

Vegas. He gave Tabish the combination. On September 15 he opened a $1 million investment account and a checking account containing $100,000. The next day he bought heroin and filled the Xanax prescription, and also met with the mayor and a real estate agent. Supposedly, he also instructed his attorney to cut Murphy out of his will, as he feared she might kill him. The day after that, he was dead.

The real estate agent, Barbara Brown, had called the house that day and learned from Murphy that Binion was quite ill and unable to come to the phone. At this time, Murphy complained about Binion's addiction. She'd met Binion in 1995 when she worked at a topless bar, Cheetah's, and had moved in after he divorced his wife. She told the police that Binion had been about to enter a drug treatment program for his addiction because it had gotten out of control. He'd often threatened to kill himself.

It seemed likely to investigators, given his eroding fortunes and strong addiction, that Binion had decided to commit suicide. In fact, two decades earlier, one of his sisters had taken her life, and she, too, had had a substance abuse problem. But then the Clark County death investigator placed "undetermined" on the death certificate. That designation indicated that the circumstances were too ambiguous to make a definite call.

The chief medical examiner believed it could have been an accidental overdose. The death had certainly not been natural, and the only other option was "homicide." At this point, however, no one was looking in that direction. But Binion's estranged sister, Becky Behnen, was pondering it. She did not believe that her brother would have taken Xanax in that kind of dose. But there were already events in motion that cast even more suspicions on Binion's death.

Just over a day after Binion died, a sheriff's sergeant patrolling Binion's ranch one night came across Tabish and two men digging on the property. Tabish claimed he was recovering the silver at Binion's behest for his daughter, Bonnie. Binion had told him that if he died, Tabish was to make sure it was sold and the funds transferred to her. Inside the vault were six tons of silver bullion, over one hundred thousand rare coins, and a stack of currency. Altogether the stash was worth somewhere between $7 million and $14 million. Why Tabish was digging at two in the morning remained a question. All three were arrested for burglary and grand larceny, pending an investigation.

By this time rumors were flying that Tabish and Murphy were acquaintances, even lovers. Some people claimed to have heard Tabish talk about killing Binion. Ted's sister Becky did not like Murphy, so she hired a private investigator, Tom Dillard, to snoop around. He called Dr. Michael Baden, a former New York City medical examiner and famed expert, to review the autopsy report. Dillard learned that Tabish not only was rumored to be Murphy's lover but was deep in debt. In addition, he learned about Binion's fear of Murphy's lethal intentions.

Toxicology reports confirmed that a lethal dose of heroin and Xanax were in Binion's body, along with traces of Valium. Baden

"BURKING"

William Burke ran a boardinghouse in Edinburgh, Scotland, during the early 1800s with his partner William Hare. They knew they could make money supplying bodies to surgeons and had a regular customer who asked no questions. The trick was to present a body that had no bruises or wounds, because it had more value, especially if it was fresh. Rather than digging up graves as other body snatchers were doing, they decided to cut some corners. They would get their target victim drunk and then either grab him from behind in an armlock around the throat or sit on his chest while holding his nose and mouth closed. Thus, they had a fresh body to deliver with no marks. This method came to be known as "burking," named for the member of this partnership who was eventually hanged for his crimes. In nine months, the two ghouls managed to kill sixteen people.

reviewed the records and thought it could have been a homicidal overdose. When Larry Sims, the medical examiner for Clark County, agreed, changing the death certificate to "homicide," Baden was going to withdraw, but then Binion's family asked him to look at the residence and death scene photos.

"I went to the ME's office to look at the photos," he said, "and I noticed petechial hemorrhages in the eyes suggestive of suffocation. I also recognized handcuff marks on Binion's wrist, abrasions around his lips, and marks on the chest that looked like shirt button compression. That alerted me to the possibility of burking."

Baden believed that one or the other person had sat on Binion's chest to prevent him from breathing while covering his mouth and nose, and the red marks left on his chest had been from the impression of his shirt buttons. Then when Baden looked again at the toxicology results, he realized that what he'd been sent contained a significant typographical error. "They'd said there was a huge amount of Xanax present, but on the original report, it was only present in therapeutic levels. So I met with the two prosecutors and said this was awkward because I didn't think he'd died of an overdose. I mentioned the marks on the body that gave me the opinion that he'd died from burking suffocation." So now they had two different causes of death from two experts. They thought about it and decided to use both opinions.

In June 1999, based largely on the reports given to them by the private investigator and an outside review of the autopsy records, the Las Vegas police arrested Sandra Murphy and Rick Tabish. The suspicion was that Tabish and Murphy had conspired to kill Binion and take his money. Murphy believed she might inherit millions, and the will did stipulate that she would get Binion's house and $300,000, for a total of over $1 million net worth.

Detectives believed that the twosome had drugged Binion with his own stash and then possibly suffocated him. The circumstances were certainly suspicious, with Murphy perhaps aware of Binion's plan to disinherit her and Tabish so quickly digging up the silver. In addition, Tabish had been implicated in an extortion plot (in which he was later convicted).

One more factor was that Binion did not ingest heroin, he smoked it, yet there was a considerable amount of morphine in his system, as if he'd been forced to ingest it. It looked as if his face had been rubbed clean prior to any officials examining the body, and the lack of vomit on him was inconsistent with suicide by drugs. Lividity suggested that he'd been facedown for a while before being turned faceup. It seemed fairly clear that he'd been handled in some manner before the paramedics arrived.

Both Tabish and Murphy insisted they were not guilty.

The trial began early in 2000, and the prosecutor proposed two possible causes of death: homicide with a forced drug overdose, and homicide by suffocation. He offered experts to support both. The pathology expert for the defense was a friend and colleague of Baden's, Cyril Wecht, the coroner from Pittsburgh. He agreed with Sims on the drug overdose but believed Binion had died by his own hand, intentionally. It was a suicide.

The jury apparently accepted Baden's version, because on May 19, 2000, after the jury deliberated nearly seventy hours, Tabish and Murphy were both convicted of first-degree murder and sentenced to life in prison. Murphy's minimum term was twenty-two years, and Tabish's was twenty-five.

After an appeal, in 2003 the Nevada Supreme Court threw out the convictions, stating that the judge should have severed the case from an unrelated extortion case involving Tabish. Both defendants were granted a retrial, which began in October 2004.

This time the outcome was quite different. Tabish actually took the stand for two days to explain his position about the silver. He asserted that he was not at Binion's house when the man died. While some members of the jury thought Binion might have been murdered, his lifestyle and drug addiction did provide enough room for a find-

Defense attorney Richard Momot (in front) talks to defendants Rick Tabish and Sandra Murphy, on trial for the murder of Ted Binion.
AP/Wide World Photos

ing of reasonable doubt. In addition, the crime scene had been contaminated, and the investigation, including some of the witnesses who came out in the first trial, could not be trusted. Tabish and Murphy were acquitted of murder, robbery, and conspiracy to commit murder, based on insufficient evidence. Baden was there to testify once again to his theory about burking, but he was the only expert to do so. Nine other medical experts stated that Binion had died from a drug overdose.

Yet Murphy and Tabish did not get free that easily. They were convicted on other charges and found guilty of attempting to steal Binion's buried silver. They had to await sentencing to find out what would happen next. Tabish received a sentence of one to five years for that act, while Murphy was cleared due to time already served.

Murphy went to court to pursue her right to inherit Binion's house, but did not get it. Tabish attempted to get out on parole for another conviction, and failed as well. Both are determined to keep putting their respective cases before the court. Murphy, now thirty-five, works in California as a fine arts dealer.

SOURCES

German, Jeff. *Murder in Sin City*. New York: Avon Books, 2001.

Howard, K. C. "Legal Try for Funds Restarts." *Las Vegas Review-Journal*, July 11, 2007.

"Judge Denies Murphy's Try for $28,000." *Las Vegas Review-Journal*, August 5, 2005.

O'Connell, Peter. "Six to Face Trial in Binion Case." *Las Vegas Review-Journal*, September 14, 1999.

Puit, Glenn. "Binion Case: Lawyers Say Tabish Key." *Las Vegas Review-Journal*, November 22, 2004.

———. "Binion Trial Verdict: Reversal of Fortunes." *Las Vegas Review-Journal*, November 24, 2004.

———. "Medical Examiners Say Binion's Death a Homicide." *Las Vegas Review-Journal*, October 26, 2004.

———. "Murder Trial: 'Loving Times' Described." *Las Vegas Review-Journal*, November 10, 2004.

———. "Murder Trial of Murphy, Tabish: Binion Jurors Explain Vote to Acquit." *Las Vegas Review-Journal*, May 8, 2005.

———. "Retrial Begins Monday: 'Old Cowboy' Has Nothing to Say." *Las Vegas Review-Journal*, October 10, 2004.

Wecht, Cyril, with Mark Curriden. *Mortal Evidence: The Forensics behind Nine Shocking Cases*. Amherst, NY: Prometheus, 2003.

Whaley, Sean. "Kidnap-Extortion Case: Tabish Denied Parole in Abduction." *Las Vegas Review-Journal*, January 6, 2006.

Private interview with Dr. Michael Baden.

nineteen

C.S.I.: "Empty Eyes": Six showgirls who live in the same house are murdered.

TRUE STORY: In 1966, Richard Speck slaughtered eight nurses in Chicago.

In a two-week period during the summer of 1966, America's sense of security drastically shifted. Charles Whitman climbed a tower on the campus of the University of Texas at Austin and starting shooting people at random, while Richard Speck entered a town house in Chicago and methodically stabbed and strangled eight student nurses. The age of modern mass murder had begun. Speck's shocking night of horror came first, in the midst of riots that terrorized residents of the city's West Side. He appeared to have no motive whatsoever, which added an extra chilling layer to what he did.

South Chicago Community Hospital used town houses in a crime-free part of the city's Southeast Side as dorms for student nurses, and eight nurses resided at 2319 East 100th Street: five American senior nursing students and three Filipino graduate nurses. All were in their early twenties, and four were engaged to be married. Six women were at the house on the night of July 13, 1966, one of which was a friend who occasionally stayed there. Three were still out, and another friend who had intended to spend the night had decided against it at the last minute.

Around 11:30 P.M., Corazon Amurao was falling asleep when she heard four sharp raps on her second-floor bedroom door. She opened it to a strange man dressed in black, waving a gun and indicating that she and her roommate, Merlita Gargullo, should go to another bedroom. They joined three other residents, also woken from sleep. Then the gunman brought in another young woman, so now there were six. He promised he would not kill them. He just wanted money so he could get to New Orleans. He allowed them to fetch their purses, one at a time, and he took all that he could find of their meager funds. Then Gloria Davy came home from a date, and she was forced to join the others.

The intruder, a homely man with a long, pockmarked face, took a bedsheet and began to cut it into strips, which he hung around his neck. Davy demanded to know what he was doing, but she soon saw what he intended when he used the strips to bind each woman's wrists and ankles. He ignored their requests to explain himself, but remained friendly and reassuring. He sat on the floor, asking odd questions and growing more agitated as he glanced at Gloria Davy. Then he stood up, as if to leave. Instead, he untied Pamela Wilkening's ankles and led her out alone. She spit on him, which may have been a deciding factor in what he would do. He indicated as much many years later in a prison video, saying that she had threatened him with identification in a lineup. In that moment he had decided that he would leave no witnesses, but before that he would take his pleasure from some of them. The others heard Pamela make a sound like a sigh, and then all was quiet. They were not sure what had just taken place.

The other two women who lived in the town house arrived home and came up the steps. Speck took them to the south bedroom. But then he forced them back out again. The bound women heard muffled screams and sounds of a struggle. Then, after silence, they heard water running in the bathroom. The intruder appeared once more at the door. He looked around and selected another woman, Nina Schmale. He took her to another room and she, too, made an odd sighing noise.

Again there was running water, and within twenty minutes the intruder was back. It was evident he was killing them, one by one.

Some of them had tried to hide under the beds, but Speck pulled them out and took each one away. Those who remained in the room did not know what to do. In fact, bound as they were, they could not do much of anything.

When only Gloria and Corazon were left, the man entered and turned his attention on Gloria. Corazon had managed to maneuver herself under a bed, and she listened in horror as he prepared Davy for rape, and then watched from her hiding place as he positioned her friend on a bed across the room. He raped her for about twenty minutes and then took her downstairs.

Corazon prayed fervently and waited for his final visit. He entered again and she held her breath. She was only four-foot-ten and knew she'd be no match for him. She listened as he rifled through the purses and pocketed the small change they had. Then he walked out. More than an hour went by as Corazon tried to free herself. She heard an alarm ring, which had been set to awaken someone at 5:00 A.M. for the morning shift. The house was otherwise silent. Still, she waited. She did not want to let the man know she was there. Then another alarm went off. It was 5:30.

Finally it became clear to Corazon that the intruder had actually overlooked her. She knew she had to get out and get help. Cautiously listening and peering about, she saw in the other bedrooms what she had feared: each of the eight other nurses had all been stabbed or strangled to death, some bearing more wounds than others. One victim had been stabbed through an eye, and there was blood splashed all over the floors.

Not daring to go downstairs, lest the man was still in the house, Corazon went to her own room and stepped over three bodies—one of which lay on top of another—to open a window in the front bedroom and scream, "Help me! They are all dead! My friends are all dead!" She pushed out the screen and climbed onto the ledge, continuing to cry and scream in her native tongue.

A neighbor who saw her called the police, and the first responding officer, Jack Wallenda, came in to find a nude blood-covered body on the living room couch. The victim had been raped, sodomized, and strangled. It was Gloria Davy. Upstairs, he found another woman on the bathroom floor, and three more in a bedroom. Walking down the hall in a growing state of alarm, he found an additional three female corpses. He knew a couple of these woman personally, which made the task harder. Then he found Corazon and took her out.

Gasping through her terror and grieving the loss of her friends, Corazon managed to describe the man who had done this. She was taken for treatment as police units went out in the immediate vicinity to try to find the killer. Even as they tried to determine his identity, a composite drawing of the intruder was published in newspapers, under blaring headlines about the unthinkable massacre. The man had blue eyes, a pockmarked face, light-colored hair, and a tattoo that read "Born to Raise Hell." Burglary detective Ed Wielosinski found attendants at two gas stations who recalled a guy with a suitcase talking about a ship. It sounded like the guy who had attacked the nurses, so Wielosinski went to the National Maritime Union Hall, not far from the town house, and learned about an angry sailor, twenty-four years old, named Richard Speck. He'd been inquiring about jobs. Acquiring a photo of Speck from Coast Guard files, they showed it to Corazon, and she made a positive identification. Several fingerprints from the house matched his as well. The police lured him to the union hall via his sister with the promise of a job, but he did not show up for his appointment.

In the meantime, Speck had hired a prostitute, and the police actually encountered him when a motel manager called them about problems with a man with a gun, but they did not yet know that this was the man they were seeking. They removed the gun and left. For his part, Speck did not yet know he had been identified.

On July 15 he heard a radio announcement about the murders and commented that he hoped they caught the son of a bitch. The next day his name was in the press. Speck heard this and bought himself a bottle of wine. Checking into a flophouse called the Starr Hotel, he lay on the grubby mattress of Room 584, rented to B. Brian, and got drunk. Then he slashed his right wrist in a suicide attempt, but two people who saw the blood alerted authorities. Under his bed lay a Chicago newspaper that bore the headline "Police Say Nurse Survivor Can Identify Slayer of 8."

The police actually took Speck to Cook County Hospital without realizing who they were escorting. It was the attending physician, Dr. Leroy Smith, who recognized the man from the papers. He looked for the identifying tattoo, found it, and demanded that the patient reveal his real name. Speck admitted who he was, and Smith called the police. Corazon Amurao confirmed that he was the man who had killed her housemates. They placed him under arrest.

Richard Franklin Speck was suspected in several murders in different states, but he always managed to stay a step ahead of the law. Born on December 6, 1941, into a family of eight children in Kirkwood, Illinois, he had been a sickly child. At age five he suffered a severe head injury from a hammer, and the following year he fell from a tree and landed on his head. Later he ran into an awning that resulted in severe repetitive headaches, and had an accident that resulted in yet another head injury.

When Richard's father died, his mother took him and his sister to Dallas, Texas. He was five. Then his mother married an ex-con, and Speck grew to resent her and her new husband. Some criminologists suggest that he felt betrayed at this young age, and the seeds of his anger toward women began to grow.

In fact, he raged against the world, and by age twelve he had a substance abuse problem with alcohol. He also got into trouble with the law for various infractions. When he flunked the ninth grade, he dropped out. All the while he suffered from fierce headaches that he claimed made him drink even more. It wasn't long before he added drugs, and both substances reduced his impulse control to almost nonexistent. While drunk, he would get mean.

When he was eighteen, Speck beat up his mother. He had come to detest women because they always disappointed him. Nevertheless, when he was twenty, he marred Shirley Annette Malone, fifteen. After they had a baby girl, Speck tattooed the child's name on his arm. Yet he could not hold down a job or a relationship, so his marriage quickly failed.

Speck spent several years in prison, one term of which was for assault on a woman with a knife. During that time Shirley filed for divorce, and Speck vowed revenge. When she remarried, he felt betrayed. He returned to Illinois, where he still had family, though he vowed one day to come back and kill his wife. Around that time, another woman he knew disappeared and was found murdered. Speck quickly left town. Landing a job on a barge, his drinking got him into trouble. In one town where he ended up, three women disappeared.

Speck returned to Chicago to try to get his life together. His siblings gave him a hand, but he seemed unable to turn their help into opportunity. He took a room in a flophouse and found a job, only to learn that he'd lost it. Frustrated, he started to drink. He then took some drugs—sodium Seconals. That was July 13, 1966.

It may be true that he was bent only on robbery when he pulled a

BRAIN DAMAGE AND VIOLENCE

Many criminalists have found that brain damage from blows to the head may have a significant influence on aggressive and violent behavior. The prefrontal cortex seems particularly implicated, in that as the executive part of the brain, damage to it can reduce impulse inhibition. This area of the brain is also involved in learning conditioned responses and developing a sense of remorse. One study has reported that children who received damage to their prefrontal cortex before the age of seven developed abnormal social behavior and an inability to control their aggression and anger.

Mass murderer Richard Speck, during one of his many court appearances.
AP/Wide World Photos

screen from the kitchen window where the nurses lived, but perhaps he had seen them when he was at the National Maritime Union Hall to look at job postings and decided on a sexual assault.

Speck denied any part in the sensational murders, and at his arraignment he entered a plea of not guilty. He said he did not remember anything after an evening of drinking and claimed that a stranger had given him an injection of speed. He was clearly attempting to use amnesia as his defense—a ploy that had worked for him in the past. Six psychiatrists selected by the prosecution and defense all found Speck to be competent to stand trial and believed he had been legally sane at the time of the murders. Some of them thought he was slick and manipulative.

The venue was changed and the trial moved to Peoria. Speck showed only boredom throughout the proceedings. Based mostly on fingerprints from the crime scene and the strength of Corazon

Amurao's defiant identification of him, Speck was quickly convicted. The jury recommended death.

But in 1972 the U.S. Supreme Court placed a moratorium on the death penalty so its constitutionality could be examined, and all inmates sentenced to death across the country had their sentences commuted. Speck received eight consecutive terms of life imprisonment. He served his time at the Statesville Correctional Center at Joliet, Illinois, and in ten years he became eligible for parole. However, no parole board ever considered letting him go free.

In 1978, Speck admitted what he had done that night to a reporter from the *Chicago Tribune*. "Yeah, I killed them," he said. "I stabbed them and choked them." He also became a subject for study by the FBI's budding Behavioral Science Unit. FBI agents Robert Ressler and John Douglas talked with him together, and he told them that he'd raped Gloria Davy but none of the others. Ressler's impression was that Speck displayed a complete callousness toward human life.

In years to come, Speck would claim that he did not know why he massacred the women. Psychiatrist Marvin Ziporyn, who spent over one hundred hours with Speck, saw him at least twice a week. He believed that Speck's behavior was indicative of brain damage suffered during his childhood: He had the IQ of a ten-year-old, acted out in sporadic compulsive rages, and had experienced numerous head injuries. He was impulsive, willful, rigid, and self-centered like a child, and reported having blackouts. Ziporyn believed that his mother's coddling as Speck grew up only exacerbated his immaturity.

To Ziporyn, Speck admitted that Gloria Davy, the nurse whom he had so viciously raped and mutilated before killing, was a dead ringer for his ex-wife, and her challenge had angered him. Ziporyn speculated that her physical appearance had triggered a rage that had snapped Speck's already eroding inhibitions.

One day shy of his fiftieth birthday at the end of 1991, Richard Speck died in prison from a heart attack. He had been repeatedly rejected for parole, at the vehement plea of friends and relatives of his victims, but he had not seemed to mind.

A clandestine film of his prison activities, discovered by journalist Bill Kurtis in 1996, indicated that he felt right at home in the prison, thanks to egregious lapses in the correctional system. "If they only knew how much fun I was having," he bragged about the prison officials, "they'd turn me loose." He was still getting drunk and taking drugs, but oddly enough, he had turned himself into a woman. The film showed him in blue women's panties, with enlarged breasts and a flabby body, acting as a sex object for other men. Through this gimmick, he received favors and gifts. He also described on the film how long it took to strangle a woman—"You gotta go at it for about three and a half minutes"—and admitted that after killing the nurses, he had no feelings. When asked for a reason why he had done it, he said, "It just wasn't their night." He stated, probably for effect, that Gloria Davy had been flirting with him.

After Speck died, Dr. Jan E. Leetsma, a neuropathologist at the Chicago Institute of Neurosurgery, acquired the killer's brain. When he cut it open, he found an abnormality. The hippocampus and amygdala appeared to be blurred together, but he did not know what it meant for Speck's behavior: One part controlled memory and the other strong emotions, including rage. He took pictures and sent tissues to colleagues, but then the samples were lost or stolen. No one was ever able to prove a causal relationship between Speck's brain and his actions on the night of July 13, 1966. Even in retrospect, mental health professionals still argue over whether he was able to control his behavior. He certainly knew it was wrong to murder, but some psychiatrists think it's doubtful that he had full control, especially if he had been drinking all day and taking drugs.

SOURCES

Altman, Jack, and Marvin Ziporyn. *Born to Raise Hell*. New York: Grove Press, 1967.

Breo, Dennis, and William J. Martin. *Crime of the Century: Richard Speck and the Murder of Eight Student Nurses*. New York: Bantam, 1993.

Fornek, Scott. "Collaring the Killer." *Chicago Sun-Times*, July 10, 2006.

———. "They're All Dead." *Chicago Sun-Times*, July 9, 2006.

———. "Was He Evil, Crazy—or Brain-Damaged?" *Chicago Sun-Times*, July 11, 2006.

Greene, Bob. "The Voice of Richard Speck." *Chicago Tribune*, December 8, 1978.

Lewis, Dorothy Otnow. *Guilty by Reason of Insanity*. New York: Fawcett, 1998.

Mass Murderers. New York: Time-Life Books, 1992.

Ressler, Robert. *Whoever Fights Monsters*. New York: St. Martin's Press, 1992.

Roeper, Richard. "Tapes Reveal Speck at His Freakish Worst." *Chicago Sun-Times*, May 16, 1996.

"The Secret Tapes of Richard Speck." A&E Network, 1996.

twenty

C.S.I.: "Chaos Theory": A student, with her bags packed to travel, disappears, leaving behind a complete mystery as to what happened to her.

TRUE STORY: Missing congressional intern Chandra Levy, whose decomposed remains were found in a park, presents an investigative conundrum.

Chandra Levy had confided to a few close friends that she was dating a high-ranking politician, but she "could not" say who it was. The secrecy worried them, although they knew she was careful—even afraid to walk the streets alone. They figured he was probably married.

Then on May 7, 2001, a congressman who represented her district in California called the police to report her missing. His name was Gary Condit, a democrat and fifty-three-year-old father of two. He was a senior member of the House Permanent Select Committee on Intelligence. He had heard from Chandra's parents, he reported, that Chandra had not arrived home as they expected, nor called them, and they wanted to know where she was. Apparently no one had seen her since the afternoon of April 30, shortly after she canceled her membership at an area health club.

She had gone to D.C. as an intern in the press office of the Bureau of Prisons, part of her master's program in public affairs at the University of Southern California. When her academic credentials expired with her approaching graduation, the internship ended, and she made preparations to return home to Modesto, California. The day before that, she went missing.

When Condit was flooded with questions about his association with her, he said he had met her when she visited his office to see a friend who was his intern. He referred to Chandra only as a "great person" and "good friend." His aides said she had visited the office half a dozen times to get information, and it had been more than a month since they had seen her. Condit did admit that Chandra had visited his apartment a few times but would say nothing more. He also had given her a gold bracelet.

Chandra's parents, Robert and Susan Levy, flew to D.C. to find out what they could about the investigation. They weren't certain why the police in Modesto had been told to stop their end of the investigation. The Levys made appearances on national talk shows. They initially said they knew nothing about a relationship with a politician and had not heard Chandra mention Condit in any context except that he was helping her get a job. A few months later, they would change that story.

When police searched Chandra's apartment at the highly secure Newport Building on Dupont Circle, ten blocks from the White House, they found reason to worry. Her purse was still there, with her cell phone, money, credit cards, and driver's license. Her suit-cases, packed in preparation to leave, stood close to the door. There was no sign that someone had entered and forcibly abducted her, and by all appearances she had left voluntarily but with the intention of being away for only a short time. The papers for canceling her health club membership from April 30 were in her apartment, so she had arrived from that errand, but her keys were gone. A key maker who worked near the health club would later say that he had seen her during the first week of May.

Detectives confiscated her computer to search for clues, but friends in Modesto had already described to their hometown reporters Chandra's e-mail from December referring to her affair with a congressman. She admitted to lying to someone else to deflect that person from guessing about the affair, saying she was dating an FBI agent.

Her last recorded e-mail was on May 1, to her parents to tell them she was checking airline prices. Police found a photograph in her apartment of her and Condit together. She had also looked up a website for Klingle Mansion in the rambling 1,734-acre Rock Creek Park, where she often went to jog, and had looked at several websites for Condit committees. After 1:00 P.M. she went out, wearing tennis shoes and a jogging outfit and taking only her keys. All of this information seemed sufficient to place her on the park's jogging trails four miles away.

Concerned friends, volunteers, and police cadets methodically walked the woods and riverbanks of the park, while police took search dogs out. Condit posted a reward of ten thousand dollars for information, and insisted that the focus should be on finding Chandra and getting her home. Despite the long hours searchers put in, it was difficult to cover the entire park, especially in areas that were heavily overgrown. They turned up nothing.

A man convicted of assaulting two joggers in May and July, Ingmar Guandique, was questioned but not detained. Both of his victims had been carrying portable radios and wearing headphones, so they had not heard his approach.

In August the police received a tip that Chandra's body was buried beneath a parking lot in Fort Lee, but within a day they had dismissed it because the tipster's description failed to correspond to any area on the army base.

That same month, Chandra's parents told news sources that their daughter had admitted she was having an affair with a married politician. She had not named the man, but Susan Levy says she managed to get it out of her and then agreed to keep it secret. Still, it bothered her that her daughter had made this unwise choice. Chandra's aunt affirmed that Chandra had talked about the affair openly with them all, and she went on *Larry King Live* to reveal it.

But Gary Condit then agreed to a nationally publicized interview with Connie Chung on ABC network's *Primetime Thursday*. It drew 24 million viewers but did not uncover much information, aside from the fact that he had been married thirty-four years. It did, however, show Condit to be defensive and unresponsive to difficult questions. A significant percentage of viewers responding to a postshow poll thought he was holding something back. Still, if he offered nothing and there were no other clues, there was little the police could do. An airline attendant launched a media campaign to reveal that Condit had had an affair with *her* and had falsely denied it.

By the end of that month, police had focused on a carnival worker. Eric Storm, twenty-four, was in Trenton Psychiatric Hospital for post-traumatic stress disorder and depression. He told New Jersey detectives that he'd witnessed Levy's murder, and they had taken him to be interviewed by the D.C. police. He'd already offered a tip leading to fourteen arrests in a drug ring, so he had some degree of credibility.

But then he said that Levy had written to him that she was an intern for Condit, which was not only untrue but uncharacteristic of her. His "information" proved to have no basis in fact.

Condit, who had hoped to run for reelection, lost support and then lost his congressional seat. Represented by attorney Mark Geragos, he finally admitted to police that he'd had an affair with Chandra, but denied any involvement in her death.

In March 2002, as the investigation heated up, Condit and three of his aides were summoned to a federal grand jury hearing, on the charges that Condit had misused his office. They also had to answer questions about Condit's alibis during April and May of 2001, when Chandra Levy disappeared. The prosecutor suspected that Condit had used his office and staff to intentionally mislead investigators, to keep them away from his various extramarital affairs. The chief of staff for Condit had allegedly tried to convince the flight attendant to deny her relationship with Condit. Condit had also gotten rid of a gift from another paramour. Even so, he managed to give no testimony under oath, and Chandra's parents alleged on television that he knew more about their daughter than he was telling.

Many people compared Levy's situation to that of Anne Marie Fahey, a young woman who got involved with a politically connected Delaware attorney, Tom Capano. Although her remains were never located, thanks to Capano's brother's recollection of a day he had helped dump a large cooler into the ocean, Capano was convicted of murder.

Soon after the grand jury hearings, the missing persons case became a full-fledged death investigation.

At midmorning of May 22, 2002, a man walking his dog and looking for turtles in a heavily wooded area of Rock Creek Park came across a skull, some bones, a jogging bra, a sneaker, and the tattered remains of a running suit. He alerted the police. The recovered bones went to medical examiner Dr. Jonathan Arden, although some were missing, and dental records supplied by Levy's dentist soon identified the remains as hers. The next step was to decide if her death had been an accident or a homicide and, if a homicide, whether she was killed where she was found or dumped there at some later time postmortem. Her body was over four miles from her apartment. Not far away was a portable walkman with headphones.

Reporters wondered why a police search the year before had not found her and the police's defense was that the park in this area was both steep and difficult to walk through. It would have been easy to miss something only steps away.

The investigation proceeded on two levels, one in the morgue and the other where the remains were discovered. In the morgue, they found very little soft tissue left on the bones, due in part to decompo-

Photos of Chandra Levy are on display during a memorial service held on May 28, 2002, shortly after her remains were discovered.
AP/Wide World Photos

---

sition and exposure to weather and to animal activity. Yet they looked for evidence of stabbing, bludgeoning, strangulation, and a possible gunshot.

At the scene, what was left of Chandra's remains were under accumulated natural debris, so it wasn't clear if someone had attempted to bury her. The trees had dropped their leaves and winter had settled on the ground between the time she went missing and the time she was found. Forensic investigators excavated the layers of dirt for blood-soaked ground and for fibers or hair from another person. They looked for signs of digging or of moving foliage from one area to another.

Another area of analysis centered on the clothing, to see if there was blood or DNA specimens from someone else. They looked for rips or bullet holes as well as fibers or foreign hairs that might still be clinging to shoes or sweatpants—especially if she had been transported there in a car, blanket, or carpet. Since Levy's keys were missing, it suggested that she had not accidentally tumbled down the slope, as keys were not an item that animals would likely drag away. In addition, the remains were in an area where a jogger would not likely go, so it appeared that she had been lured or forced there. Also, her ring and bracelet were missing.

Guandique was questioned a second time, thanks to a tip from a fellow inmate that he had confessed to the murder, and he was given a polygraph, which he passed, so once again he was not detained or charged. Then on May 29, a week after the discovery, Dr. Arden announced that the manner of death was homicide: Chandra Levy, as feared, had been murdered. This conclusion was based on how far she was from her apartment, the nature of her disappearance, and spandex leggings found at the scene that appeared to have been removed, turned inside out, and tied into restraints. She would not have done this herself.

However, the exact cause of her death remained unknown, and there was no clue about who had done it. She might have been targeted by someone who knew her, or she might have run in the wrong area at the wrong time and been the victim of random violence. Since the leggings were removed, there was unproven speculation that she had been sexually assaulted before she was killed.

Two weeks after the first grisly discovery, the left tibia was recovered by an investigator hired by the Levy family. It was only fifty feet away from the site where the body was found and bore a number of marks that looked like animals had chewed it. Nearby was a piece of wire bent into the form of a figure eight. The D.C. cops were thoroughly embarrassed by the discovery, especially those who had taken cadaver dogs to the site. Then two smaller bones, identified as foot bones, were located. By then Dr. Arden had examined some small neck bones that suggested Chandra had been strangled.

In July the Levy family hired a team of celebrity investigators: former Manhattan medical examiner Michael Baden, criminalist Henry Lee, and Pittsburgh pathologist Cyril Wecht. However, nothing new was found—no fibers, no hair, no foreign DNA. It seemed that the homicide would likely go unsolved. The only hope was to get information from a snitch or a confession.

In August, Condit's wife told a writer from *Esquire* magazine that her husband had absolutely not had an affair with Chandra Levy—despite the fact that he had supposedly admitted as much to the police a year earlier, and his admission had been reported in newspapers across the country. "I don't think I'm naïve," Carolyn Condit said. "I don't think I have a cover over my head." She called the idea ludicrous; it was based on someone's apparent need to destroy a man who had a successful career.

Then in October the investigation turned back to Ingmar Guandique, a Salvadoran immigrant, who reportedly had fresh scratches on his face and a swollen lip around the time Chandra disappeared. On May 7, 2001, he'd been arrested for a break-in. He said his girlfriend had hit him, but she denied it. She also took investigators to a spot in Rock Creek Park, a mile from where the remains were found, where she had gone with him. An inmate who had met Guandique in jail said Gaundique had admitted to killing Chandra. However, the evidence was circumstantial at best and insufficient to press charges.

Chandra Levy's remains were finally buried on May 28, 2003, over two years after she went missing.

Then in 2005, Condit apparently decided to go public with his story. Reporters had repeatedly said he had admitted to police in July 2001 that he had carried on an affair with Levy, although he had not said so publicly. Dominick Dunne devoted a *Vanity Fair* article to the case, accusing Condit of the affair, and Condit retaliated with an $11 million lawsuit for defamation. Dunne apologized and settled for an undisclosed amount.

Truth has been elusive in this case. Thus far, the nature of Chandra's relationship with Condit and the identity of the person who killed her both remain equally unclear. The case, while cold, remains open.

SOURCES

El-Faizy, Monique. "Chandra Murdered, D.C. Coroner Rules." *New York Daily News*, May 29, 2002.

Fischer, Marc. "The Mysterious Case of the Student and the Congressman." *Bergen County Record*, June 28, 2001.

Jurkowitz, Mark, and Don Aucoin. "The Media: After Condit, Chung Is Back." *Boston Globe*, April 25, 2001.

Kennedy, Helen. "Chandra's Body Found in Park." *New York Daily News*, May 23, 2002.

———. "Chandra's Kin Hire Star Forensic Team." *New York Daily News*, July 21, 2002.

———. "D.C. Cops Mystified as Intern Vanishes." *New York Daily News*, May 16, 2001.

———. "Psych Patient May Hold Clues to Chandra." *New York Daily News*, August 29, 2001.

Lathem, Niles, David K. Li, and Andy Geller. "Condit Is Ducking Grand Jury." *New York Post*, April 28, 2002.

———. "Missing Intern Left Clue: E-Mail to Pal Is Pointing to Congressman." *New York Post*, May 18, 2001.

"Levy's Parents Say Chandra Admitted Affair." CNN.com, August 1, 2001.

Marzulli, John. "Experts Say Bones May Be Keys to Puzzle." *New York Daily News*, May 24, 2002.

"Progress in Probe of Intern Killer." *Pittsburgh Post-Gazette*, October 4, 2002.

Sherman, Mark. "Evidence Suggests Levy Murdered." *Newark Star-Ledger*, May 24, 2002.

twenty-one

C.S.I.: "Table Stakes": A dazzling couple run a black-tie fund-raiser at the home of an absent socialite. The couple claims to be house-sitting, but they're selling off the homeowner's possessions. She didn't pack to leave, suggesting that she's dead and they're grifters.

TRUE STORY: Grifter mother-and-son team Sante and Kenny Kimes murdered a New York socialite and took over her property.

The last time Irene Silverman's employees had seen her was on July 5, 1998. A widow of some fifteen years, she had turned her Versailles-inspired home on Manhattan's Upper East Side into an apartment building for wealthy tenants. Among them was Manny Guerin. He had presented himself to the widow quite recently as a polished young man fresh out of college and managed to quickly ingratiate himself. He was also able to fork over the six-thousand-dollar-per-month rental fee. Mrs. Silverman saw him going in and out with an older woman he called his "assistant," and she soon decided she did not like his type in her building. She let him know she meant to evict him.

Because she was a wealthy philanthropist living near Central Park, the eighty-two-year-old Silverman was a vulnerable target. In fact, she never left the building without a member of her domestic staff. Her friends watched out for her, and when no one could find her all afternoon and into the evening of July 5, her staff filed a missing person's report. She was last seen on Sunday morning in her nightgown near her office in the gray limestone mansion at East

Sixty-fifth Street. An investigation turned up a trail of blood spots outside her building that suddenly ended. A maid told police that Mrs. Silverman had threatened Guerin that morning with eviction, and he had argued with her.

Also missing was Manny Guerin and his green Lincoln Town Car. The police released a sketch of this man and soon learned from another officer that "Manny" was already in custody. His real name was Kenny Kimes, and he was a wanted grifter in league with his sixty-three-year-old mother, Sante Kimes.

By coincidence, on the evening of July 5, a federal warrant for the Kimeses for passing a bad check in April in Utah had resulted in their arrests, via a tip from an FBI informant. They had called this man and sent him a plane ticket to come to New York to manage an apartment building for them. Instead, he alerted law enforcement, went to the meeting at the New York Hilton in a bulletproof vest, and allowed the police to nail them.

A search of their stolen Lincoln Town Car turned up Irene Silverman's passport, a pair of handcuffs, several syringes, a Glock 9mm handgun, stun guns, loose ammunition, wigs, suitcases containing nearly $30,000, and papers that suggested that the two had planned a con on the elderly lady so they could take over her $7.7 million building. But there was more.

A call from California, thanks to news reports, revealed that Sante Kimes was wanted there in association with the March 14 murder of a businessman. The man had been shot and dumped into a trash bin near Los Angeles International Airport. In fact, mother and son had a record of arrests for such things as theft, arson, forgery, insurance fraud, and had even enslaving Mexican immigrants. Sante had been arrested fourteen times and had even served a prison term. Kenny, a muscular young man, had convictions for robbery and assault.

Apparently, as Sante and Kenny traveled around, posing with various aliases, people began to disappear. In the Bahamas, a banker who had kept a dinner appointment with Sante had vanished that day. In California, sixty-three-year-old David Kazdin had been shot in the back of the head before being dumped in the trash. It seemed likely he'd met his fate when he'd refused to assist the Kimeses with a scam in Las Vegas.

The scheme was as follows: The pair listed Kazdin as the new owner of a house on the golf course that Kimes had owned with her now-deceased husband, which came with a renter. In Kazdin's name and with the help of a notary who was apparently willing to file false papers, they took out a $280,000 mortgage, wiring the money to an offshore account. Then they "sold" the house to the renter, an unwitting homeless man through whom they obtained fire insurance. Directly afterward, they torched the place for the considerable insurance payout and tutored the renter in how to act as their front man.

However, arson was suspected and calls were placed to Kazdin, who was unaware of the scheme and adamant that he had taken out no such mortgage. Soon, he turned up dead. The Kimeses held the renter captive to keep him from spilling the beans, but he escaped and notified police. By that time they had found Kazdin's body, but the Kimeses had already fled the state, via the Lincoln Town Car for which they'd given a fraudulent check. They then drove through the south to Florida, where they learned about Irene Silverman's apartments for the wealthy. They considered rich elderly people easy targets, and it wasn't long before they had concocted yet another scheme, installing "Manny Guerin" as a tenant in Mrs. Silverman's building.

GRIFTERS

People known as grifters are con artists, or "confidence men," who intentionally deceive others with the goal of personal gain, usually financial. They may utilize aliases, swindle scenarios, confidence games that confuse their targets, or tricks involving romance, gambling, or charity. They exploit the naïve and trusting as well as the greedy. Often they work with accomplices, known as shills, who assist in the manipulation. To cover their tracks, some resort to murder.

Sante Kimes was a born con artist, with thefts and fraud dating back to at least 1961. She had no sense of boundaries and even got her children involved in her schemes. Once well-off via properties she and her husband owned and managed, Sante fell onto hard times after he died. Determined to be rich again, Sante had persuaded her two sons to work grifts with her. Kent Walker, her oldest son, remembers life with Sante in *Son of a Grifter*, in which he tries to make sense of why he rejected a life of crime while his younger half brother Kenny (the son of the husband who died) did not. Throughout his childhood Kenny had been terrified of his mother and hated her intensely, yet nevertheless went along with whatever she demanded.

Sante was a charmer, Walker states; she worked people with great skill. Her sons believed she would do anything for them, which was one reason they were so easily influenced. She knew how to present herself as a first-class type of person, and people usually bought it. Mistaken during her youth for Elizabeth Taylor, she was well aware of how easy it was to manipulate others. Having no roots, she could slide away quickly from paying the consequences. In her world, there was no truth except her sense of entitlement.

"I've met a lot of good liars in my day," Walker says. "None of them are as good as my mom." He writes that there was no one easier to love and no one easier to hate. She had once used him to escape arrest by punching him hard in the mouth and directing the police against a store clerk who had accused her of theft. They arrested the clerk while Sante took Kent to the doctor. After he was arrested at age twelve for theft, he decided to turn his life around. He would not become his mother's partner, he vowed, so she turned to his half brother, Kenny.

After the New York arrest, a senior law enforcement officer told a reporter for the *New York Times* that the Kimeses were "the most ingenious, evil con artists we've seen in a long time." Fifty detectives were assigned to the Silverman case. Some had already checked out reports of body parts in dumps in New Jersey, and others had looked up and down the New Jersey Turnpike but had turned up nothing.

They feared that Irene Silverman was dead. They tested items from the car that yielded DNA, but none were linked to the missing socialite. They looked to the Kimeses to find clues in their criminal habits.

Mother and son had traveled the country together, making fraudulent purchases, shoplifting, or cheating someone out of something, and staying a step ahead of the law as much as they could. Most everyone who spent enough time with them realized they were not what they initially seemed, which is why they moved on so quickly from one scheme to another.

An investigation of the dealings the Kimeses had with Irene Silverman mirrored the type of arrangement they had tried to finagle with David Kazdin. It was a complicated scheme that relied on a notary who agreed to help, but in this case the notary who saw Irene's signature on a legal form had wanted her to be present. That was a problem, so the Kimeses had resorted to trying to forge the signature themselves. Irene's decision to evict Kenny had forced them to act faster than they'd planned, so the subsequent work was sloppy. On July 5, Kenny grabbed Irene in the hallway outside his apartment and pulled her inside, where Sante administered a stun gun to her head. Then she commanded Kenny to strangle the woman and when Irene was dead, Kenny wrapped her in multiple layers of plastic bags. Sante told him to go put her into a Dumpster. He took the body to his car, placed it in the trunk, and drove to New Jersey. When he saw a construction site outside Hoboken, he placed the corpse in a large Dumpster. Sante was correct that no one would find her. But the police found other items that she hadn't counted on.

There was a new development toward the end of July. Sante had placed a duffel bag in the care of the concierge at the Plaza Hotel just before she was arrested. Inside were more papers as well as tapes of phone calls she had made while in the Silverman building. It seemed that she had been trying to scam the elderly woman into revealing her social security number. There was also a deed that ceded Silverman's building over to Kimes, via a corporation, for less than 10 percent of its market value. How she had believed she would get away with this fraudulent transaction and forgery was a mystery, since no one who knew Irene would accept it—especially if she was missing. The deed was contained inside a manila folder on which had been written "Final Dynasty." With these papers, at any rate, was evidence of someone practicing Irene's signature. That would help if they went to trial. The best evidence was fourteen spiral notebooks filled with the incriminating details of the plan, penned in Sante's hand.

But Irene Silverman's body was not found. That made the case much more difficult. In addition, the Kimeses' attorneys were stating that Irene had other enemies, and no one could prove the Kimeses had done anything to her.

Nevertheless, the case seemed to be circumstantially strong against both grifters, especially with the notebooks, so it went to trial in the spring of 2000. Even without a body, the jury found that there was sufficient evidence to convict this notorious team of first-degree murder. The jury found Sante Kimes guilty of fifty-eight different crimes and Kenny of sixty. They were given multiple life sentences, with Sante getting 120 years and Kenny 125. The judge called Sante a "sociopath of unremitting malevolence." Sante asked her son, "Is this the end of everything for us?" He urged her to stay strong and assured her it would be all right. To reporters she called the verdict a "temporary setback." Apparently so used to getting away with crime, she was certain an appeal would eventually free her.

After their New York trial, the Kimeses were scheduled to be extradited to California to face charges in the Kazdin murder, but in the summer of 2001, Kenny took a hostage in prison—a Court TV reporter—and held her for four hours to try to force a deal that would prevent officials from sending his mother to California. It didn't work, and he got eight years in disciplinary confinement. As a

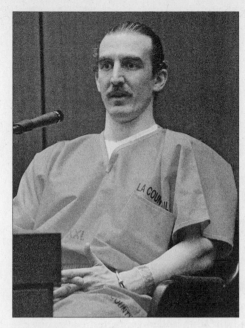

Kenneth Kimes confesses in open court to the murder of Los Angeles businessman David Kazdin, the elderly Irene Silverman in New York City, and a banker named Sayed Bilal Ahmed in the Bahamas, all committed for the love of his mother, Sante.
AP/Wide World Photos

way to reduce that time, on November 16 Kenny admitted that Irene Silverman was indeed dead, and he tried to help officers locate the body, but this long after the incident they were unable to find anything.

Sante suddenly stopped fighting extradition to California, and she and Kenny were flown to Los Angeles, where a grand jury indicted them. At the 2004 trial, Kenny admitted to the murder of Irene Silverman and provided full details of how it was done. He also said he had killed Sayed Bilal Ahmed, the banker in the Bahamas, by drugging and drowning him in a bathtub. He then dumped the weighted body into the ocean. Then in exchange for a life sentence, he pled guilty to killing David Kazdin. In a surprise move, perhaps to make a preemptive strike against *Sante's* possible betrayal, Kenny implicated his mother in court as the person who had ordered him to kill each person. She glared at him the entire time, and he avoided her eyes.

When she took the stand, Sante declared she was innocent. In an almost pathetic attempt to con the jury, she showed an abundance of

In Los Angeles, Sante Kimes testifies at her trial for the murder of David Kazdin. Her son, Kenneth, who had already pleaded guilty, testified against her.
AP/Wide World Photos

---

photographs of herself during better times to prove they didn't need the money, so there was no motive for scamming, let alone killing, anyone. Despite all her screaming in the courtroom over the lack of justice, she was nevertheless convicted, receiving another life sentence. Wisely, she had never pulled the trigger but had manipulated her son into doing the dirty work, so she did not get a death sentence. Nevertheless, for a woman who had once been a multimillionaire, she had sunk to the lowest possible point. Called out quite publicly as a compulsive grifter (even portrayed in a movie by Mary Tyler Moore), it's unlikely she'd ever again manage to con someone into much more than an extra dessert or a postage stamp for a letter from prison.

SOURCES

Boven, Sarah van. "A Mystery in Manhattan." *Newsweek*, July 20, 1998.

Caruso, Michell. "How They Killed Irene." *New York Daily News*, June 23, 2004.

Drew, Christopher. "Lawyers Link Slain Client to Suspect in Disappearance." *New York Times*, July 16, 1998.

Gregorian, Darah. "Court Slaps Sante." *New York Post*, December 8, 2006.

"Grifter Serving Life Faces Another Trial." *New York Times*, June 6, 2004.

Havill, Adrian. *The Mother, the Son, and the Socialite*. New York: St. Martin's Press, 1999.

"Kimes, Son Get Life Sentence in L.A. Murder." *Washington Post*, March 22, 2005.

Kocieniewski, David. "Deed Ceding Widow's House to Suspects Found, Police Say." *New York Times*, July 25, 1998.

———. "Lawyers Defend Suspects in Disappearance." *New York Times*, July 14, 1998.

———. "Mother and Son Face Questioning in Socialite's Disappearance." *New York Times*, July 8, 1998.

———. "Police Hope Clues in Car Lead to Missing Woman." *New York Times*, July 15, 1998.

———. "Police Say Socialite Signed Papers Before She Vanished." *New York Times*, July 9, 1998.

Lueck, Thomas. "Murderer Reveals New Details in Slaying of Socialite." *New York Times*, June 4, 2004.

McFadden, Robert, and Frank Bruni. "A Twisted Tale of Deceit, Fraud and Violence." *New York Times*, July 14, 1998.

McQuillan, Alice. "Mother and Son Guilty on 118 Counts in Death of New York Millionairess." *New York Daily News*, May 19, 2000.

Risen, James. "In the Ashes of a Las Vegas House, Investigators See Clue to a New York Case." *New York Times*, July 11, 1998.

Sachs, Susan. "In a Life of Improvisation, a Sudden, Troubling Exit." *New York Times*, July 11, 1998.

Stockstill, Mason. "Jury Convicts Sante Kimes in Murder of LA Businessman." *Associated Press*, July 7, 2004.

Walker, Kent, with Mark Schone. *Son of a Grifter*. New York: Avon, 2001.

Yeoman, Barry. "Bad Girls." *Psychology Today*, November–December 1999.

twenty-two

C.S.I.: "Sounds of Silence": A boy found dead is traced to a school for the deaf, and one of the other students becomes a suspect.

TRUE STORY: Two murders occur at Gallaudet University, a school for the deaf, and a student is the suspect.

Students who lived on the first floor of Cogswell Hall at Gallaudet University in northeast Washington, D.C., noticed that the door to 101, Eric Plunkett's room, was closed all day on September 28, 2000. Those who saw this realized it was unusual. The nineteen-year-old generally liked it open so that he could see who was walking by and invite people in. He enjoyed having other students hang out with him. Toward the end of the day, the student across the hall, Joseph Mesa Jr., told the dorm's resident adviser that he smelled a bad odor near Plunkett's room and thought someone should check. Around eight that evening, the RA stood outside Eric's door but did not smell anything unusual. Just to be sure, he used a master key to enter.

The sight that greeted him was a terrible surprise. Eric lay on the floor, bludgeoned to death. There were clear bruises on his head and neck. School officials were called to the scene, as were the police, who believed that someone had beaten Eric with a chair. Given the heavy security on campus due to the school's being situated close to some questionable neighborhoods, it seemed most likely that the homicide had been committed by another student who had access to the dorm. The next day the provost alerted the student body to Eric's death, and a crisis team was organized.

With a congressional charter signed by Abraham Lincoln in 1864, Gallaudet University is the world's only four-year school to tailor classes and services specifically for the deaf and hearing impaired. At this time, the student population numbered about two thousand.

The crime shocked the university. The campus was considered a safe haven for young people who often experienced social prejudice and ostracism from the hearing world. But the situation was about to grow worse.

Freshman Thomas Minch, eighteen, had come to Gallaudet from Greenland, New Hampshire. He'd quickly made friends with Eric and expressed both shock and grief over the murder. He joined in the efforts to compose a public memorial, even posting a dedication on his website. But then the police arrived on Tuesday to bring him in for questioning. With the help of an interpreter, detectives asked about his relationship with Eric and soon placed Minch under arrest. He'd admitted that he'd argued with Eric the day before and had even hit him, but he denied killing him. The detective, with six years' experience, decided this was a confession. They charged Minch with second-degree murder. The students were stunned, and they came in droves to his preliminary hearing. It seemed impossible that Minch would have killed anyone, let alone Eric.

At the arraignment, the U.S. Attorney's Office dropped the charges against Minch, citing insufficient evidence. Apparently the cops had made an assumption about things Minch had conveyed, but had failed to gather evidence for a case. However, the police did not clear Minch. They simply believed there was more work to be done. While Minch was freed that day, he knew he remained the chief suspect. In fact, Gallaudet suspended him, citing safety issues, so he went home.

Seven detectives were assigned to continue the investigation, but by Christmas they were unable to make a case, and Plunkett's murder remained unsolved. His parents were heartbroken, but they prepared

The campus at Gallaudet University, the nation's only liberal arts college for the deaf. The insular community was rocked by two murders in September 2000 and February 2001.
AP/Wide World Photos

to come to campus the following semester to help the healing process along.

At the end of January, a grand jury convened to hear the evidence thus far, but on February 3, 2001, tragedy struck again. A fire alarm went off in Cogswell Hall during the early morning hours, and the fourth-floor RA checked the rooms and came across Benjamin Varner, a nineteen-year-old resident there. He'd been murdered, stabbed multiple times in the head, chest, and neck. Like Plunkett, Varner had lived alone.

The police processed the scene but failed to locate a murder weapon in the room or dorm. Yet they did find a blood trail leading away from the room, an indication that the killer had been injured. They collected samples to run tests for comparison should they identify a suspect.

The FBI entered the investigation, and a reward of ten thousand dollars was offered for information leading to an arrest. There was talk around campus of a serial killer haunting the dorm, but the similarities between the crimes seemed superficial: The victims had lived in the same dorm, both were nineteen, and both lived alone. Unlike Plunkett, Varner had kept to himself and was not involved in many campus activities. He'd hoped to become an accountant and toward that end had studied hard to make good grades. Plunkett had been bludgeoned with a weapon found in the room, while Varner's killer had seemingly come prepared with a knife.

Nevertheless, it was too soon to say one way or the other. The statistics on how rare it was for a murder to occur on a college campus indicated that there could be a connection. From 1997 through 1999, there had been fifty-three homicides on college campuses around the country, according to statistics gathered by the U.S. Department of Education; and in 1999, only three of eleven had occurred in dorms.

The university beefed up security, including requiring twenty-four-hour identity checks on anyone entering campus and closing all gates except the main entrance, as they had done following Plunkett's death. They recorded the license plate numbers of anyone coming or going from campus. Students had to use their key cards to enter the dorms, and more staff members were recruited for overnight stays. Cogswell Hall was closed and its residents reassigned to other dorms. Understandably, many students and their parents were worried about the campus. Eric Plunkett's mother arrived from Minnesota to plead with the teenagers not to leave, because that would only compound the tragedy. Nevertheless, five withdrew.

The police interviewed a number of students to learn if anyone in the dorm that night had seen a stranger, especially near Varner's room. They wanted to know who had set off the fire alarm, although it was clear that by the time this incident occurred, Varner had been dead for at least a day. The investigation was complicated by the need for interpreters for every interview, but officers painstakingly worked their way through the list of students who'd known Varner. They kept an eye out for someone who had suffered recent injuries.

*   *   *

It did not take long to make an arrest. A search of the grounds recovered a bloodstained jacket and knife in a trash bin beside a dormitory. The team of crack detectives determined that the day before he was found, Varner had failed to meet with two friends and had not gone to class. He also had not kept a doctor's appointment. Bank records where he had an account showed that he had visited the bank on Friday to cash a check. It could not have been Varner, so detectives requested the bank's videotape. After viewing it, they now knew by sight the young man who had probably committed the crime. But they did not know his name.

Secret Service handwriting experts said the check had been written by someone other than Varner, and it was made out to Joseph Mesa, a freshman at the university who'd lived in Cogswell Hall. When detectives located him in the adjacent Krug Hall, they recognized the young man on the bank surveillance video. Mesa, age twenty, was from Barrigada, Guam. He was also under arrest.

Thus, only ten days after the murder, the police had a solid suspect in the Varner murder, and several factors pointed to Mesa as the culprit in Plunkett's as well: He had lived across the hall from Eric Plunkett and had been the first to alert the RA to the incident. He'd said there was an odor when there wasn't, an indication that he knew about a body and wanted it found.

Mesa had fresh scratch marks, as if he'd been in a fight, and his handwriting matched that on Varner's check. His fingerprints were also lifted from Varner's room. While the police awaited a blood analysis, they believed they had apprehended a serial killer. Had he not been caught, he might have killed again, as do most such offenders who murder for self-enrichment. In fact, he would soon admit as much himself.

After several interviews in which he was confronted with the evidence thus far, Mesa admitted to the crimes. "To be honest with you," he said to a detective, "I did it." The story he then told police over the course of almost four hours was that he had gone into Varner's room during the night of February 1 to rob him. Varner was there and the two of them struggled. Mesa grabbed a four-inch paring knife from the room and stabbed Varner to death. He then took a check from Varner's checkbook and wrote a check to himself for $650. He also admitted to killing Plunkett and said they both had seemed like easy targets. He'd taken Plunkett's debit card to go shopping.

Police got a warrant to search Mesa's dorm room. They found bloody shoes and clothing, which they confiscated, as well as bank cards from both victims. One shoe matched a bloody footprint found outside Varner's room.

Further investigation indicated that Mesa had been quite familiar with Plunkett's room. Plunkett's sister, online with him via live-action camera just before he died, recalled having seen Mesa in her brother's room, taking a videotape. Plunkett had referred to him as "my friend." Only a few days later, he was murdered.

Charged with two counts of felony murder, one while armed, along with several charges of robbery and burglary, Mesa was held without bail for his preliminary hearing. He showed no reaction, but like the thief in the night that he was, he already had plans to slip away from his responsibility. Both sets of parents of the victims were overwhelmed by their inability to have protected their sons, and while they were glad for an arrest that looked as if it would stick, they did not feel closure over the senseless nature of the killings.

This arrest exonerated Thomas Minch, who was officially welcomed to return (he declined), but students who knew Mesa were shocked. One told reporters that he'd attended high school with Mesa and believed he was not the kind of person who would kill anyone. Others described him as a nice guy, but records showed that he'd often been in trouble in high school. Good impressions from acquaintances clearly did not tell the whole story about this young man.

The trial was set for May 2002, but there were still revelations to come.

*   *   *

In April the investigation took some heat from reporters at the *Washington Post*, who had tracked the records back to the first arrest. Apparently the detectives had missed some key evidence during the Plunkett investigation that could have prevented the second murder. Had they done basic police work, they would have uncovered important information. "We are accountable," Executive Assistant Police Chief Terrance W. Gainer acknowledged. "We need to do better."

Among the problems was the fact that Eric's wallet had been missing, which might have pointed toward robbery as a motive and alerted police to look for financial transactions. In fact, Eric's debit card had been used on the day he died, yet no one followed up on this obvious clue. Mesa already had a suspension for a debit card theft, and he was the one who had helped discover the body by alerting the RA to the odor. (A basic rule of police work is to check out the first person at the scene.)

The mistakes began almost immediately. The case was assigned to an investigator who'd solved only half of his cases over the six preceding years and had three arrests dismissed for lack of evidence. He had bungled the interview with Minch, assuming that an admission of having an argument with someone was tantamount to a confession. To worsen the situation, this officer's supervisor had accepted his judgment call without asking for corroborating evidence—basic with any confession.

The police had also interviewed Mesa at the time, since he lived across the hall, but had not requested a background check, which would have revealed the suspension for theft and illegal use of a debit card. They also did not investigate the fact that Mesa's report about an odor was unfounded. It suggested that he wanted the body to be found, perhaps for a thrill.

There had been no routine inventory of Plunkett's possessions in his room, which would have red-flagged the missing items. The police also did not follow up on purchases made with Plunkett's debit card. Thus, no one requested videotapes from the stores where the purchases were made until months later, after the videotapes had been erased. Even after the first detective had been removed from the case, a new team accepted Minch as the suspect without question and failed to look for new clues. It was a classic case of tunnel vision: They were all thinking inside the theory the first detective had proposed, despite his obvious errors. No one even tried to establish a timeline leading up to the murder.

Varner's parents were in anguish when they learned about these errors. Their son might still be alive had the case been correctly investigated. Second-guessing is easy, but everyone involved in a supervisory capacity admitted the investigation had been bungled.

Mesa underwent psychiatric examinations at St. Elizabeth's Hospital, and while he was detained he apparently wrote a lot of letters. In March and April 2002, he communicated with his girlfriend, Melani de Guzman, asking her to lie for him to beef up his case for mental illness. "It isn't true," he wrote, "but I hope it will work, anyway." He also sent a letter to his brother-in-law in Guam to persuade him to destroy certain pieces of evidence not yet in police hands. Investigators who learned about these communications confiscated Melani's letters, although defense attorney Ferris R. Bond moved to have them suppressed. He lost.

The trial required an interpreter for Mesa, which meant the proceedings would take much longer than normal. All comments had to be relayed to him, and he had to have time to communicate with his attorney. A partition was set up for private conferences, conducted in sign language, and the courtroom windows were covered. The federal prosecution team was Assistant U.S. Attorney Jeb Boasburg and Assistant U.S. Attorney Jennifer M. Collins. Their argument was simple: Mesa had methodically selected specific individuals to rob and kill so that he could purchase items for himself and his girlfriend.

Defense attorney Bond's argument was more surprising. A lifetime of frustration over his inability to communicate had triggered Mesa's bad behavior. He'd had directions to kill in his head, not from voices, as hearing people might, but in sign language. Supposedly the image of two hands directed his behavior, and he could not stop. Thus, at the time of both murders, Mesa had been legally insane. (Bond apparently had no explanation for Mesa's lack of remorse afterward.)

As the trial progressed, during which the jury watched Mesa's taped confession to the police, it was clear that he had targeted Plunkett because the boy had cerebral palsy, which weakened him. Mesa practiced going into Plunkett's room—the door of which was usually open—to see if he could sneak in without being noticed. Then he entered one night, grabbed Plunkett in a choke hold from behind, and squeezed until he fell to the floor. Mesa then used a chair within reach to beat him repeatedly until it was clear he was dead. With Eric out of the way, Mesa rifled the unlocked desk drawers and grabbed a debit card. He went out the next day to purchase some items, such as matching T-shirts for himself and his girlfriend.

Not long after, he considered killing his roommate, but changed his mind because it would throw suspicion on him, and so he looked for someone else. He did steal the roommate's credit card. After Christmas, Mesa was running out of money, and when he noticed that Varner lived alone and heard he had money, Mesa decided that Varner would be his next target. Varner was larger, so this time before he went, Mesa armed himself with a knife. Varner did put up a struggle, and Mesa stabbed him seventeen times, leaving the room in such haste he left items behind, including the knife. But when there was no mention of Varner's death, Mesa returned to the room the next day to grab his possessions and to take Varner's checkbook. He put his bloody jacket and the knife into a bag and dumped them into a trash bin, but he failed to clean up the blood trail he'd left or wipe clean his fingerprints. Thus, he was caught. Still, he was quick to say he had confessed out of guilt and to bring the school community some peace of mind.

But then he claimed he couldn't help it. He'd had a devil on his shoulder urging him to do it so he could get money. He'd also had an angel urging him to stop. This cartoonish rendition of "voices in my head" probably swayed few who heard it. In fact, theft is a far cry from murder, so if the "devil" was urging him to steal, that did not explain the rest of his actions. According to one reporter, throughout the confession Mesa appeared to alternate between being disturbed and being indifferent. When it was over, he even placed a fast-food order.

Three psychiatrists who examined Mesa for the prosecution found him to be depressed and antisocial, but sane and malingering—faking a mental illness. Yet one defense expert indicated that Mesa suffered from a rare condition known as intermittent explosive disorder. This expert described Mesa's childhood difficulties with a father who had beaten him over his inability to communicate, the result of which was that he felt compelled by forces he could not control to fly into fits of rage and do terrible things.

To top it off, Mesa took the stand in his own defense, testifying

INTERMITTENT EXPLOSIVE DISORDER

An impulse control disorder in which a person fails to resist aggressive impulses that are out of proportion to the provoking situation. Sufferers often describe the episodes as being precipitated by uncontrollable tension or rage: Their thoughts race, their body tingles or tightens, they feel intense pressure in their heads and overwhelmed by the need to act out; and the episode is followed by a sharp decline in arousal and a feeling of relief. After acting out, they often express shame or remorse. This disorder is found most often in young males and can take the form of such conditions as road rage, domestic abuse, or compulsive sexuality. While the syndrome is controversial among clinicians and not always accepted in court, to be thus diagnosed, a person must have experienced several serious episodes that cannot be accounted for as another mental disorder.

via an interpreter, to explain to the jury the nature of his experience with his illness. This was far more interesting than anything the psychiatrists had said. He described a pair of hands gloved in black leather that had forced him through sign language to commit the murders. "I felt as if they were more powerful than I am," he claimed. He said he had resisted the evil hands by going to a bank he knew had a surveillance camera to cash Varner's check, thus ensuring he would be caught. Once in jail, he wouldn't be able to kill again. In fact, he added, the hands had already directed him to kill both the lead prosecutor and himself.

Boasburg spotted an opportunity in this admission. To prove that Mesa did in fact have control over these impulses, he said, "But you haven't killed me, have you?"

Mesa quickly signed, "Not yet."

At some point in the trial Mesa identified the hands as those of a professional wrestler known as the Undertaker, but also said the hands had been signing to him in his mind since childhood. At their instigation, he had taken a baseball bat and beat to death the family cat and her kittens. The hands had also shown him exactly how to kill the two Gallaudet victims.

In the end, Mesa's defense, unique though it was, did not prevail. The jury deliberated only three hours before they found him guilty of first-degree murder. As the interpreter conveyed to him his fate, he showed no expression. In July 2002 he was sentenced to life without parole.

Thomas Minch, who did not return to the school, filed a lawsuit for false arrest and defamation of character. Cogswell Hall was converted from a dorm into a general-use building, and a memorial was set up on campus to honor the victims.

SOURCES

Berke, Jamie. "Gallaudet Murder Redux—Death at a University for the Deaf." Deafness.about.com, February 3, 2001.

Boule, Margie. "One Door Closes as Another Opens in Case of Slain College Student." *Oregonian*, March 15, 2001.

Diaz, Kevin. "From Silence to Friendship to Murder?" *Minneapolis Star Tribune*, May 19, 2002.

———. "Suspect in Gallaudet Slayings Says Images of Hands Told Him to Kill." *Minneapolis Star Tribune*, May 15, 2002.

Donohue, Andrew. "Charges against Classmates Dropped in Beating Death of Gallaudet Freshman." *Minneapolis Star Tribune*, October 5, 2000.

Fernandez, Manny. "At Gallaudet, Pain and Perseverance." *Washington Post*, May 15, 2004.

Healy, Patrick. "College Calm Pierced by Freshman's Slaying." *Boston Globe*, October 7, 2000.

Santana, Arthur. "Ex-Student Convicted of Gallaudet Murders." *Washington Post*, May 22, 2002.

———. "Jurors See Confession in Gallaudet Killings." *Washington Post*, May 8, 2002.

———. "Mental Illness Blamed in Two Killings." *Washington Post*, May 3, 2002.

Thompson, Cheryl, and Manny Fernandez. "Clues Missed in First Slaying at Gallaudet." *Washington Post*, April 22, 2001.

Watson, Traci. "Gallaudet Reels at Arrest of One of Its Own in Killings." *USA Today*, February 15, 2001.

twenty-three

C.S.I.: "35K O.B.O.": An assailant accosts a couple returning to their car after an anniversary dinner, slitting the woman's throat and stabbing the man. The SUV is stolen but turns up abandoned, with a female body inside. A bloody handprint on a T-shirt becomes the most significant clue for solving the crimes.

TRUE STORY: The "Universal CityWalk Murders" in Los Angeles, committed on Mother's Day 1995, involved the stabbing of two women in a parking lot. A handprint was the key piece of evidence in a sordid tale that had several twists.

It was shortly after eleven o'clock in the evening. Paul Carasi had bought a Mother's Day dinner for his mother, Doris, and former girl-friend, Sonia Salinas, who was the mother of his two-year-old son, Michael. They had dined at the Country Star Restaurant on the street of shops and eateries known as Universal Studios' CityWalk, and despite the late hour they had included the toddler. The disagreements they'd had lately seemed forgotten as they laughed that evening and generally had a good time. But when they reached the car parked in a shadowy area on the top floor of the five-story parking garage, something went desperately wrong.

It was Carasi who found a security guard, telling him that two women had been attacked and lay dying or dead. He said he'd been knocked out and then held down by a man while another man stabbed his companions. He had feigned unconsciousness to save himself since he could not help the others. The guard followed him to where Doris and Sonia lay in a pool of blood next to the blue Chevy Caprice, both of them stabbed repeatedly in the face, chest, and neck. Their throats were slashed through to the spinal cord, and there was evidence of a considerable struggle. Carasi's son was in the car, unharmed and strapped into his car seat, screaming, "Mommy! Mommy!" It was a horrendous sight.

The guard phoned the police, who were already investigating another incident about four miles away. A 911 call from a woman named Donna K. Lee had directed highway patrol officers to a stranded red Chevrolet Beretta on the Hollywood Freeway. They found the forty-four-year-old woman lying next to the car, stabbed in the back and abdomen clear through to the intestines, but she was alive. She said that she had pulled off the freeway because she felt ill and someone had then tried to rob her. Oddly, her car was locked.

She was transported to Panorama City Hospital, and once she was sedated, she was unable to answer questions. An officer stayed with the car to search the area and soon located two fanny packs, some bloody clothing, and a knife thrown over the embankment. One pack belonged to Doris Carasi and the other to Paul Carasi, who had just claimed at the other scene that they had been stolen. Yet here they were, near where another woman had allegedly been robbed. And there was more. With the fanny packs were a bloody washcloth, a pair of bloodstained latex and cotton gloves, a jacket, a sweater, and a brown purse containing identification for Sonia Salinas. Then inside the Beretta, investigators collected plastic bags with blood on them and a bloody fanny pack belonging to Donna Lee that contained twenty-four dollars. Her cell phone was there as well, but she had claimed that someone robbed her. One more interesting item was a parking stub from the Universal CityWalk garage, stamped an hour earlier. Clearly there was more to both stories than either Lee or Carasi were telling. In fact, these two knew each other intimately.

Lee was Carasi's current girlfriend, and they had been living together for the past month in an apartment in the same North Hollywood building that Doris Carasi, sixty-one, had managed. She lived two doors down from them and reportedly disapproved of their relationship because Carasi had abandoned Sonia, the mother of

Doris's grandchild. Doris had recently assisted twenty-nine-year-old Sonia to garnish Carasi's wages for $375 a month in child support, and Sonia was a frequent visitor to Doris's apartment. Carasi, Lee, and Salinas all worked in the same branch of the Bank of America in Los Angeles. Lee and Carasi had met there. Given these suspicious circumstances, it did not take detectives long to start asking questions in the apartment building and at the bank.

Some residents of the apartment building claimed to have seen Carasi leave on the fateful evening with his mother, son, and Salinas, and they had all looked happy. However, one neighbor stated that Doris had verbally reproached her son about moving in with Lee, and not long before the double homicide they had fought over this issue.

The police examined tapes from surveillance cameras from the CityWalk parking lot to see if they could identify the alleged culprits, but were unable to find any suspicious groups of men such as Carasi had described. The double homicide itself had occurred in a blind spot, during a time when none of the regular patrols were in the area, and it was possible that the assailants had been aware of the surveillance weak spots and taken advantage.

The initial reports indicated that Carasi, thirty, was not a suspect in the slayings. He claimed he had not seen the attackers so he could not offer a description to help identify them. He had been held from behind, he stated, and thrown to the ground, where he'd passed out. While the victims' purses were missing, along with Carasi's pack, the superficial cut on Carasi's hand alerted investigators to reconsider his story. It made little sense that an assailant bent on robbery would cut the throats of two women but merely slash at the hand of the male member of the party and hold him on the ground. He would have been the greater threat and thus the most likely target of deadly force. Yet he escaped relatively unscathed. The idea that these same attackers had located Carasi's girlfriend's car and stabbed her in an unrelated attack seemed too preposterous to accept. Something was clearly fishy.

*   *   *

By May 19, four days later, the picture was coming together for detectives, and as Lee left the hospital, they arrested her for murder. Half a dozen witnesses had placed her at the CityWalk that night, and the ticket stub proved she had been in the parking lot. She was clearly a suspect. Carasi was questioned and released, despite failing a polygraph examination, because there was no physical evidence against him. Yet he remained a suspect as investigators awaited the results of lab tests from the crime scene.

Lee made several inconsistent statements about the attack against her, initially saying that she was attacked on the highway near where she placed the call, but changing that to being attacked at the CityWalk parking lot. She was considered uncooperative, as she withheld details about just who had stabbed her, and how. Asked why she had not notified a security guard at CityWalk to make a police report and get medical attention, she said it hadn't occurred to her. She claimed that the details about how she was stabbed were blurry to her. She knew nothing about the items found on the highway and said she had been nowhere near the stabbing incident on the top floor.

Yet the evidence indicated otherwise. Investigators speculated that Lee had assisted with the attack, was unexpectedly stabbed during it, and had then driven away to dump the items. But she had locked herself out of her car, so she'd been forced to call the police for help. Now in a jam, she had fabricated the story about a robbery. In other words, things had not gone according to plan, so she had figured out a story that she thought would sound plausible.

Carasi issued a statement saying that neither of them was guilty, and Lee quickly got a lawyer. At her preliminary hearing, she pled not guilty. But then in August, the lab analysis came back. Now Carasi was under arrest, and both were bound for trial. To the press, Deputy District Attorney John Gilligan stated, "None of the stories they tell are even remotely consistent with the physical evidence."

Paul Carasi, before opening statements in his trial for the murder of his mother and his ex-girlfriend (the mother of his child), a crime committed on Mother's Day.
AP/Wide World Photos

Among the incriminating items of evidence was a splotch of blood on Carasi's shirt. He claimed that he had slipped in the pool of blood and fell, and also that he'd touched the victims to see if they were still alive, then wiped his hand on his shirt. But the blood analyst said the handprint was not his; the angle indicated it was from one of the victims, perhaps grabbing him as she was dying. There was blood spatter on his shirt as well, which he could only have received had he been close to one of the women during the attacks.

At their arraignment, both defendants pled not guilty. Since they had allegedly committed multiple murder, the DA's office decided to go for the death penalty.

Jury selection began in Santa Monica in November 1997, and reporters speculated over whether Lee would stand by Carasi or turn on him and save herself.

The prosecution announced plans to call approximately seventy witnesses, including security guards, medical experts, criminalists, and coworkers. During opening statements, prosecutors John Gilligan and Phil Stirling contended that Carasi and Lee had planned the attack and killed the victims so they could get sole custody of Carasi's young son and avoid child custody payments. Apparently Carasi's credit card debt was so extensive that he'd decided it was better to kill Salinas than pay her. Reportedly, Carasi had said he would "get" Salinas one day for taking his money, and he wanted her dead.

In support of this motive, the physical evidence told an incriminating story: Carasi had stabbed the two women and Lee had assisted, but before dying, Sonia had managed to turn the knife against Lee, stabbing her. Lee then left in her car and concocted the story about a robbery. But clearly, no one had robbed her.

Lee's attorney, Henry Hall, contended that she was a victim as well, of battered woman's syndrome. In contrast, Carasi's attorney, public defender Ralph Courtney, portrayed her as cunning and obsessed, pressuring Carasi to protect their money. Gilligan argued that Carasi and Lee had been inspired to kill Doris and Sonia by the barrage of media attention over the slaughter by stabbing of Nicole Brown Simpson and Ronald Goldman on June 12, 1994. The trial of O. J. Simpson had been showing on television in 1995, every day, all day. Anyone pondering murder could not help but compare their situation to this one and see how to do it.

The most telling evidence was the blood, and sheriff's department senior criminalist Elizabeth Devine used it to reconstruct the crime. It had started in the car. The toddler had been strapped in, and Salinas was in the front passenger seat when she was initially stabbed. She scrambled toward the driver's side door but could not get out before she was stabbed again in the left side. Doris Carasi was in the backseat, behind Sonia, being stabbed as well. That meant there were two assailants, because one or the other could have escaped had there been only one. Both women got out or were pulled out of the car and their throats were cut. Salinas had grabbed Carasi's shirt as he attacked her. Devine said they were able to match the hand imprint on the shirt against the injuries on her palm, and she demonstrated with a mannequin wearing a similar shirt how it had been done. She also showed how Lee had held down Sonia's feet as her throat was being slashed. Droplets of Sonia's blood had sprayed onto Carasi's jacket as he lifted his arm to strike.

On a knee of Lee's jeans they had found blood from Doris, which directly contradicted Lee's claim that she had not been at the scene. In addition, there was blood from Lee on Salinas's shoe, indicating that Salinas had placed her foot against Lee's bleeding abdomen. Defense lawyers accused crime scene workers of missing crucial evidence and mixing up the blood samples they'd collected. Apparently the Simpson trial was on everyone's mind, since the defense in that trial had used a similar argument—and won.

Donna Lee took the stand and was asked to explain how she had received a stab wound to her stomach while in the parking lot, yet had not sought assistance there. Instead she had driven away. "I don't remember physically being stabbed anywhere," Lee said, unable to clarify whether her attacker had been male or female. "Just being grabbed by my arm and then my stomach hurting. Then me driving the car away."

Her attorney said she had been attacked by the same knife as the other two victims, so it was probably the same attacker. Her story was that she had gone to CityWalk to talk with Carasi, and as she sat in her car, pouting over being stood up, she was attacked. She had believed she was being carjacked, so she had driven away. The incident had happened too fast, she stated, for her to realize what was occurring or what she should do. When she realized she was cut, she tried to drive herself to a hospital but was forced to pull over.

Los Angeles prosecutors rarely seek the death penalty against a female defendant. Between 1992 and 1998, only six had been prosecuted in a capital case, making eight on death row altogether versus 464 men at that time. Statistics in 1998, as this trial was in progress, indicated that 18,645 men had been executed in the United States, but only 511 women. In part, this is because juries are less likely to vote to execute a woman.

In keeping with her attorney's strategy, she described her relationship with Carasi as one of abuse, in which he beat her at least once a week. She said she had never loved him, but he was all she had, so she remained in the relationship.

After three months of testimony, on March 23, 1998, both Lee and Carasi were convicted of planning and executing the double homicide, leading into the sentencing phase, with victim impact statements from relatives. Then the panel deliberated for over four days before recommending death for Carasi on April 14 (causing him to weep), but the jurors deadlocked over Lee, voting 10-2 in favor of recommending death. The holdouts said they had doubts over just how involved Lee had been in the crimes, and one woman had been sympathetic because of the abuse Lee had allegedly suffered, but all thought she had lied when she said she had not been near the crime scene.

While the judge considered calling a mistrial for Lee's penalty phase, the DA's office accepted life without the possibility of parole. In May the office issued a statement to the effect that it would not retry the case in order to seek the death penalty for Lee. Both Carasi and Lee were sentenced shortly thereafter.

SOURCES

Blankstein, Andrew. "Death on Mother's Day." *Los Angeles Times*, November 10, 1997.

Finz, Stacey. "Prosecutors' Call for Death Penalty Rare for Women." *Los Angeles Daily News*, January 13, 1997.

Hartlaub, Peter. "Carasi Jurors Call for Death." *Los Angeles Daily News*, April 14, 1998.

———. "DA's Office to Drop Pursuit of Death Sentence for Slayings." *Los Angeles Daily News*, May 12, 1998.

———. "Jurors Told of Simpson Case Tie." *Los Angeles Daily News*, January 6, 1998.

———. "Woman Refuses to Implicate Companion." *Los Angeles Daily News*, March 3, 1998.

Larrubia, Evelyn. "Carasi Given Death Penalty." *Los Angeles Times*, April 14, 1998.

——. "Evidence Tests Were Bungled, Defense Says." *Los Angeles Times*, March 14, 1998.

——. "Expert Reconstructs Scene in Slayings at CityWalk Garage." *Los Angeles Times*, February 18, 1988.

——. "OJ Case Called Model for Slayings." *Los Angeles Times*, January 6, 1998.

Tamaki, Julie. "Carasi, Girlfriend to Stand Trial in CityWalk Slayings." *Los Angeles Times*, August 22, 1995.

——. "New Charge in CityWalk Murders Crime." *Los Angeles Times*, May 23, 1995.

——. "Slaying of 2 at CityWalk Investigated Violence: Slashing of Third Woman Nearby Is Included in Inquiry." *Los Angeles Times*, May 16, 1995.

——. "Woman Pleads Not Guilty in CityWalk Slayings." *Los Angeles Times*, May 24, 1995.

twenty-four

C.S.I.: "Fallen Idols": Two high school kids go missing from a basketball game, and blood drops are found near their jackets. This leads through a labyrinthine story that ends in one boy's body being found with a teacher with whom he'd been having sex.

TRUE STORY: While not clearly associated with an actual incident, a twist in this episode was based on the growing number of female teachers getting sexually involved with their underage students, with negative, even fatal, consequences.

A physical education teacher who drew media attention was Pamela Rogers Turner in McMinnville, Tennessee. Her brief marriage to a basketball coach had terminated in 2005, by which time the twenty-eight-year-old woman had already seduced a thirteen-year-old boy who loved to play basketball. She initiated contact, sending him a text message that she thought he was cute. While it's not clear what he thought of this breach in professional propriety, he sent her a response—he thought she was "hot."

Words turned into action, and they met secretly to consummate their mutual attraction. It lasted three months, with sexual incidents occurring at school, at Rogers's home, on the way to a basketball game, and even at the boy's home, but once the affair was discovered, Rogers was arrested. What she viewed as a relationship was in fact a crime. Not only that, it was a violation of community trust.

Rogers faced 15 counts of sexual battery by an authority figure and 13 counts of statutory rape. She initially pled not guilty, but on August 12, 2005, to avoid a trial, she agreed to plead "no contest" to four counts of sexual battery and to serve nine months in the Warren

County jail (she was out in six). With a suspended eight-year sentence, Rogers was to serve just over seven years of probation.

The directives also stipulated that she could not purchase or possess pornography, could not profit from her crimes, could not use the Internet, must register as a sex offender, and had to leave the boy she had molested alone (including having no contact with his family or via third parties). In addition, she had to give up her teaching certificate and make no sexual contact with any other minor. Rogers accepted the terms, served her time, and then quickly reestablished contact with the boy.

In March 2006 the former homecoming queen sent video images of herself in black lingerie to his cell phone (which made it onto several Internet websites), as well as nude photos. In addition, to get to him she communicated with his sister, both by phone and via blogs on her MySpace website, which he could access as well. She used his basketball number, 32, to send clandestine messages.

Clearly, Rogers had become obsessed. She asked the boy if he still loved her and if he would wait for her, vowing she could wait for three years if necessary. She created a new e-mail address and gave him the password, then in a bout of insecurity, questioned him about his relationship with other girls. She also wrote, "Thank u 4 making me the happiest person in the world." She kept sending videos and photos, some of them involving her in sexual activity (unspecified in the warrant), apparently to keep him interested. At the same time, she was seeing a counselor for her sex crimes and appearing in court to assure officials that she was abiding by the probation stipulations.

On April 24, 2006, after police officers found the MySpace page, Rogers was arrested again and her phone records collected. Coming before the same official, circuit court judge Bart Stanley, she pleaded for mercy and apologized to all whom she had harmed, admitting that what she did was wrong. Rogers claimed she was willing to rehabilitate herself, but the judge did not believe her. She had already misjudged herself on that score, or had lied outright, so there was no good reason to give her another chance. He ordered her to

Teacher Pamela Rogers Turner appears in court with her attorney, charged with having had sexual relations with a thirteen-year-old student.
AP/Wide World Photos

serve the rest of her sentence—seven years—at the Tennessee State Prison for Women. When Rogers pled guilty to sending nude photos of herself to the boy, she received two more years.

Mental health experts indicated that Rogers was sexually immature and probably addicted to sex. Many of the teachers who have been caught over the past decade in erotic entanglements with their students share a similar psychological profile. They find the idea of a secret sexual escapade alluring, often feel entitled to take what they want, naïvely believe it's a victimless crime (and not, therefore, truly criminal), and generally delude themselves with the idea that the student they target is "mature for his age" and can make adult decisions. Since in their minds they're "soul mates" with the targeted student, anything that keeps the two together is justified.

What these teacher-predators fail to consider is that seducing an underage child, male or female, makes them sex offenders, no different in the eyes of the law than males who seduce an underage child (although some judges have viewed what a woman does as a lesser offense). Despite the claim by many of them that they're following the course of "true love," some are repeat predators of vulnerable children, more closely resembling pedophiles. They're among the women called "cougars"—older women seeking younger sex partners—but their predatory behavior is criminal.

It's not only boys who are victims. Several female teachers have

FEMALE SEX OFFENDERS

A study of these women reveals that they are generally self-centered and needy. They fail to take into account a child's vulnerability and probable inability to make adult decisions about sex. These women seek their own goals and seem unable to fully comprehend what they are doing. Most, in fact, were married at the time they decided to sexually abuse a minor, thus harming their families. After getting caught, they've often described how good it felt to be admired by the boys. That's probably the source of the addiction.

Females represent 10 percent of sex offenders, and many are mothers molesting their children. A high percentage suffer from anxiety or depressive disorders, have troubled relationships with their fathers (and husbands), and have a grandiose image of themselves. Their husbands fail to give them the attention they crave (they say), so they turn to hormonally charged boys who will tell them what they want to hear about how beautiful and desirable they are. Being with a boy also makes them feel younger.

Most of these offenders are immature, dependent, and sensitive to rejection, so they gravitate toward younger people rather than peers. The risk of rejection with this group is less likely and the possibility of being admired highly likely. They also create a situation in which they exert control, especially if they feel controlled themselves by their husbands. The child follows their lead, sometimes even when he doesn't want to. Despite the popular perception that boys who are thus seduced are "lucky," in fact some have felt frightened and even violated.

been caught having unlawful sexual contact with girls. Amy Gail Lilley, thirty-six, got involved with a fifteen-year-old in Florida, for which she received house arrest and eight years' probation. In Michigan, Elizabeth Miklosovic pled no contest to assaulting a fourteen-year-old girl, whom she said she had "married" in a pagan ceremony.

The number of female teachers targeting students is increasing. These women initiate the activity with a flirtatious overture, taking advantage of boys who are sexually stimulated and flavoring their crime with a romantic tone. The female teachers generally use a style of seduction known as grooming, in which they gradually get a child into position to respond to their overtures. They might even "groom" the child's family, to prevent them from becoming suspicious. While we don't yet know if there are lasting effects on boys from these encounters, statistics are emerging that indicate they have trouble in later relationships and difficulty trusting authority figures. Some even go on to molest children who are the age they were when the teacher molested them.

While the idea that such boys are victims is controversial, there was one case in which this issue is in no doubt. Sean Powell, 18, believed that his thirty-year-old teacher loved him. Erin McLean was an intern at his high school, and he was certain she'd leave her husband, Eric McLean, and their two children to marry him. So certain was he that on the evening of March 10, 2007, he arrived at the McLean home in Knoxville, Tennessee, and sat outside with his car running.

Eric, 31, was outside when Sean approached. Eric asked him to leave but Sean ignored him. This annoyed Eric, who was already angry about the boy's obsessive attention to his wife and aware that they'd been having an affair, but he'd been unable to leave the woman he loved. Frustrated, Eric called 911 to report the young man as an intruder, then went to retrieve a newly purchased rifle from his truck, apparently to show he meant business. Just seven minutes later, Erin called 911 and said that her husband had just shot Sean in the head, killing him.

McLean fled but was soon under arrest. He claimed he did not know exactly what had happened, and relatives said he'd desperately wished to save his marriage. McLean had a reputation as a good father and a good neighbor. The sudden violence seemed entirely uncharacteristic.

Sean's birth mother, Debra Flynn, talked with reporters from *Knox News*, claiming that from what she had learned from Sean, Erin had "led him on." Flynn had discovered the text messages that Erin had left on a cell phone, urging Sean to come to her. She spoke with him on the phone almost every day, and quite often each day. To Flynn's mind, the teacher was a predator, teasing Sean—a deeply insecure young man—with the possibility of marriage. She said he had admitted the affair and told Flynn he'd asked Erin to marry him.

The affair allegedly began when Erin started teaching English as part of a graduate internship at West High School during the fall of 2006. She met Sean, a senior, there, and enticed him. He had a substance abuse problem that annoyed his adoptive parents to the point of kicking him out of their home, so Erin asked Eric to help Sean, and Eric had tried to persuade his own parents to take the boy in. They declined. Afterward, Eric began to suspect there was more to Erin's interest in Sean than helping a boy in trouble. Sean went to live with his birth mother in another town, dropping out of school, but soon returned to Knoxville to see Erin.

In jail, Eric agreed to an interview with NBC's Matt Lauer. He admitted shooting Sean but insisted it had been an accident. It had bothered him that his wife spent so much time on the phone with Sean, and then his two young sons told him that Erin and Sean had been holding hands. Eric's attorney explained that when the incident occurred, he'd been trying to bluff Sean into leaving. But the loaded rifle had gone off.

Four days after the shooting, Erin attempted to commit suicide, but she was rushed to a hospital and saved. At this writing, Eric's charge of second-degree murder has been changed to first-degree murder, and his trial is pending. Mystifying as it may seem, the kind of bond that often occurs in these situations can inspire emotion so blind that such consequences are never foreseen. But just as in the episode, the first step taken toward becoming illicitly involved can become a life-and-death decision.

SOURCES

"Affair between Student and Married Teacher Leads to Teen's Murder in Tennessee." Foxnews.com, March 18, 2007.

De la Cruz, Bonna. "Sex Abuse of Boys Not Only Trait Duo Share." Tennessean.com, April 7, 2006.

Hazelwood, R., and A. Burgess, *Practical Aspects of Rape Investigation*. 3d ed. Boca Raton, FL: CRC Press, 2001.

Hislop, Julia. *Female Sex Offenders: What Therapists, Law Enforcement and Child Protective Services Need to Know*. Ravensdale, WA: Issues Press, 2001.

"Husband Got Gun Two Weeks before Teen Shot." Associated Press, March 27, 2007.

"Jail for Teacher in Sex Case." CBSnews.com, August 12, 2005.

Kuehl, Michael. "Women as Rapists and Pedophiles." ipce.info, 2004.

Lakin, Matt. "'Love Triangle' Murder Trial Delayed until September." Knoxnews.com, December 14, 2007.

Lowe, Caroline. "Inside the Mind of a Female Sex Offender." *Special Reports*, wcco.com, February 23, 2006.

Matthews, Frederick. *The Invisible Boy: Revisioning the Victimization of Male Children and Teens*. Canada: National Clearinghouse on Family Violence, Health Promotion and Programs Branch, 1996.

"MySpace Page Puts Teacher Back in Jail." Associated Press, April 12, 2006.

Shoop, Robert. *Sexual Exploitation in Schools*. Thousand Oaks, CA: Corwin Press, 2003.

State of Tennessee v. Pamela Joan Rogers Turner. F-10178, April 10, 2006.

"Teacher's Husband Says He Shot Teen." Associated Press, March 22, 2007.

Young, Cathy. "Double Standard." *Reasononline*, June 2, 2002.

twenty-five

C.S.I.: "Gentle, Gentle": An infant is found dead, laid in a blanket on a golf course, and most of the evidence suggests an inside job, not the work of a home intruder. There is another child in the home, and a suspicious ransom note.

TRUE STORY: The murder of six-year-old beauty queen JonBenét Ramsey in 1996 in Boulder, Colorado, was a complicated investigation that threw suspicion on the parents.

It was the day after Christmas 1996, at 5:52 in the morning, when JonBenét Ramsey's mother, Patricia "Patsy" Ramsey, called 911 and shouted to the dispatcher that her six-year-old daughter had been kidnapped and a ransom note left in the home. In response to questions, she read parts of the note, and then insisted again she needed help. She sounded frantic and distraught.

It was a normally quiet day in the affluent Colorado town, but the Boulder police sent Officer Rick French to 755 Fifteenth Street shortly after 6:00 A.M., and Patsy met him at the door. She was clearly upset, although her husband, John, seemed relatively calm and emotionally controlled. They had another child in the home, they said, nine-year-old Burke, who was still in bed.

Patsy told French that she had gone into JonBenét's second-floor bedroom to prepare her for a planned holiday trip and was surprised to find her bed empty and the child nowhere on the second floor. Patsy went down a back staircase to the first floor to look in the kitchen, and there on a lower step she found a three-page note, written in black felt-tip pen on white legal paper and laid out with the pages alongside one another. She picked them up and read them, realizing at once it was a note about JonBenét, and it was directed to her husband, "Mr. Ramsey." The author or authors demanded certain conditions, including that he not call the police and that he prepare to pay $118,000 for his daughter's return. Otherwise she would die.

A patrol supervisor, Paul Reichenbach, arrived, as did four of the Ramseys' friends. Fleet White and his wife had seen them the night before in the White's home for a Christmas dinner. They were among the last to have seen JonBenét.

A crime scene evidence team was directed to the home and a trace put on the phone line for incoming calls, with the expectation of a scheduled call from the kidnapper. Reichenbach walked through the house, looking in each room for the missing child. He saw no sign of forced entry, although when Fleet White went on his own into the basement for a cursory inspection, he noticed a broken window. John Ramsey admitted that he had broken it a few months earlier when he'd forgotten his key. He had not yet fixed it, although there was a grate over it. It appeared not to have been disturbed. A minister arrived, and Burke was woken and moved to another location.

Since the house was not secured, and many different people were allowed to go in and out, the scene was compromised. The note had been moved and touched, and the Ramseys' friends were allowed to move through the home without restriction or accompaniment. No scent dog from the K-9 unit was utilized to try to determine if the missing child had walked through the downstairs and out the door. In retrospect, there would be a lot of criticism.

John Ramsey called his attorney to discuss getting the ransom money. Oddly, the deadline for the kidnappers' call came and went with no communication, but no one seemed to know what to do. During questioning, Patsy seemed confused as to whether she had gone to JonBenét's room first or found the note first.

Two members of the Boulder County Sheriff's Department standing guard at the Ramsey family home the day after six-year-old JonBenét Ramsey was found murdered.
AP/Wide World Photos

By noon, of the official personnel who'd come, only a detective, Linda Arndt, was still at the scene, but seven civilians were present. Arndt directed John Ramsey to take a friend with him to search the house from top to bottom, just in case. At 1:00 P.M., he and White went directly to the basement, when they spotted a suitcase near the broken window and wondered if an intruder had put it there. Ramsey could not recall doing it.

Around 1:20, Ramsey opened the door of a darkened, windowless room situated within another room and discovered his daughter's body on the floor. Apparently everyone else who had come down to the cellar had overlooked this area. The Ramseys called it their wine cellar. The child lay on her back, her arms bound over her head with a cord, while another cord was wrapped tightly around her neck, and a white blanket wrapped her torso. A piece of black duct tape was over her mouth. Although she was dressed in the clothing she had worn the evening before, close by lay her favorite pink nightgown.

Instead of alerting the detective to get her downstairs, John Ramsey immediately ripped off the duct tape, removed the blanket, and tried to take off the binding. Then he carried the body of his daughter upstairs. Arndt took the dead child and laid her on the floor, placing a blanket over her. At this time the body was in a full state of rigor mortis, although there was no expert present to give a proper assessment of its progress. Because of the holiday, the coroner, Dr. John Meyer, did not arrive for over six hours. At eight that evening, he examined the body and had it moved to the morgue.

Meyer began the autopsy on the morning of December 27. At that time he found chunks of pineapple in JonBenét's upper digestive tract, which meant that investigators had to find out when her last known meal had been and precisely what she had eaten.

Meyer removed the ligatures from the neck and right wrist, finding that the one around the neck had been tightened with a short stick broken off of something else. Abrasions were present on the right cheek, the left side of the neck, the right shoulder, and the left lower leg. A ligature bruise was on the right wrist. There were also dotted-pattern injuries to her cheek and torso, which some experts believed could be bruises from a stun gun. A spot of blood was inside the panties and around the vagina, and Meyer noted petechial hemorrhages from asphyxiation on the eyelids, lungs, and neck. In addition, there was a large hemorrhage on the right side of the skull, over an eight-inch fracture and a bruised area of the brain.

The cause of death was determined to be asphyxiation by strangulation, but the child had also suffered blunt force trauma to the head, after strangulation.

It turned out that she had not eaten pineapple for dinner, and no one recalled her eating a snack before bed, since she'd reportedly been asleep when carried inside, but there was a bowl of cut pineapple in the kitchen that yielded fingerprints from Patsy and Burke.

How and when JonBenét had consumed this remained a mystery, as did the actual time of her death. During the autopsy, Meyer was unable to definitively establish it.

The ransom note became one of the most crucial pieces of evidence, although it had been handled quite a bit. It proved to have been written on a tablet in the Ramsey home, with a pen from inside the home that was replaced back in its container. There was evidence that the letter writer had made a few false starts on the tablet that Patsy normally used. The note said:

Mr. Ramsey,

"Listen Carefully! We are a group of individuals that represent a small foreign faction. We ~~do~~ respect your bussiness but not the country that it serves. At this time we have your daughter in our posession. She is safe and unharmed and if you want her to see 1997, you must follow our instructions to the letter.

"You will withdraw $118,000.00 from your account. $100,000 will be in $100 bills and the remaining $18,000 in $20 bills. Make sure that you bring an adequate size attache to the bank. When you get home you will put the money in a brown paper bag. I will call you between 8 and 10 am tomorrow to instruct you on delivery. The delivery will be exhausting so I advise you to be rested. If we monitor you getting the money early, we might call you early to arrange an earlier delivery of the money and hence a earlier ~~delivery~~ pickup of your daughter.

"Any deviation of my instructions will result in the immediate execution of your daughter. You will also be denied her remains for proper burial. The two gentlemen watching over your daughter do not particularly like you so I advise you not to *provoke them. Speaking to anyone about your situation, such as police, F.B.I., etc., will result in your daughter being beheaded. If we catch you talking to a stray dog, she dies. If you alert bank authorities, she dies. If the money is in any way marked or tampered with, she dies. You will be scanned for electronic devices and if any are found, she dies. You can try to deceive us but be warned that we are familiar with law enforcement countermeasures and tactics. You stand a 99% chance of killing your daughter if you try to outsmart us. Follow our instructions and you stand a 100% chance of getting her back. You and your family are under constant scrutiny as well as the authorities. Don't try to grow a brain John. You are not the only fat cat around so don't think that killing will be difficult. Don't underestimate us John. Use that good southern common sense of yours. It is up to you now John!*

"Victory!

"S.B.T.C"

The opening paragraph included misspelled words, but other more sophisticated words had been spelled correctly. The author mentioned "a small foreign faction," although foreigners do not view themselves as foreign. The amount of ransom demanded suspiciously matched that of John Ramsey's bonus that year. The author projected a deferential tone toward John Ramsey, but referred to him in both a formal and familiar manner. The inconsistencies were confusing and seemed to indicate a person who knew John Ramsey but was not very bright.

Also, there were issues with how the body had been arranged, and where. The offender had wrapped JonBenét in a white blanket, and her favorite pink nightgown lay next to the body. Linda Haufman-Pugh, the Ramseys' housekeeper, believed the white blanket and possibly the nightgown had been in a dryer the last time she saw them. That meant that if an intruder committed the crime, he knew that this nightgown was JonBenét's favorite and had rummaged around to find it. Thus, he either knew her pretty well or was uncannily lucky in his guesses and discoveries.

Yet clearly he'd come unprepared. He wrote the ransom note there in the house, taking a good amount of time, and found items for the garrote in the cellar—a paintbrush from Patsy Ramsey's art supplies. If he'd brought a stun gun to subdue the child, he was not thinking very clearly, as a stun gun would hardly be the way to keep her quiet. To the police, the evidence was consistent with someone familiar with the house's layout and the family's habits.

Yet some investigators believed there was also evidence that pointed to a stranger. A boot print found in the basement did not match the Ramseys' shoes (although later it would seem to match one of Burke's boots), there was an unidentified fingerprint (which might be unrelated to the incident altogether), and the marks on the child suggested the possible use of a stun gun.

To try to understand how JonBenét would have crossed the path of a killer, a victimology was done, which involved compiling a biography of JonBenét's brief life and a timeline of her movements on the days leading up to the murder.

The Ramseys had arrived in Boulder when JonBenét was one year old, moving into a four-story Tudor-style house of approximately five thousand square feet. There were two staircases to the second floor (the closest to JonBenét's room was a spiral staircase), and the master bedroom was on the third floor. The home had recently been part of an open-house tour in the area to benefit a charity, and the Ramseys employed housekeepers. Thus, there was some exposure to outsiders, but there was much more that could have drawn a stranger's attention.

JonBenét had been homeschooled and attended a church preschool. She spent summers in Michigan, where she participated in sports programs. She also was in beauty pageants for children, and had quickly won a local title. Her mother bought her expensive lessons for stage manners, but did not hire a specific trainer. Her mother said JonBenét had loved performing in the shows. Teaching young girls poise, confidence, and manners was a common Southern tradition, and among JonBenét's awards were the Colorado State All-Star Kids Pageant at age four, the division title in America's Royale Tiny Miss contest at age five, and Colorado's Little Miss Christmas award just eight days before her murder. It is possible that these public exposures may have drawn the attention of a child molester attending the pageants. However, most child molesters are known to their victims and prefer to "groom" them, seducing them with affection and gifts.

Patsy Ramsey, thirty-nine, had long kept a bedroom next to Jon-Benét's, as she suffered through chemotherapy for ovarian cancer, but by the time of the incident she had returned to the master bedroom one floor up. The home had no intercom system. Patsy had been involved in the world of beauty pageants herself; she was John Ramsey's second wife, and they'd been married sixteen years. With him, she had two children.

John Ramsey, fifty-three, was a successful and wealthy CEO, running a computer distribution company. During the incident, at his attorney's suggestion, he retained a lawyer as soon as the police asked him to come to the police station for an interview. He'd experienced the loss of a twenty-two-year-old daughter in an auto accident in 1992, and was the father of two other adult children, who were away from the house at the time.

The neighborhood where the Ramseys lived was an affluent, low-crime area, populated by luxury homes and estates. John Ramsey had so little concern in that regard that he had not even bothered to fix the window he'd broken to get into the house.

During Christmas day, before the murder occurred, the family had spent the morning opening gifts. They were also preparing to fly to their vacation home in Michigan before going to Florida. They went to the home of friends, the Whites, for dinner, leaving there around 8:30 in the evening. They made two stops along the way home to deliver gifts to other friends, arriving at the house around 9:00. JonBenét reportedly fell asleep in the car and was carried to bed. Patsy said she had prepared her and tucked her in. She never woke up. Patsy and John went to bed and reportedly heard nothing during the night. They retired late and were going to rise early.

Despite strong suspicions and a lengthy grand jury hearing, no one was charged in the murder. Eventually Patsy succumbed to cancer and died, but not before she became aware of a man who would soon claim to be the killer.

Nearly a decade after the murder, American investigators swept into Bangkok on August 17, 2006, to question John Mark Karr. He did not say much, but as they were leading him through a throng of reporters and cameras, the forty-one-year-old schoolteacher admitted to the media, "I was with JonBenét when she died," adding, "I am so very sorry for what happened to JonBenét. It's very important for me that everyone knows that I love her very much, that her death was unintentional, that it was an accident."

It turned out, however, that he was lying. His DNA, supposedly left behind when he "tasted her blood," was no match for the slight amount of unidentified DNA found on the child's underwear. In addition, his family, including a former wife, claimed he was with them in Alabama on the day of the murder. They could not understand why he was saying these things.

Karr countered by saying that the DNA test was untrustworthy and his family was just protecting him. He continued to connect himself to the crime, and there were open questions about the "S.B.T.C." signature on the ransom note—similar to those on letters to his first wife. Nevertheless, there was too much evidence *against* his being involved to accept his claim—despite transporting him back to Colorado at great expense.

False confessions are common in high-profile cases: the Lindbergh kidnapping, the Black Dahlia murder, and even the Nicole Brown Simpson/Ronald Goldman slaughter all collected voluntary false confessions. Clearly Karr was seeking attention, since he said that he hoped Johnny Depp would play him in a movie made from his manuscript—which he believed would earn a "billion dollars." Karr had also initiated an association with a journalism professor, Michael Tracey, who'd made several documentaries about the murder. Sending explicit and revealing e-mails to this man risked exposure, but he did it anyway. It seems likely that he was toying with getting caught.

Karr was obsessed with the Ramsey murder for several years and reportedly knew every detail. If he genuinely sought to take responsibility for it, why did he get it wrong? He claimed that JonBenét was a willing "lover" and that her death was an accident during sex, but the autopsy revealed that the little beauty queen had a bad crack on her skull, had plenty of bruising, and was strangled with a garrote— hardly an accident. Nor had there been evidence of the type of sexual penetration Karr described.

Perhaps in his long-running, demented sexual fantasies, Karr— like a stalker—romanticized a violent connection with JonBenét, saw himself as her killer (her "deliverer"), and in the process of ruminating he diminished the brutality so he could assure himself he'd meant no harm. There's little doubt that he was partly—if not mostly— motivated by the desire to be associated with her.

Karr's background has all the earmarks of a child molester who was mentally rehearsing for an opportunity. He claimed that as a boy in Alabama he played only with girls and remarked that this was still his "peer group." In other words, mentally he never grew up. At age nineteen in 1984, he forced a thirteen-year-old girl to marry him, but she managed to get this association annulled. When Karr was twenty-four, he married a sixteen-year-old who gave birth to twins, which Karr delivered himself at home. But they died at birth, and before he buried them he named them Angel and Innocence. In one e-mail he claimed to like dolls, so it's no wonder that given JonBenét's stage trappings and doll-like makeup, Karr perceived her as his "goddess."

Karr became a teacher, but a colleague sensed something wrong when she saw him down on a classroom carpet with the girls. While some supervisors said they heard no complaints, others evaluated Karr as a poor teacher. For one job, he moved to Petaluma, California, the town in which Polly Klaas was abducted and murdered in 1993. Karr became obsessed with this crime as well and wrote to the girl's killer, Richard Allen Davis. Karr told several people he was writing a book about men who kill children.

Fired in 2002 after an arrest for possession of child pornography, Karr fled overseas and started to travel, falsely claiming in résumés that he'd held prestigious child care and teaching jobs in various places. He was a secretive, paranoid loner who behaved so inappropriately with the landlord's wife and young stepdaughters in his rented abode in Costa Rica that he was told to leave. Reportedly

STALKERS OF CHILDREN

Most child molesters are adult males. Some are aggressive, others passive, some charming, others inept. They arise in all socioeconomic, racial, and ethnic groups. A few are psychotic and some even stop after only one encounter, but the most dangerous types, and the ones most likely to repeat, are those who seek to hurt children and those stuck in an adolescent mind-set who claim to "love" their victims. Repetitive fantasies that develop through adolescence grow into a fixed mental blueprint, influencing victim type, preferred sexual activities, and the plan of approach. Persistent offenders tend to be intelligent and compulsive, and may satisfy their needs without considering the consequences. They commit their full resources to their fantasies, often using the Internet to remain anonymous while they seek out vulnerable children.

he said that, sexually, he was "like a wolf." When he posted his vita for teaching jobs, he included a photo of him with a young girl.

Over the years, Karr became an elementary school teacher, once applied for a day-care license, and was willing to undergo a sex change operation to become a nanny. But he didn't just profess a sexual fetish for young girls. He apparently viewed himself as a child killer, once claiming falsely to another person that he was wanted in four states for child abuse and child murder. Karr seemed to romanticize the violence he said he committed on JonBenét, and he aspired to be the "most wanted killer in history."

Held for the child pornography charges, Karr was eventually released because the police in California could not find the evidence they'd once collected against him. Despite the number of experts who claimed that the events surrounding Karr's confession strongly suggested that Boulder investigators did believe an intruder had committed the crime, there are still questions over why key items seem more consistent with a crime committed by someone familiar with the house and family.

SOURCES

Douglas, John, and Mark Olshaker. *The Cases That Haunt Us*. New York: Scribner, 2000.

"Ex JonBenét Ramsey Murder Suspect John Mark Karr Arrested for Domestic Violence." Associated Press, July 7, 2007.

Kher, Unmesh, and Simon Montlake. "John Mark Karr's Strange Life as a Teacher." *Time*, August 18, 2006.

Lee, Henry, and Jerry Labriola. *Famous Crimes Revisited*. Southington, CT: Strong Books, 2001.

McCrary, Gregg. "Profile of the Murder of JonBenét Ramsey." Crimelibrary.com, September 2007.

"No DNA Match, No JonBenét Charges." CNN.com, October 23, 2006.

Schiller, Lawrence. *Perfect Murder, Perfect Town: The Uncensored Story of the JonBenét Murder and the Grand Jury's Search for the Final Truth*. New York: Harper, 1999.

Thomas, Steve, and Donald A. Davis. *JonBenét: Inside the Ramsey Murder Investigation*. New York: St. Martin's Press, 2000.

ABOUT THE AUTHOR

Dr. Katherine Ramsland has a master's degree in forensic psychology from John Jay College of Criminal Justice, a master's degree in clinical psychology, and a Ph.D. in philosophy. She has published thirty-two books, including *Beating the Devil's Game: A History of Forensic Science and Criminal Investigation*, *The Human Predator: A Historical Chronicle of Serial Murder and Forensic Investigation*, *Inside the Minds of Serial Killers*, *The Science of Cold Case Files*, *The Criminal Mind: A Writers' Guide to Forensic Psychology*, and *The Forensic Science of C.S.I.* Her *Vampire Companion: The Official Guide to Anne Rice's Vampire Chronicles* was a bestseller, and she has been translated into ten languages. With former FBI profiler Gregg McCrary, she coauthored *The Unknown Darkness: Profiling the Predators among Us*, and with law professor James E. Starrs, *A Voice for the Dead*. In addition, Ramsland has published over four hundred articles on serial killers, criminology, and criminal investigation, and was a research assistant to former FBI profiler John Douglas for *The Cases That Haunt Us*. She wrote many features for Court TV's Crime Library, currently contributes editorials on forensic issues to the *Philadelphia Inquirer*, pens a regular feature on historical forensics for *The Forensic Examiner*, and teaches forensic psychology and criminal justice as an associate professor at DeSales University in Pennsylvania.